DOUBLE-CONSCIOUSNESS AND THE RHETORIC OF BARACK OBAMA

Studies in Rhetoric/Communication
Thomas W. Benson, Series Editor

Double-Consciousness
—— *and the Rhetoric of* ——
BARACK OBAMA

The Price and Promise of Citizenship

Robert E. Terrill

The University of South Carolina Press

© 2015 University of South Carolina

Published by the University of South Carolina Press
Columbia, South Carolina 29208

www.sc.edu/uscpress

Manufactured in the United States of America

24 23 22 21 20 19 18 17 16 15
10 9 8 7 6 5 4 3 2 1

Library of Congress Cataloging-in-Publication Data
can be found at http://catalog.loc.gov/.

ISBN 978-1-61117-531-8 (cloth)
ISBN 978-1-61117-532-5 (ebook)

For Debbie

Contents

Series Editor's Preface

In *Double-Consciousness and the Rhetoric of Barack Obama*, Robert Terrill discovers in the rhetoric of Barack Obama a consistent practice of "double-consciousness," a concept traced to the work of W. E. B. Du Bois, but applied by President Obama, claims Terrill, with a new range of effects and potentials. In *The Souls of Black Folk* (1903), Du Bois wrote that the circumstances of African American life had prompted the development of "double-consciousness," not a "true self-consciousness," but a "sense of always looking at one's self through the eyes of others. . . . One ever feels his two-ness,—an American, a Negro; two souls, two thoughts, two unreconciled strivings; two warring ideals in one dark body, whose dogged strength alone keeps it from being torn asunder." The rhetoric of Barack Obama, notes Terrill, is not directly derived from nor identical with the double-consciousness described by Du Bois, but it is analogous to it in the sense that Obama typically credits alternating perspectives and points of view. From Obama's practice, using a mode of critical analysis he calls "inventional criticism," Terrill develops the concept of *democratic double-consciousness*—an attitude and practice productive of democratic civic engagement. Democratic double-consciousness, as it is demonstrated by Barack Obama, is not simply a tactic in a zero sum game of competitive persuasion, nor even an effort to create a transcendent synthesis, so much as it is a habit of recognizing the legitimacy of opposing sides, of rejecting false binaries, choosing outcomes that solve problems while preserving dualities. The democratic rhetoric of double-consciousness is energetically engaged, but also reflective, hesitant, modest, and open to a multiplicity of perspectives. Such a rhetoric is likely to be deplored by those who enter political or rhetorical engagements seeking merely victory, unity, and moral certitude.

Professor Terrill guides us through the theoretical underpinnings of double-consciousness and in a series of case studies of the speeches of Barack Obama he shows what democratic double-consciousness looks like in practice, with variations adapted to the contingencies that shaped speeches on race, religion, rights, peace and war, health care reform, the economy, and the responsibilities of democratic citizenship.

THOMAS W. BENSON

Preface

This book has its genesis in two rather commonplace and overlapping observations: the study of rhetoric fosters particular forms of duality, and effective democratic citizenship also requires particular forms of duality. This book, fundamentally, is an attempt to begin to work out some possible points of connection between these two apparently parallel notions.

The interdependence of rhetoric and democracy has long been noted, of course, often described in terms of a sort of baseline rhetorical competence that is required if citizens are to participate in civic culture. But I was intrigued by a particular component of rhetorical competence, one associated less with instrumental advantage and more with the extent to which the gaining of rhetorical competence entails the cultivation of attitudes or perspectives that are of particular value to democratic practice. In other words, I was interested in exploring the idea that the foundational necessity of rhetoric to democracy has more to do with the doubled habits of thought and speech that it cultivates than with the fact that studying rhetoric can improve the ability of citizens to present themselves effectively.

I spent a good deal of time thinking about ways to make this connection. The ancient rhetorical canon of *invention* emerged as a fertile locus of inquiry because it requires a doubled attention to self and to audience, an oscillation between the motives of interpretation and production, that seems particularly valuable to civic discourse. It became evident that the foundational pedagogical practice known to rhetoricians as *imitatio,* especially as it is implicated in the cultivation of an inventional facility, also was significant in this regard. I returned, as I so often do, to the work of W. E. B. Du Bois, and in particular to his discussion of double-consciousness[1] in his monumental work *The Souls of Black Folk,* which reinforced my conviction that any discussion of duality and democratic citizenship must engage race. And as I explored the literature on practices of democratic citizenship, it became clear that some sort of duality often was evoked as a trait of the ideal citizen.

But the sort of rhetorical criticism that I practice requires an object of study, a collection of texts, a representative figure. In one of the documents I

Preface

had produced for my tenure case, I had described a future project as consisting of a loosely connected collection of analyses of various manifestations of political duality in public and popular culture. I pursued that for a while, but quickly I discovered that to produce a coherent argument I needed instead to focus on a single exemplar rather than a scattering of case studies.

And then, as if on cue, came the ascendancy of Barack Obama. And I initially took little notice. By spring 2008 I was aware of him, of course, but wasn't following him closely. National elections tend to bring my inner cynic to the surface, for one thing, and, besides, Hillary Clinton was still the presumptive Democratic candidate. While Obama's growing reputation was built primarily on his oratorical skills, what I had heard from him thus far had not impressed me. When Obama came to Bloomington in April, my family and I joined the crowds gathered on Kirkwood Avenue, and my son reached out and shook his hand, but otherwise he occupied only the periphery of my consciousness.

Then one afternoon late in that semester, a graduate student, Kathleen McConnell, came into my office, and in the course of talking about other matters she asked me if I had seen or read the speech that Obama had given on race back in March. She knew that I had been thinking about duality and citizenship, and she thought I might find that Obama had said something interesting about those topics in his address. Several weeks later, when I finally got around to reading the transcript, I found, unsurprisingly, that she was correct. I began to take notice and then notes and discovered that Obama presents himself, not only in that speech but also habitually, as a sort of icon of duality, both a speaking embodiment of a doubled attitude and an idealized democratic citizen, so that he and his public discourse presented an ideal opportunity to explore the issues which had come to be of interest to me.

And so, while I did not set out to write a book about Barack Obama, I have done so. But I think that this book is better than the book that I did originally set out to write, inasmuch as it is an extended reflection on the interdependency of rhetoric, duality, democracy, and race. I position my work among that which has focused on Obama, distinguishing my approach as a work of *inventional criticism* animated by the purpose of locating in Obama's public discourse the resources of citizenly address. Rather than trying to understand Obama's discourse as the outward symptom of his inner self or to appreciate its artistry or appeal, I aim to draw from his discourse resources that may be of value to citizens who are attempting to invent ways to address one another. Some of these ideas about the relationship between rhetorical invention and rhetorical criticism were worked out in essays written in tribute to two of my most important academic mentors, Janice Rushing and Michael Leff, both of whom passed away during the long period of time leading up to this work; the essays are titled "Going Deep" and "Learning to Read," and are listed in the bibliography.

The particular resources that I draw from Obama's discourse are doubled tropes and figures that characterize a style of speech that fosters and sustains a dual perspective, cultivating in its hearers an ability to hold two or more points of view simultaneously and to speak accordingly. I align this style of speech with Du Bois's notion of double-consciousness, discuss its implications as a mode of address rooted in African American experience, and locate analogous formulations in other descriptions of U.S. citizenship. I introduce the term *democratic double-consciousness* to refer specifically to the manifestation of duality as a resource for rhetorical invention in a democratic context. A preliminary discussion of the relationship between duality and citizenship is in my essay "Mimesis, Duality, and Rhetorical Education," listed in the bibliography.

The speech to which Kathleen directed me, titled "A More Perfect Union," is taken as an exemplar of democratic double-consciousness. Delivered at a moment of crisis in Obama's presidential campaign, it has been widely acknowledged as among the most eloquent and vivid explorations of race to come from a major-party candidate for office but has not been widely recognized as an especially rich and potent resource of citizenly invention. This analysis is foundational to my argument because it is within this speech text that Obama presents a rhetorical mechanism through which Du Boisian double-consciousness is transformed into democratic double-consciousness. The analysis is developed from my essay "Unity and Duality in Barack Obama's 'A More Perfect Union,'" listed in the bibliography.

There are limitations inherent in the use of "A More Perfect Union" as an exemplar, however. For one thing, that speech actually is not representative of Obama's public address when he is speaking about race. In fact, he tends to avoid speaking about race at all, but when he does so it generally is within the context of the African American civil rights movement of the 1960s. Other instances of Obama's race talk, extending through the 2008 presidential campaign and into his first term in office, illustrate the way that Obama negotiates the extraordinarily narrow confines set out in our public culture regarding talk about race, as well as the implications of those confines for the propagation of democratic double-consciousness.

Three prominent addresses that exhibit a doubled style, inviting the audience toward double-consciousness, do so without explicitly addressing race. These speeches—on health-care reform, war and peace, and the economy—provide an opportunity to assess the reach of democratic double-consciousness. They also indicate the significance of democratic double-consciousness as a form of address that is most effective when associated with an exemplary speaking subject. My essay "An Uneasy Peace: Barack Obama's Nobel Peace Prize Lecture," listed in the bibliography, was adapted here to further this particular exploration.

I conclude with a brief discussion of the implications of duality as it is manifest in Obama's public address and its connections to the forms of duality that seem to be components of rhetorical competence. Most significant, when Obama's discourse invites us to experience our own duality as an inventional resource for addressing the divisions of contemporary civic culture, when it invites us to cultivate a doubled consciousness that recalls Du Bois's famous formulation, it asks us to recognize the burdens of democratic citizenship but also the potential for those burdens to animate a more inclusionary democratic idiom.

Acknowledgments

I must begin by thanking my wife, Debbie, to whom this book is dedicated. Throughout the long weekends, late nights, and early mornings that were taken over by this project, she remained preternaturally supportive, patient, and encouraging. She forgives my neglect of uncountable matters of duty and protocol, offers careful and honest assessment of my ideas no matter how inarticulate, and always pulls me back to the surface before I sink too deeply into self-doubt. There is simply no way I could have finished this, or started or finished anything, without her. My son and daughter have grown toward becoming young citizens while I have been working on this book, and whatever optimism it contains largely is an effect of their presence in my life.

I have been blessed with wonderful colleagues throughout my career at Indiana University. Bob Ivie and John Lucaites, in particular, have strongly supported me from the very beginning and continue to offer guidance and opportunity far beyond what anyone should expect from senior colleagues. Phaedra Pezzullo has been a valued friend and interlocutor from the day she arrived on campus. They all are strongly present in this book, though perhaps in ways that they will not recognize. I am deeply indebted to Jim Denton, at the University of South Carolina Press, for seeing promise in this project, and to the anonymous reviewers who offered challenging and tremendously helpful suggestions. The press has been remarkably supportive and responsive throughout, and the book is much better, as a result, than it might have been.

And of course I must thank my students, both undergraduates and especially graduate students, for the humbling privilege of learning together with them.

CHAPTER 1

Inventional Criticism

On January 20, 2009, almost 2 million people braved the cold in Washington, D.C., to watch Barack Obama deliver his inaugural address. Many more around the world watched the new president live on television or streaming over the Internet, and still more watched later on their DVRs or on YouTube or Whitehouse.gov. It was the culmination of a presidential campaign season that promised to be historically significant whatever the outcome: the Democratic Party primaries eventually had come down to deciding whether the nominee would be a white woman, Hillary Clinton, or an African American man; the Republican Party nominated for vice president a white woman, Sarah Palin, to join the war hero and self-styled "maverick" John McCain on the presidential ticket. The campaign prompted the problematics of representation that tend to roil just beneath the surface of U.S. political culture to break repeatedly into the open. It may not be surprising, then, that so much of the commentary on Obama's address, on the crowds that filled the National Mall, and on the balls, concerts, and parades that accompany the spectacle of the peaceful transfer of U.S. executive power, in corporate media broadcasts as well as in uncountable blog posts, Twitter feeds, and Facebook updates, included pronouncements about the significance of Obama's race.

A nation that 150 years earlier had divided itself in a civil war fought fundamentally over African slavery had elected an African American president. Some observers were impressed that it had come to pass so soon; generations of Americans had wondered if it might happen in their lifetimes, and here it was at last. Others reminded us that the century and a half that had passed should have been time enough for any number of African Americans to have risen to the nation's highest office. And, for many, Obama's election seemed to usher in a postracial era, a time when race would be no longer politically significant, when finally it could be said that the great movements for equality of rights and opportunity had reached their conclusion. The United States had come together to elect a black man as president and in the process perhaps had seemed to erase racial divides that had been significant in national politics for centuries.

But this latter sort of optimism easily was unsettled by details of biography and demography. For one thing, Obama is biracial, as his mother, Stanley Ann Dunham, was a white woman from Kansas, a fact that Obama drew upon repeatedly throughout the campaign and that no doubt contributed to his appeal among some white voters. Obama also is not directly descended from slaves, as his father was a foreign exchange student from Kenya. Together with his being born and raised for much of his life in Hawaii, where attitudes about race may differ somewhat from those in other parts of the United States, these points encouraged some of his critics to question whether he had lived through or could represent an authentic African American experience and thus the extent to which his election could be imagined to redress racial wounds. And even a cursory analysis of the election results suggests not so much that the country had come together to elect its first black president but instead that it still was deeply divided by race. Obama won the election with 365 electoral votes, well above the 270 required, but just under 53 percent of the popular vote; while almost all of the African Americans who voted had voted for him, fewer than half of the white voters had done so. His opponent, John McCain, won handily across the former Confederacy, receiving, for example, 85 percent of the white vote in Mississippi; McCain lost North Carolina and Indiana by just one percentage point each, lost Florida by two points, and won Missouri by one—in each case, he fared far better in precincts that were overwhelmingly white.

A good part of the address that Obama delivered to this divided electorate was relatively standard inaugural boilerplate. An inaugural address, as Karlyn Kohrs Campbell and Kathleen Hall Jamieson have reminded us, is expected to unify the audience, rehearse "communal values drawn from the past," and set out the "political principles that will govern the new administration," and it is clear that Obama's address had been crafted to satisfy these expectations.[1] He reminds his audience, for example, that though we find ourselves "in the midst of crisis," this also is a time "to reaffirm our enduring spirit" because we are "keepers of [a] legacy," and "guided by these principles once more we can meet those new threats that demand even greater effort, even greater cooperation and understanding between nations."[2] Obama is a savvy public speaker known to mine the oratorical history of the United States while composing his most important speeches, so we can assume that he and his staff are well aware of the norms, precedents, and generic constraints governing presidential inaugurals.

The citizens addressed by these generic elements of Obama's inaugural are assured that the new administration will not entirely discard old practices, reminded that the apparent divisions in the present will be overcome in the future, and invited to recall and endorse vaguely described but purportedly fundamental values. These rather staid assurances suggest perhaps a fairly passive or

2

spectative mode of citizenship, one characterized by an invitation to gaze upon traditional norms, to witness the peaceful transfer of power, and to behold the promise of the new administration to launch programs and initiatives.

Of course, Obama's address offers more than that. It is, in fact, a discourse on citizenship and offers in particular a depiction of the web of interdependence and reciprocity that sustains democratic culture. He asks his listeners, for example, to recall those who have "struggled and sacrificed and worked till their hands were raw so that we might live a better life." "For us," Obama continues, "they packed up their worldly possessions and traveled across oceans in search of a new life. For us, they toiled in sweatshops, and settled the West, endured the lash of the whip, and plowed the hard earth. For us, they fought and died in places like Concord and Gettysburg, Normandy and Khe Sanh." The repeating of the phrase "for us" at the beginning of each of these clauses, a rhetorical figure called *anaphora,* links these sacrifices thematically and also logically, setting these varied experiences beside one another as coequals in emphasis rather than in a linear series or in chronological order. Immigrants, laborers, settlers, slaves, farmers, and soldiers, separated by centuries and thousands of miles, all are brought together so that we might feel their continued presence.

Unusually for an inaugural address, the speech invites us to recall the particularities of race that have fractured our polity in the past and that continue to do so in the present, suggesting even that this history might be a source of hope for the future, for "because we have tasted the bitter swill of civil war and segregation, and emerged from that dark chapter stronger and more united, we cannot help but believe that the old hatreds shall someday pass." The communal "we" invites his audience to cross time and to figuratively share in those past sacrifices and to place his own election within that context.

The ideal U.S. citizens Obama is addressing are to remember these sacrifices, past and present, military and civilian, slave and free, "with humble gratitude." But they also are to emulate them, not merely to observe past actions but to contribute their own so that they can see, like those who have come before, that the United States is "bigger than the sum of our individual ambitions" and, as such, embodies a "spirit" that must "at this moment, a moment that will define a generation, . . . inhabit us all." This address asks its hearers to experience not only an obligation to feel the burden of the past but also a responsibility to bear that burden in the present, to recognize one another within a web of reciprocity that at the same time is informed by the discord and distrust that remain a part of the legacy of race in the United States. We are asked to recognize that the burdens borne by our fellow citizens and the shouldering of similar burdens ourselves can be a source of renewal. "This," Obama concludes, "is the price and the promise of citizenship."

In this book I explore the potential for Obama's public discourse to provide for citizens of the United States a resource upon which they may draw as they attempt to negotiate this price and promise. This is a work of rhetorical criticism, which I understand as an effort to render public discourse as a resource for a more robust enactment of citizenship. Through the close examination of key speeches from Obama's campaign and first term as president, I define and characterize the inventional resources they offer. In other words, I situate Obama's public address as an inventional resource for citizenship, as a rhetorical storehouse that might inform the ways that citizens address one another and recognize themselves as being addressed.

The particular resources I am searching for are those that present and that would foster in their hearers a doubled discourse, a way of speaking characterized by figures and tropes that encourage a stereoscopic view, a balanced perspective that presents the world as consistently characterized by duality. This is the style evident in Obama's inaugural, for example, as it encourages us to acknowledge our obligations to one another while also sustaining our individual identity, to feel the burdens of the past while also addressing the opportunities of the present, to see ourselves from the point of view of others without relinquishing our self-interest. It is a mode of speech that, like that inaugural address, acknowledges the impress of race on American citizenship. It explicitly articulates habits of citizenship, particularly as they are manifest in a doubled manner of address through which people may recognize and engage with one another as citizens.

Puzzling Obama

While this book draws upon Obama's public discourse in order to suggest contributions to practices of democratic citizenship, most of the extant literature on Barack Obama positions its subject as a puzzle to be solved and his public address as among the clues that can be used in the solving. A quick review of some of these studies is useful as a way to clarify the distinctiveness of my own approach. Many popular books on Obama treat his discourse as a fog of clever words and well-crafted phrases that obscure the true, and usually sinister, character that lurks beneath; many academic studies, conversely, regard his public speeches and statements as an archive of clues to the man's inner psyche, or they attend to various features of his discourse in an attempt to decipher its meaning, decrypt its eloquence, or account for its persuasive effect.

Dinesh D'Souza, one of Obama's harshest critics, describes him as "an enigmatic figure, a puzzle both to his adversaries and to his supporters" and "certainly the least-known figure ever to reach the presidency."[3] D'Souza's strategy for solving this puzzle is "to discover Obama's own narrative, one that makes psychological sense of the man, and that helps to explain his policies and his deepest beliefs," and in this way to discover the "interpretive key that unlocks the mystery and helps us understand" him.[4] Jerome R. Corsi, another Obama critic, promises "to fully document all arguments and contentions" and to "extensively footnote all references," in an effort to puncture "the façade of personality that Obama has constructed in his two books."[5] For Sasha Abramsky, in a largely appreciative study, the task similarly is to "understand Obama the man, rather than Obama the myth," though Abramsky adds a more ethnographic approach, interviewing "the men and women who knew him" at various stages in his life.[6] This mode of critique may be motivated, in part, by a general distrust of eloquence or by a suspicion that a talented orator like Obama might be able to craft a benign persona that is attractive to the uninformed while it hides a more ominous truth. The trick, then, is somehow to get past the flood of discourse that Obama has produced ever since becoming a public figure—his intensely personal autobiography, a somewhat less personal but still revealing political memoir, many hours of interviews, and innumerable speeches and public statements—to discover the "the little man behind the curtain," as the *Pittsburgh Post-Gazette* columnist Jack Kelly puts it.[7] Such studies are inherently unsatisfactory, of course, not only because mostly what one discovers behind the public discourse of a public figure is more public discourse but also because they begin with the premise that such discourse is unreliable and thus discount from the outset their primary source of evidence.

A complementary set of studies treats Obama's public discourse as an outward symptom of his inner nature. His oratorical performances, for example, may be understood as clues to "the unconscious thought processes that might be influencing them"; thus their analysis has the potential to "profoundly enhance our understanding of Obama's character."[8] The study of Obama's oratory might illustrate "his progression as a thinker and rhetorician,"[9] or it might allow "the discerning critic" to "track the development and refinement" of his discourse over the course of his career, revealing "marker[s] of the mind—the thought processes—of Obama."[10] James T. Kloppenberg's goal, for example, in his impressive and important study, is "understanding him as a writer, and as a politician." For Kloppenberg, this "requires placing his ideas in the deeper and broader contexts of the American political tradition," and particularly within the American pragmatist tradition.[11] Extending back to William James and John Dewey, this tradition informs the work of several of the faculty who were at the Harvard Law School during Obama's time there, including Cass Sunstein and Laurence Tribe. In fact, Kloppenberg argues that when Obama entered Harvard Law, in the fall of 1988, the faculty was in the midst of an intense conversation about the meaning of pragmatism and its relevance to the practice of law and that his public discourse bears the continuing mark of that conversation.[12]

Richard W. Leeman, a rhetorical scholar, does not disagree with Kloppenberg's analysis but adds an interest in accounting for Obama's rhetorical appeal. He notes that audiences repeatedly reported that Obama's discourse was uplifting and inspirational, especially during the 2008 campaign, and quite reasonably suggests that that reaction was not a result of Obama's indebtedness to philosophical pragmatism. Leeman discerns, instead, what he refers to as a "fundamentally teleological" character in Obama's public discourse, meaning that it embodies and enacts the development of "an overarching purpose or end" that guides decision making and judgment. Obama's discourse inspires, in this reading, because it encourages its audience to reach for ideals just beyond its grasp, draws its hearers toward a goal, and engages them in achieving a purpose. Leeman's perspective thus provides an important supplement to Kloppenberg's, as it explicitly recognizes Obama's public address as *rhetorical,* crafted with the intention of constituting and affecting an audience.

However, like Kloppenberg, Leeman frames his analysis as a means toward the discovery of Obama's inner nature, noting that "teleology is a critically important element of Obama's worldview" and in fact "that Barack Obama's character is teleological."[13] Documenting the influences of intellectual traditions that are evident in Obama's discourse and seeking to account for its appeal contribute substantively to our understanding of Obama as an individual as well as the cultural and political implications of his rise to prominence. At the same time, however, such studies attend to Obama's discourse primarily as a means to discovering an underlying condition.

Inventional Criticism

This book is driven by a rather different set of motives. Again, I regard Obama's discourse as a repository or archive of modes of speech that are particularly well suited to democratic citizenship and my critical task as rendering those modes of speech available as inventional resources. This book is an effort to reveal what is in these texts, but for the purpose of proposing what might come of them, not to account for how meaning was made but rather to suggest and to demonstrate some of the ways that it might be made. Rather than an effort to understand Obama's discourse as the outward symptom of something hidden within or to appreciate its artistry or account for its appeal, this book seeks to draw from Obama's public address inventional resources that may be of value to citizens who are attempting to address one another as citizens.

These motives are manifest in a particular inflection of rhetorical analysis that I refer to as *inventional criticism*. Rather than being animated primarily by a concern for theory, method, or object, inventional criticism is animated by purpose; it is a critical practice that is characterized by a commitment to rhetorical analysis as a medium through which public texts are rendered inventional resources for citizenly discourse.[14] As Arthur Walzer reminds us, "it is not an exaggeration to characterize the history of rhetoric as a twenty-four-hundred-year reflection on citizen education."[15] And so it may be that the purpose I am describing is an underlying or tacit motivation of much rhetorical criticism, and to that extent my project is distinguished by making this purpose explicit and bringing it to the fore as primary.

The story about rhetoric that generally is told reminds us that in the Western tradition, it traces its rise as an object of study and focus of pedagogy to the emergence of democracy as a form of government in ancient Athens.[16] The story is one of opportunity and circumstance: in the fifth century B.C.E., self-governing democratic citizens needed to acquire the skills that would enable them both to produce public discourse and to respond to the public discourse of their fellow citizens, and teachers of rhetoric emerged to fulfill that need. It was valuable to identify and codify features of effective speech and theories developed of argument, arrangement, style, memory, and delivery, as well as other elements of public oral discourse such as the use of humor, the presentation of self, the role of probability, and the nature of public opinion. The first work of inventing what eventually came to be recognized as rhetorical theory was begun by the itinerant teachers known to us as the Sophists, and then Isocrates and Aristotle established the most influential Athenian schools in which students could study rhetoric. This story emphasizes the need for democratic citizens to become skilled in the production and critique of public discourse and positions the study of rhetoric as able to develop that faculty.

This account emphasizes the cultivation of a sort of baseline eloquence as an instrumental democratic skill—citizens have opinions to express, interests to protect, organizations to form, leaders to support and condemn, and values to reinforce and critique and therefore must be able to participate productively in civic culture. Democratic citizens must exhibit what Gerard Hauser refers to as "*rhetorical competence,* or a capacity to participate in rhetorical experiences."[17] There is no denying this requirement or its continuing importance; indeed, it easily can be argued that contemporary citizens require even more robust training in rhetoric than did their ancient forebears, as they now navigate multiply mediated and interactive public spheres that are thoroughly saturated in discourse. If the citizens of ancient Athens required training in the production and critique of public discourse at a time when orality was the primary communication medium and "citizen" was a largely an elite status bestowed upon a homogeneous subset of the population, then certainly in the twenty-first-century

United States, where an increasingly diverse citizenry is presented with new media at a giddy rate, a rhetorical education is simply mandatory.[18]

I am far from the first to make this assertion, of course, as not only rhetorical scholars but also a growing number of political scientists and others have made a similar case. Bryan Garsten, for example, has acknowledged that the art of rhetoric is essential to a "a well-functioning republican polity" and "a healthy political life." "Politics naturally gives rise to controversy," he observes, and the art of rhetoric teaches "citizens how to engage in controversy through speech rather than force."[19] Iris Marion Young has suggested "rhetoric" as among the modes of citizenship that might be understood as vehicles through which democracy might become more inclusionary. Rhetoric, as she defines it, "refers to the way claims and reasons are stated," to the manner in which things are said, and notes that increasing sensitivity to the power of rhetoric can help to explain "how some people can be excluded from the public by dismissal of their style." Thus, rhetoric is "a feature of political expression to which we ought to attend in our engagement with one another, rather than an aspect of expression we try to bracket in order to be truly rational."[20] Elizabeth Markovits also calls for a "home for rhetoric in political theory," because she believes that an acknowledgment of rhetoric as "a quality of all (human) language use, one that is thoroughly intertwined with any utterance," might help to ameliorate our more exaggerated collective allergy to stylistic artfulness in public discourse.[21]

Views such as these help to restore rhetoric to its rightful place at the core of the practice and study of civic life, but they still present important limitations and neglect important aspects of the rhetorical tradition. While Young, for example, acknowledges the value of rhetoric, she also limits rhetoric to the "affective, embodied, and stylistic aspects of communication" that might render a message more salient or affective.[22] Similarly, Markovits appreciates the important contributions that rhetoric can make to contemporary practices of citizenship but also limits its function to serving as a "practical complement to truth, a legitimate way of transmitting truth to others."[23] Specifically, these views neglect the *inventional* capacity of rhetoric: its ability not merely to enhance discourse already crafted through other means or to transmit ideas already discovered in other ways but also to constitute the very process through which discourse is crafted and truths are articulated. This extends the significance of rhetoric beyond the development of a sort of baseline eloquence and marks it out as a sensibility or *habitus,* manifest in the capacity to produce effective persuasive speech in a civic context, to the development of a capacity for discursive invention through which citizens might craft the identities and relationships that constitute the political communities of which we all are a part.

Richard McKeon defined *rhetorical invention* with deceptive simplicity as "the art of discovering new arguments and uncovering new things by argument."[24] Invention is the first of the five ancient canons of rhetoric, the others being arrangement, style, memory, and delivery, so one might be excused for assuming that it also is the least complex.[25] The concept of "invention" with regard to verbal skill suffers in comparison with invention as scientific discovery. "It is unusual, but understandable," Arabella Lyon points out, "to say, 'Late last night, in my laboratory, I invented a new polymer chemical.'"[26] We would take this to mean that the scientist has produced something entirely new, something previously unknown. It is somewhat more puzzling to hear a speaker to say, for example, "I invented a metaphor." Rhetorical invention cannot refer to the creation of something entirely novel, because if rhetoric is to find an audience it must be at least to some extent familiar. Rita Copeland notes that the Latin term for rhetorical invention, *inventio,* "literally means a 'coming upon,' a discovery of that which is there, or already there, to be discovered. The term has little to do with originality or with creation *ex nihilio.*"[27] Deities create; humans invent.

Of course, in an age such as ours that so strongly valorizes the entirely or seemingly new, invention, understood in this proper sense as the entirely human activity of making use of what comes ready to hand, inevitably loses some of its sheen. Paradoxically, however, this is the quality of rhetorical invention that renders it civically potent. The central problematic of discursive invention in a civic context, what makes it so challenging, is that it must culminate in discourse that is at once both novel and familiar. Rhetoric has to begin with and then contribute to the discursive forms that already are available. Rhetorical invention requires, in other words, thoughtful and critical engagement with the discourse of others, and it is this essential engagement, this interpretive or perhaps hermeneutical work to communicate with others, that marks rhetorical invention as a fundamental practice of citizenship. A rhetorician working in a civic context must perceive the members of an audience not as passive reservoirs to be filled or as recalcitrant obstacles to be moved but as dynamic and embodied souls, afflicted with reason, passion, prejudice, tolerance, and any number of other human attributes out of which political communities might be formed; it requires a rather radical interpretive flexibility, an ability and propensity not for the sort of analysis that might be performed from the relative security provided by the pretense of objectivity but rather for the embodied and dialogic engagement that opens the rhetor to the influence and perspective of the other.

The greater the extent to which citizens gain facility in rhetorical invention, the more receptive they may become "to alternative modes of expression, engage in active interpretation to understand what is being said and how it relates to them, and be open to change."[28] The more apt citizens become in the interpretive and productive practices associated with the invention of public discourse, the more likely they are to become engaged and critical participants in civic culture. Discourse invented from within the role of citizen entails speaking in the idiom of another about a common good (or ill), with the dual purpose of recognizing other individuals as fellow citizens and also of inviting those fellow citizens to recognize themselves. Rhetoric is the medium of citizenship.

The mode of rhetorical analysis that I refer to as inventional criticism is motivated by two contributions to the development of a facility in rhetorical invention. First, it is self-consciously inventional, addressing public discourse as an opportunity for rhetorical invention. James Jasinski has provided an elegant summary of four different senses of rhetorical invention: inspirational, systematic, imitative, social. Of these, the mode of rhetorical criticism I am describing is most closely associated with the imitative. This sense of invention explicitly "locates speakers and writers in a world of *other texts and voices* that help to shape the generation of discourse."[29] Imitation, in this sense, refers not to "the mere repetition or mechanistic reproduction of something found in an existing text" but rather to "a complex process" through which artifacts of public discourse "serve as equipment for future rhetorical production."[30] Imitation, then, properly understood within a rhetorical context, is an effort to produce not another discourse or artifact identical to an original but instead a new discourse that is set in dialogue with and that bears the imprint of the original.

As a critical approach informed by this tradition, then, inventional criticism proceeds through an endeavor to identify within the public discourse that is under analysis particular features or characteristics that are worthy of emulation, and it culminates in neither a description that would duplicate the original artifact nor in the production of a generalized theory that might be applied to any cultural artifact but rather in a new discourse that emerges through an interpretive engagement with a particular artifact. The new discourse—the critical work—is thoroughly influenced by and connected to the artifact under analysis, because it is governed by the self-conscious realization that all discourse is bound to other texts and voices and that it is through the critical engagement with such discourse that new discourse is invented.

The influence of the tradition of *imitatio* and its fundamental assumptions about intertextuality enable inventional criticism to avoid the agent-centered biases of much public-address scholarship. It is axiomatic that no public discourse can have a unitary source. As a consequence, inventional criticism assumes and fosters productive habits that disrupt the notions of transparency and authenticity commonly associated with assertions of agent-centered discourse; it assumes, in other words, a notion of rhetorical agency as "promiscuous and protean," in Campbell's terms.[31] Throughout this book when I refer to the public discourse of Barack Obama, I do not mean to assert or assume that all of the words under study are the product of his personal creative genius. I also do not explore the problematics of ghostwriting or the relationship between Obama and his writing staff. In that sense, though this book takes the public oratory of Obama as its archive, it should not be understood narrowly as being *about* Obama, at least not in the way that many other projects are. Again, the critical purpose here is not to discover Obama's inventional skill but to make available from his discourse inventional resources that may contribute to the efficacy of democratic engagement.

When engaged in inventional criticism, a critic cannot take refuge behind the fiction of neutrality or objectivity, sustaining a so-called and ultimately illusory critical distance from the object of study, because the critical work is not guided by the goal of merely describing the discourse or accounting for its resonance, circulation, or effects. Because this mode of analysis presents itself not as an extra-rhetorical reporting of findings discovered through other means but as a rhetorical and inventional performance, the knowledge invented cannot be separated from the critical practice within which it is invented. It takes as its goal an intervention in public discourse rather than merely a description of it. Inventional criticism understands critical rhetorical work as a mode of rhetorical production and rhetoric as a manner of engaging in civic culture and thus rhetorical criticism as one such form of engagement.[32]

While the first inventional motive that informs this mode of criticism is situated at the point of contact between the critic and the public discourse under study, the second motive is situated between the critical work and its readers. The critical work—in this case, this book—makes available the inventional resources that emerge from critical engagement with public discourse at the same time that it models the interpretive approaches through which that discourse might be engaged. Though the analyses in this book are a species of close reading, inventional criticism is methodologically agnostic; it is distinguished by its purpose rather than its method. It culminates in a critical text that has been invented through an engagement with public discourse that is analogous to the ways that citizens might engage the discourses of other citizens, and of course such engagements might be analogous to any number of critical methods.

Kirt Wilson has provided a succinct and thoughtful review of some of the debates that shaped rhetorical criticism in the last decades of the twentieth century and that continue to inform critical practice in the present; he concludes that "public address criticism is not terribly distinct from the act of public address itself."[33] It is possible to extend this analogy too far and thus elide the very qualities that distinguish an understanding of discourse as rhetorical, including a sensitivity to the differing audiences, purposes, goals, and ethos that generally differentiate the scholarly production of rhetorical criticism from the vernacular production of rhetorical discourse. Rhetorical critics, in other words, should be especially sensitive to the ways that the criticism of public address is not precisely like the production of public address. But no analogy is precise, and the value of Wilson's point is in no way diminished by this caveat, for he draws our attention to fundamental similarities in both rhetorical modalities, including the fact that both public discourse and the rhetorical criticism of public discourse present interpretive responses to public discourse. All rhetorical production is, at least to some degree, a "hermeneutical performance,"[34] not only the specialized work of the rhetorical critic but also the vernacular discourse produced by citizens as they respond to one another and to the issues of the day. Inventional critique depends upon this parallelism, as it enables understanding the inventional work done by the critic as analogous to the inventional work being encouraged by the critic.

Antecedent examples of and models for inventional criticism might be located throughout the rhetorical tradition, as I understand it to be a foundational rhetorical practice that pervades that tradition. Isocrates, the most important and influential teacher of rhetoric in fourth-century-B.C.E. Athens, provides an especially vivid exemplar. As it has been masterfully reconstructed by Jeffrey Walker, Isocrates's pedagogy was deeply and radically inventional, in the sense of being inventional at its root. Isocrates began by presenting to his students exemplary orations either of his own or drawn from recent public oratorical performances that would serve "as models for analysis and imitation."[35] As Walker explains, students would learn "the fundamental elements of rhetoric" through "hearing the teacher's explanation of them and through the careful reading and detailed discussion of sample texts."[36] The assumption here, common to both Isocrates's critical practice and my own, is that rhetorical theory is best understood not as it is delineated in precept and treatise but as it is performed and embodied by actors engaged on a civic stage. Isocrates and probably many teachers of rhetoric, then as now, would lead students through public texts, attending particularly to the verbal forms or persuasive tactics that were effective or eloquent, before asking his students to compose new discourses that drew upon this analysis of exemplars.[37] "With the goal of invention in mind," as Arthur Walzer describes it, "an analysis of these speeches would readily yield the special topics that are the basis of political judgment," and this is the goal of a rhetorical pedagogy.[38]

Like the Isocratean model and like many practices of rhetorical pedagogy that have persisted through the centuries, inventional criticism attends to public discourse in an effort to locate resources that will foster further rhetorical invention. Public discourse is imagined as a reservoir of rhetorical possibility, and the critic/pedagogue renders these possibilities available to individuals who might engage one another as citizens. Public discourse is not served raw, as it were, but mediated through an analysis that employs rhetorical lore as an interpretive vocabulary; then that hermeneutical performance itself provides a model that can be taken up by citizens as they engage and respond to the multiple discourses encountered in a civic sphere. But inventional critique breaks rather sharply with its root analogues in Isocratean and other premodern rhetorical pedagogy and indeed with much of the history of rhetorical pedagogy, because its focus is on enhancing the inventional capacity of ordinary citizens rather than of elite orators.[39] With regard to Obama's oratory, I am much less interested in discovering his own rhetorical prowess than I am in working to make that oratory, through critical analysis, an inventional resource for others. Inventional critique is basically democratic, then, and aims to make a contribution to the rhetorical education of democratic citizens.

The overarching motive is an effort to render public texts as what Kenneth Burke referred to as "equipment for living,"[40] specifically equipment for the invention of discourses well suited to living as a democratic citizen. It might seem that this is a narrowing of Burke's more expansive notion and that an emphasis on civic action sets limits on the rhetorical project and thus constrains its potential reach and its potential to ameliorate problems in public life.[41] I see it, however, as a frank acknowledgment that however remotely we may sense it, we are members of political communities.[42] Equipment for living, at least mostly, and more specifically, is equipment for living as a citizen. Of course, the influences upon us and our effects upon others are not limited to the boundaries of the political community of which we are citizens; it has been and remains a fact that we are not all citizens to the same degree, do not all share similar degrees of agency, and do not all act as citizens all of the time. Still we require ways to recognize and address one another as citizens that might most strongly enhance democratic practice, and my aim in this book is to explore the potential for Obama's public discourse to contribute appropriate equipment for doing so.

Rhetorical Citizenship

This book concerns itself with citizenship as it is discursively enacted or performed, a conception of citizenship suggested by what Robert Asen describes as a "discourse theory of citizenship" or by what Christian Kock and Lisa S. Villadsen refer to as "rhetorical citizenship."[43] This draws our attention to the ways that citizens address one another as citizens, the way that they recognize and identify with one another, as well as the way that they are addressed as citizens by institutions, offices, and persons in power. A focus on the discursive habits of citizenship supplements conceptions of citizenship as a legal status; while certainly it is true that "citizenship cannot be earned simply by acting as a citizen ought to, or as most citizens seem to,"[44] it also is true that the ways in which citizenship is enacted are its most legible manifestations. Whereas any number of visual, aural, and even tactile experiences might be understood as participating in these modes of citizenly address, this book is focused on speech. As Peter Meyers reminds us, *speaking to one another in public* is the single most important activity of the democratic Citizen. *Speech* is what positions us. *Speaking* is how we carve out our positions."[45]

This conception of citizenship also takes into account the fluidity of citizenship, the fact that not everyone is addressing others or being addressed as citizens during every waking moment. Citizenship is imagined as process and performance more than as possession, as "something one can take up, rather than as a condition that is always or never present."[46] Citizenship, in fact, even might be "enacted by non-citizens," as Asen puts it, meaning that in particular situations individuals who do not possess the legal status of citizenship might be addressed as though they were citizens or might seize the opportunity to draw upon the available models and resources and speak as citizens.[47] The citizenly role "makes everyday life with others possible," Meyers continues, adding that "sometimes we choose this role, sometimes we fall into it. It is just as easy, indeed easier, to fall out of it."[48]

Understanding citizenship as a public role that is both invented within and enacted by rhetoric brings to mind Edwin Black's acknowledgment of the first and second personae that are indelibly present in rhetorical address. The "first persona" is the "implied author," a role that entails and may be defined by the production of public speech. Like citizenship, as I am describing it, the "first persona" is a role that is taken on when one engages in public address, embodied and enacted in the moments of its production, rather than imposed or awarded as a status that is stable regardless of circumstance. The first persona of citizenship is enacted when an individual is engaged in speaking like a citizen. The "second persona," as Black describes it, is the "implied auditor" of public address. This is not necessarily the actual auditor but rather the auditor that can be extracted from an examination of the discourse itself, particularly of the "stylistic tokens" present in such discourse. The actual auditors who hear the address are presented not merely with a discourse directed to them but also with a discourse that presents "a model of what the rhetor would have his real auditor become."[49] To recognize citizenship as a mode of rhetorical speech is to recognize it also as constituted in and through rhetorical speech. Citizenship, in this mode, is the role into which a discourse invites its audience, signified by the particular discursive resources through which the invitation is offered and the stylistic tokens that the discourse provides as ways through which to enact this role.

The brief analysis of Obama's first inaugural address with which I began this chapter presents several stylistic tokens that might be made available as inventional resources of citizenship. The past, for example, is presented not merely as a backdrop or precursor but as constitutive of the present; the present not only has been shaped by the past but is depicted as depending for its existence upon the sacrifices of those who have lived in the past. Further, the present is a site where these past sacrifices should be not merely remembered but actually reenacted, not merely recalled but also taken as models to be emulated. Obama's address sustains a distinction between sacrifices willingly made by intrepid pioneers and those forcefully imposed on African slaves, offering a discourse of citizenship that draws these experiences together but does not equate them, rejecting reductive melting-pot metaphors for something more visceral, complex, multifaceted, and respectful. He evokes the weight of the past as among the burdens of citizenship and supplies a language through which citizens might articulate that burden to one another.

Inaugural addresses are expected to lay out the political principles that will characterize the new administration, and the section of Obama's speech where this generic obligation is most evidently fulfilled is shaped by a set of balanced rhetorical figures. Antithesis, for example, is the figure in which contrasting words or ideas are put alongside each other, often in grammatically parallel phrases. One of the best-known appearances of this figure is John F. Kennedy's call in his own inaugural to "ask not what your country can do for you; ask what you can do for your country." The figure may be particularly fitting for inaugurals because its grammatical parallelism suggests continuity at the same time that its ideational contrast suggests change. Obama includes several examples of this figure, as when he sets the question of "whether our government is too big or too small" against the question of "whether it works," a contrast that is extended in his urging to provide "opportunity to every willing heart—not out of charity, but because it is the surest route to our common good."

Antithesis invites us to see two options as essentially comparable and then to shift our attention from one to the other—not this but that. Obama's speech also contains several figures that present a more complex doubled form, inviting the copresence of different ideas rather than a choosing among them. Isocolon, for example, is a form of grammatical parallelism among phrases of a common length that can have the effect of establishing equal emphasis among the ideas or assertions thus articulated. In Obama's speech, this figure links the collective "size of our gross domestic product" with the personal "reach of our prosperity" and sets the "missiles and tanks" of military might on an equal footing with the "sturdy alliances and enduring convictions" of diplomacy; we are asked not to choose one over the other but to look upon both items and determine that both are equally important. Perhaps the highest emotional summit in this generally earthbound oration is gained by the parallel phrases that continue this thought, as Obama praises those who have come before because "they knew that our power grows through its prudent use; our security emanates from the justness of our cause, the force of our example, the tempering qualities of humility and restraint."[50] Power and prudence, justness and humility, force and restraint—all balance each other in carefully weighted pairs that emphasize their interdependence and that depend upon their equal significance.

The disposition or arrangement of Obama's address reinforces these dualities, especially with respect to the relationship between the present and the past. After dispensing with the tradition of placing the new president within the long line of presidential succession, his address concentrates on the challenges of the present. He reminds his audience that "we are in the midst of a crisis" characterized by a "sapping of confidence" and a "nagging fear that America's decline is inevitable." Of course, he must provide a way out of the morass, and though Obama tells his audience that "the time has come to 'set aside childish things,'" that "the ground has shifted," and that "the world has changed, and we must change with it," this speech as a whole is informed less by an antithetical logic in which we are urged to choose not the past but the future and more by a recursive logic through which we are brought back repeatedly to the well of the past as a way to address the future. The "Founding Fathers" are made to speak to the "governments watching today," their "principles" are brought to bear on "new threats," and a "patchwork heritage" will enable "a new era of peace." The past and the present are brought into dialogue, each always distinct and yet both always in sight.

These figures could be said to articulate a certain political ideology; they surely are informed by the literature, history, and legal scholarship with which Obama is familiar; they may provide a glimpse into the workings of his mind; they very likely contribute to the resonance of his best oratory; and they may, in turn, account as well for some aspects of both his political successes and his failures. But they are, fundamentally, ways of speaking. Obama is modeling figures and tropes and schemes of speech upon which citizens might draw when called upon to address one another and through which they may recognize themselves as addressed. These are rhetorical forms that themselves draw upon and contribute to the embodied storehouse of rhetorical invention that characterizes civic culture. They are particularly conducive to democratic citizenship to the extent that they encourage auditors to cultivate a duality that situates them within an interdependent network of others. They model a manner of address in keeping with the importance of public speech to democratic practice and open up the possibility for a proliferation of perspectives.

Any work that discusses U.S. citizenship, however conceived, must address the issue of race. This is perhaps especially true for a book like this one, in which citizenship is construed as a discursive practice, because our difficult racial past has a profound effect on the way that we talk about citizenship. Citizenship in the United States is deeply implicated in the politics of race. Citizenship as a legal status has been defined repeatedly along racial lines, through court decisions, executive orders, and legal statutes reaching back to the drafting of the Constitution itself. But, more important for the purposes of this project, the practices of citizenship also have been implicated in racial politics and experiences—the modes of discourse through which individuals enact their own citizenship and recognize the citizenship of others are inflected by the official and unofficial strictures on citizenship. It may seem either counterintuitive or self-evident, depending on one's perspective on human nature, that in response to the litany of stereotypes, caricatures, and exclusionary politics that characterize the discursive policing of U.S. citizenship there might arise rhetorical resources that both bear the impress of this history and offer a mode of addressing them productively in the present. That is the argument in the next chapter, in which I situate the doubled discourse that characterizes Obama's public address within a tradition that finds its most vivid articulation in the work of W. E. B. Du Bois.

CHAPTER 2

Democratic
Double-Consciousness

As a young man "trying to reconcile the world as I'd found it with the terms of my birth," Barack Obama went to the library and "gathered up" books by African American authors to "corroborate this nightmare vision" of a world divided by race and himself divided with it. As the incident is portrayed in his memoir, *Dreams from My Father,* he seems disappointed in the resources afforded by this literature, finding in it "the same weary flight, all of them exhausted, bitter men, the devil at their heels." Even the *Autobiography of Malcolm X,* by which Obama is particularly moved, was tainted by Malcolm's "wish that the white blood that ran through him, there by an act of violence, might somehow be expunged." Obama realizes that he could never feel that way about the white blood in his own veins and wonders "what else I would be severing if and when I left my mother and my grandparents at some uncharted border."[1] In the next scene of his memoir, Obama is playing basketball with some older black men who express their admiration that "Malcolm tells it like it is," while at the same time asserting their rejection of some of Malcolm's most fundamental commitments, saying "you won't see me moving to no African jungle anytime soon. Or some goddamned desert somewhere, sitting on a carpet with a bunch of Arabs." Obama catches his friend Ray laughing at this and calls him out as having never himself read Malcolm's autobiography, to which Ray responds: "I don't need no books to tell me how to be black."[2] In the memoir, Obama next describes his grandmother, whom he called Toots, being so unsettled by an aggressive black panhandler that she refuses to ride the bus to work. After his grandfather agrees to take her and they leave, Obama sits on the edge of his bed and realizes that though his grandparents had never "given me reason to doubt their love . . . yet I knew that men who might easily have been my brothers could still inspire their rawest fears."[3]

Presentations of doubleness tumble through these scenes: the mixture of hope and despair in African American literary classics; Obama's own mixed response to Malcolm X, which is paralleled by the simultaneous admiration and rejection voiced by the older black men on the basketball court; the border at which he fears he might be asked to leave his white family; the assertion of a sort of black authenticity that Obama, though black, cannot claim; his grandparents' expression of both familial love and racial fear. Regarding the memoir as a form of public address—though itself a form of address with its own affordances, as I will note in later chapters—I quote these passages not as evidence that Obama *is* doubled but instead as evidence that he often *portrays* himself and others as doubled. These are tropes that seem to cluster around Obama, in his self-descriptions, in his own discourse addressed to others, and in others' discourse about him; he is something of an avatar of two-sidedness, a clearinghouse for depictions of duality, a binary star at the center of a galaxy of orbiting doubled figures. This makes his public discourse an unusually rich site for the exploration of doubled talk as an inventional resource.

In this chapter, I situate the sort of doubled address enacted by Barack Obama within the racial problematics of U.S. citizenship. I begin by correcting some common misconceptions about the sort of duality presented in Obama's discourse, framing it not as dialectical but instead as paratactic. His discourse, in other words, does not enact a synthesis of dichotomous ideas but instead invites the maintenance of multiple perspectives. I then align these discursive habits with *double-consciousness* as it was articulated by the African American theorist and critic W. E. B. Du Bois. While it is clear that Obama came into contact with Du Bois's work and while it is reasonable to conclude that Obama was influenced by Du Bois, my argument here is that the habits of speech and thought that can be developed as inventional resources in Obama's public discourse are analogous to Du Bois's ideas and thus can be brought into more vivid relief through a comparison with them.

I then propose *democratic double-consciousness* as a term to describe a specific variation of double-consciousness that is inflected explicitly toward democratic citizenship, as an attitude or perspective, manifest in discourse, that is particularly productive for democratic civic engagement. This concept is given more theoretical depth by articulating it with the work of contemporary political theorists who both emphasize the racial tensions fundamental to conceptions of U.S. citizenship and attribute to effective democratic citizenship qualities that recall double-consciousness, either implicitly or explicitly. The purpose of this chapter is to position Obama's public address as presenting discursive practices that are rooted in the racial problematics of U.S. citizenship and that may in turn serve as resources for the invention of effective citizenly speech.

Nondialectical Duality

Cassandra Butts, a friend of Obama's from his time at Harvard Law School, suggests that "Barack has become a kind of human Rorschach test" and that people "see in him what they want to see."[4] Obama himself, in the prologue to his second book, *The Audacity of Hope,* suggests that he is something of a "blank screen on which people of vastly different political stripes project their own views."[5] This assessment is supported, in part, by the review in the previous chapter of some of the existing literature on Obama, which does show that critics, pundits, and scholars are able to locate a variety of influences and perspectives in Obama's public persona and public discourse. But at the same time, Obama does not seem to be entirely a tabula rasa, because the views projected upon him tend to assume a distinct bifurcation. Many observers tend to experience Obama not as an empty receptacle but specifically as a doubled figure.

Terms suggesting paradox and duality fairly inundate the discourse that people use when describing Obama. Sasha Abramsky notes, for example, that Obama's friends refer to him variously as "a pragmatic idealist, a radical moderate, or, sometimes, a moderate radical."[6] "Depending on whom you talk to," he says elsewhere, "Obama is either a pragmatist in the garb of an idealist or an idealist hiding behind a mantle of pragmatism."[7] Similarly, Carlin Romano describes Obama as expressing in his speeches and statements "a rich moral idealism tempered by astute pragmatism."[8] The journalist Fareed Zakaria calls Obama a "practical idealist."[9] Richard Wolffe notes a "peculiar combination of risk and self-discipline, of high-minded dreams and practical details, of restlessness and roots."[10] Newton Minow, former chair of the Federal Communications Commission in the Kennedy administration who came to know Obama in Chicago, describes him as "a universalist who doesn't deny his particularity."[11] Jonathan Alter suggests that Obama exhibits a "compassionate dispassion" in his interactions with others.[12]

Many of these observations go beyond merely acknowledging that Obama's commitments can be difficult to pin down to attributing a special advantage to Obama's doubleness, generally having to do with a perceived ability to understand issues, situations, or people from multiple perspectives. As Bakari Kitwana puts it, "Obama points to himself as an example of a person who in his personal life has had to straddle both sides and implies that voters should trust that he has a vested interest all around."[13] David Remnick, similarly, quotes one of Obama's college friends who describes him as "someone who was able to straddle things," not only racially but between and among various groups and identities.[14] Justin A. Frank suggests that Obama has learned to manage his racial duality and even to cultivate it as an advantage, so that "his split parts have evolved into different self-states that convince most audiences—and at times even himself—of his total authenticity."[15] Ben Wallace-Wells, in *Rolling Stone,* describes Obama as "at once an insider and an outsider, a bomb thrower and the class president." "I'm somebody who believes in this country and its institutions," Wallace-Wells reports him saying. "But I often think they're broken."[16]

Some associate this tendency to "straddle" things, to stand as an outsider and as an insider, to be both supporter and critic, builder and bomb thrower, with Obama's apparent facility with the fundamental political art of compromise. Remnick, for example, suggests that "Obama's predilection . . . is to reconcile possibilities" and that "conciliation [is] his default mode, the dominant strain of his political personality."[17] Abramsky notes that "Obama is, both by personality and as a strategic political choice, a conciliator, a community builder," and Shelby Steele acknowledges that "one thing Obama instinctively knows is the art of bargaining."[18] To "be a successful politician you had to make a few compromises along the way," and, as Remnick points out, "Obama rarely failed to make them."[19]

Others see the tendency to compromise as a political liability. In an insightful piece in the *New York Times,* for example, titled "Why Is He Bi?," Maureen Dowd laments Obama's tendency "to be on both sides at once," to participate "in all political identities" without seeming "deeply affiliated with any side except his own."[20] David Maraniss notes that Obama "came from all sides and no sides," and Remnick describes Obama's second book, *The Audacity of Hope,* as designed "not so much to straddle the ideological divide as to embrace the entire landscape of political opinion all at once."[21] Justin Frank, in a chapter titled "Accommodator in Chief," pathologizes Obama's proclivity toward compromise, referring to it as an "obsessive bipartisan disorder" and suggesting that it is "the sometimes puzzling outward manifestation of a fundamental organizing principle of his psyche, which he must protect from challenge in order to maintain his sense of calm and self."[22] Paul Krugman, writing in April 2011, deep into Obama's first term in office, captures at least some of the collective anxiety and disappointment among Obama's supporters when he asks, "What happened to the inspirational figure his supporters thought they elected? Who is this bland, timid guy who doesn't seem to stand for anything in particular?"[23]

These observations suggest that the political art of compromise is itself two sided, a revered skill without which little can be accomplished in public life that when thought to be carried too far, past some indefinable limit, can become a symptom of confusion or, worse, wimpiness. As many of these observations come from midway through his first term in office, they may also tell us something about the perhaps overinflated sense of hope with which many imbued Obama's election.[24] Most important, they illustrate that Obama's duality is not only a self-presentational conceit; while it certainly is a part of the public persona that he carefully crafts, it also invites particular responses from his audience. This doubled persona can itself be thought of as a form of address, then, neither merely a faithful expression of Obama's inner psyche nor a communicative action. More than a cautionary tale about the possible perils of compromise in the face of great expectations, these observations suggest that Obama's public persona models figures of identification that can be recognized and, perhaps, emulated.

Rhetorical analyses of Obama's discourse have drawn our attention to these doubled tropes as a mode of address but tend to cast them as evidence of his dialectical frame of mind. Donovan S. Conley suggests, for example, that Obama's "signature move . . . involves juxtaposing and then surpassing the extremes of U.S. political debate—individualism and compassion, religion and science, collective security and individual rights, patriotism and shame (and so on)."[25] Martin J. Medhurst, similarly, observes that Obama's "narrative signature" entails a wide variety of "dialectical opposites, with ordinary/extraordinary, easy/hard, seen/unseen, right/wrong, few/many, rise/fall, and past/future being chief among them." He frequently introduces "policy that transcends the extremes," Medhurst continues, "often by incorporating the best features of each into a reconceptualized whole," which "has the effect of making Obama appear to be the more reasonable of the contending parties, because he is seen as considering both sides before issuing a Solomonic decision that often splits the difference."[26] David Frank, drawing in part on Medhurst's work, calls our attention to "Obama's treatment of binary oppositions with dissociative strategies, his embrace of paradox, and his understanding of the contradictory impulses of human nature," characteristic of "a rhetorical strategy that links particular truths to a larger, more universal value."[27]

Other observations, however, suggest that, though Obama does have a tendency to organize the world into dualities, he is motivated not by transcendence but by a more nuanced multiperspectivalism. Laurence Tribe, "Obama's intellectual mentor at Harvard,"[28] recalls working with him on an essay that Tribe eventually published, and he praises especially Obama's ability to keep "both values in mind" as they worked through the legal arguments.[29] Remnick notes that when he was teaching at the University of Chicago, Obama "insisted that students learn to understand and argue all sides of a question."[30] Alter describes Obama as having "a knack for getting inside the heads of others and seeing things from their perspective, even if that perspective (whether it was Tom Coburn's or an anti-Obama protestor at a town meeting) struck his friends as irrational."[31] Kloppenberg suggests that the particular brand of pragmatism to which Obama was exposed at Harvard emphasized "the importance of hearing all sides of a dispute before forming a judgment. He had learned that leaders in crisis situations should follow a few rules of thumb: Listen to diverse points of view. Weigh rosy projections against worst-case scenarios. Above all, put yourself in the other person's shoes."[32] In a 2004 interview for *The New Yorker,* Obama himself argues that teaching constitutional law "keeps you sharp" because "you need to be able to argue both sides. I have to be able to argue the other side as well as Scalia does. I think that's good for one's politics."[33] This is a habit of thought characterized not by the dialectical resolution of binaries but by the appreciation of duality.

This latter habit of mind, as described by Obama's friends and associates, most closely corresponds to the doubled discourse that is the focus of this book. While his addresses do frequently juxtapose the extremes of contemporary U.S. political culture, these extremes rarely are absorbed into a universal frame that dissolves their opposition. His addresses frequently present differing points of view and observations on political life, not as incompatible or as necessitating compromise or synthesis but instead in a way that preserves the integrity of each of them. In the 2009 inaugural, for example, Obama "reject[s] as false the choice between our safety and our ideals," arguing instead that "the rule of law and the rights of man" as stated by the "Founding Fathers" do not have to be given up "for expedience's sake." The tension between ideals and expediency is not challenged but allowed to stand. There is no Solomonic splitting of differences or dissolution of division in the warm bath of universal value but instead a perspective that acknowledges both the tension and the opposing values that animate it and urges us to keep both sides in view. Similarly, in that same address, while "the question before us [is not] whether the market is a force for good or ill," we are not asked to substitute some more transcendent or universal question; instead, we are asked to recognize both that capitalism's "power to generate wealth and expand freedom is unmatched" and that, "without a watchful eye, the market can spin out of control." We are not being asked to decide whether the market is good or bad but instead are being encouraged to understand that the market is both good and bad. This is not a contradiction that must be resolved; in fact, it is quite often Obama's argument that an attempt to resolve such tensions is what causes the trouble in the first place.

Stanley Fish is correct to call this a *paratactic* style, one characterized by "the placing of propositions or clauses one after the other without indicating . . . the relation of co-ordination or subordination between them."[34] Richard Lanham refers to parataxis as a "syntactic democracy," meaning that it sets the various items it addresses all upon a single plane, without explicit order or hierarchy.[35] Generally a rhetoric of compromise or synthesis requires connectives to indicate the relationship between ideas, but within a paratactic logic every idea, perspective, and tradition gets equal say.[36] Parataxis, of course, begins with duality, as there have to be at least two things set aside each other; this is not a dialectical duality that is destined to be resolved but instead a coincident duality that brings two voices or positions into view at the same time and holds them there, before the eyes of the audience, without guidance as to their relationship. Importantly, though parataxis begins with duality, it is not limited by duality. Whereas a dialectical logic presupposes two categories, perspectives, or traditions, parataxis is not limited by binary logic; any number of things might be addressed paratactically, and as a result this is a logic that scales freely, spawning additional duality and coincidence in a geometric progression toward multiplicity. Still, it is this initial duality and the potential of Obama's discourse to invite it that are of central concern in this book.

Double-Consciousness

Among the literature that Obama gathered up from the library when he was a young man looking for ways to understand himself was the work of W. E. B. Du Bois. Obama told Wolffe that when he visited Africa for the first time, to come to terms with his father's legacy, he came to a new understanding of "what W. E. B. DuBois [sic] wrote about one hundred years ago, the sense of displacement, the sense of being on the outside."[37] And Kloppenberg finds that "elements of W. E. B. DuBois's [sic] seminal *Souls of Black Folk* surface both in Obama's discussions of his divided consciousness concerning race . . . and in his penetrating analysis of the tragic inevitability of slavery's poisonous legacy, the inherited prejudices and social practices that doomed radical Reconstruction."[38] It is not especially surprising that Obama should be familiar with Du Bois or that an African American of mixed race might particularly seek out and draw upon Du Bois's work on double-consciousness as a resource to help parse out some of the problematics of his own identity. In fact, it would have been difficult for anyone in the United States who came of age intellectually in the 1980s and 1990s, as Obama did, and who was interested in race relations in the United States, to avoid some experience with Du Bois, given the number of books and articles focused on him, and on double-consciousness, that were published during that time period.[39]

What is important for the purposes of my argument is not the extent to which Obama was directly influenced by Du Bois; it is enough to suggest that the reference is not implausible. For, regardless, the citizenly resources that can be invented through a critical engagement with Obama's public discourse are usefully illuminated by Du Bois. Throughout the remainder of this chapter and the remainder of the book, when I note points of intersection and resonance between Obama and Du Bois it is to illustrate the critical utility of a Du

Boisian vocabulary, not to assert that Du Bois had a direct or explicit influence on Obama. The focus of my argument is that Obama's public discourse offers inventional resources for democratic citizenship and that the work of elucidating and enhancing these resources is facilitated by extending Du Bois's double-consciousness as a heuristic. The next section of this chapter characterizes these particular resources as precipitating a *democratic double-consciousness,* but at this point a brief explication of Du Boisian double-consciousness will both locate the key terms that I am borrowing from Du Bois and illustrate the extent to which I am modifying them for the purposes of my analysis.

Double-consciousness is widely recognized as Du Bois's "most important gift to the black literary tradition."[40] He introduces the idea in his monumental *The Souls of Black Folk,* published in 1903 and recognized today as both a literary classic and a theoretical touchstone. The central place of this work in the African American canon and its place in the literary canon of the United States more generally is, for all intents and purposes, universally recognized. It is a work of profound variety and astonishing range—comprising essays, memoirs, fiction, polemic, and snippets of song—but duality courses through the volume as a recurrent theme, as an organizational pattern, and perhaps especially as a literary style.[41]

Double-consciousness manifestly and figuratively infuses the book, melding the various genres and topics into a coherent whole.[42] The precise meaning of the term "double-consciousness" has been and continues to be the focus of discussion and debate; critics and theorists disagree about what Du Bois actually may have intended by it, upon what sources he may have drawn in formulating it, and to what specific life experiences he may have been responding; all have been thoroughly explored.[43] But almost everyone begins by quoting in full the following passage, from near the beginning of "Of Our Spiritual Strivings," the first essay in *The Souls of Black Folk:*[44]

> After the Egyptian and Indian, the Greek and Roman, the Teuton and
> Mongolian, the Negro is a sort of seventh son, born with a veil, and
> gifted with second-sight in this American world,—a world which yields
> him no true self-consciousness, but only lets him see himself through
> the revelation of the other world. It is a peculiar sensation, this double-
> consciousness, this sense of always looking at one's self through the eyes
> of others, of measuring one's soul by the tape of a world that looks on
> in amused contempt and pity. One ever feels his two-ness,—an Ameri-
> can, a Negro; two souls, two thoughts, two unreconciled strivings; two
> warring ideals in one dark body, whose dogged strength alone keeps it
> from being torn asunder.

> The history of the American Negro is the history of this strife—this longing to attain self-conscious manhood, to merge his double self into a better and truer self. In this merging he wishes neither of the older selves to be lost. He would not Africanize America, for America has too much to teach the world and Africa. He would not bleach his Negro soul in a flood of white Americanism, for he knows that Negro blood has a message for the world. He simply wishes to make it possible for a man to be both a Negro and an American, without being cursed and spit upon by his fellows, without having the doors of Opportunity closed roughly in his face.[45]

It is perhaps fitting that double-consciousness, in Du Bois's formulation, is itself doubled. He seems to mean two things at once, each of which has significance with regard to Obama's public discourse.

On the one hand, of course, double-consciousness is a burden, a particularly vivid sort of alienation that, as Adolph Reed notes, Du Bois understood as "arising broadly from blacks' contradictory and marginal position in American society."[46] Double-consciousness is a response to and a marking of the racial problematic of U.S. citizenship, through which invitation and rejection are insolubly linked in a presentation of citizenship that is tantamount to a form of torture so severe it threatens to tear the individual asunder. Under such circumstances a coherent identity can be fashioned only through dogged individual will, and even then it is under the constant threat of dissolution. Double-consciousness relies upon a conception of citizenship as an active and self-constitutive practice, something that is invented by those who are and would become citizens—always already constrained by cultural and political structures—rather than something that is conferred. Double-consciousness presumes, in other words, some degree of agency; indeed, it is the frustration of this agency that provokes it. Double-consciousness results from a longing to join with others in a civic culture that is characterized by contempt, pity, and strife, so that Du Bois recognizes citizenship as a mode of engaging with self and others that is embodied, enacted, and rife with affect—it is a "sensation." It entails as well the doubled sense that not only would one's personal position be improved through inclusion but also that inclusion would begin to ameliorate some of the discord and disease of the larger political body. It arises from the hard work of attempting to join that larger political body coupled with the humiliation that accrues as these attempts repeatedly are rejected by that body, like a parasite or an infection. Double-consciousness derives from the power of a dream that never is diminished in its constitutive force even as it seems forever deferred.

Double-consciousness is intimately implicated in ways of seeing, as Du Bois deploys tropes of sight, perspective, and point of view. Double-consciousness, as he describes it, is the "peculiar sensation" of always being forced to view "one's self through the eyes of others." Double-consciousness permits, as Du Bois puts it, "no true self-consciousness," in that an individual afflicted with double-consciousness cannot experience an unreflective authenticity, the thorough and unself-conscious presence that is bestowed only on those members of the dominant culture who need not be concerned with how they are viewed by the other. "From the double life every American Negro must live," Du Bois writes elsewhere in *Souls,* "as a Negro and as an American . . . from this must arise a painful self-consciousness, an almost morbid sense of personality and a moral hesitancy which is fatal to self-confidence."[47] To be a person of color in the United States, Du Bois suggests, is to be always conscious of the fact that one's identity is in part imposed by the white others who gaze upon one's body.

Taking Obama's memoir, again, as a form of public address, we can see him evoking this experience when he describes the reaction of people who discover his mixed-race heritage "searching . . . my eyes for some telltale sign" or guessing at his "troubled heart . . . the mixed blood, the divided soul, the ghostly image of the tragic mulatto trapped between two worlds."[48] This passage depicts Obama being defined by the gaze, an identity being thrust upon him through the power of looking, as others—he does not identify their race—search his body for evidence to support their own assumptions. The doubled motive evident in Du Bois's conception is evident here as well, as Obama recognizes this as not only a personal experience but also as a moment that evokes the racial problematic of U.S. citizenship. In his memoir, he shows himself pointing out, in an interior monologue, that "no, the tragedy is not mine, or at least not mine alone, it is yours, sons and daughters of Plymouth Rock and Ellis Island, it is yours, children of Africa . . . so that you need not guess at what troubles me, it's on the nightly news for all to see."[49] Obama dismisses a romantic or transcendent effort to treat his troubled heart by mending the divisions of his soul and instead recasts the observation as an opportunity to bring into focus a telling tension inherent in contemporary U.S. public culture. It is this deferment of the merely personal in favor of the public, born from the denial of the privilege to see oneself as fully self-constituted, self-possessed, and self-confident, that is the price of citizenship.

On the other hand, the capacity for this deferment also is the promise of citizenship. Though Du Bois recognizes that African Americans are motivated by a need "to merge [their] double self into a better and truer self" and thereby resolve the ambiguity and alienation inherent in double-consciousness, the merging that he recommends actually resists this motivation. "In this merging," he explains, he "wishes neither of the older selves to be lost." In this way the burden of double-consciousness also seems a sort of blessing, a gift of second sight; the reference to the folklore about seventh sons and children born with a caul possessing preternatural or extrasensory abilities emphasizes the idea that African Americans possess particular powers of perception not granted to those to whom society grants a true and unmediated self-consciousness. To the extent that this second sight is valuable, the double-consciousness that enables it must be retained. "Double-sighted, double-conscious," David Levering Lewis concurs, "the African-American must neither reject America nor vanish into it."[50] While African Americans strive to develop a coherent identity, they should not wish entirely to abandon the split imposed by the dominant culture. As Du Bois describes it in *Souls,* Lewis writes, "the divided self would not remain flawed, compromised, unstable, or tragic. It would become in time and struggle stronger for being doubled, not undermined—the sum of its parts, not the dividend."[51] What Du Bois "wished to eliminate," according to Ernest Allen Jr., "was not the two-fold character of African-American life, but rather its most alienating, imposed characteristics."[52] Du Bois was influenced by Hegel, but the duality that he described was not a binary to be resolved or transcended; Du Bois wished to retain the duality but to recast it over time so that it became more of an adaptive advantage.[53] What is less often noted is that the advantages that may accrue to double-consciousness are public as well as private. Double-consciousness is a resource valuable not only for its potential to address the alienation experienced by marginalized individuals who would gain full recognition as citizens but also for its potential to help repair the rent fabric of civic life by providing perspectives and attitudes that contribute to the practices of citizenship itself. "Pressing the logic of Du Bois's formulation," as Thomas Holt puts it, "suggests a radical proposition: that African-Americans should celebrate their alienation, for *it* is the source of 'second-sight in this American world.'"[54]

An evolution in the presentation of double-consciousness from individual burden to collective contribution is evident in the way that Obama portrays himself in his memoirs. In his first book, *Dreams from My Father,* he tells us that as a teenager he "learned to slip back and forth between my black and white worlds, understanding that each possessed its own language and customs and structures of meaning," and yet he remained motivated by a conviction "that with a bit of translation on my part the two worlds would eventually cohere."[55] This youthful faith in a sort of transcendence was rattled, however, by a persistent "feeling that something wasn't quite right" about the fact that white girls sometimes mentioned in the middle of a conversation that they liked Stevie Wonder, or that people he didn't know sometimes asked if he played basketball, or that the school principal told Obama that he was "cool." "There was a trick there somewhere," he recalls his younger self thinking, "although what the trick was, who was doing the tricking, and who was being tricked, eluded my conscious grasp."[56] The trick, of course, was that the divisions Obama felt—in himself or in the worlds between which he learned to move—could never be fully transcended because he could never be racially neutral. People always will recognize him as black, and so the privilege of transcending race can never fall to him; the sacrifices of double-consciousness present primarily a personal adaptation deployed to address the resultant alienation.

In his second book, *The Audacity of Hope,* written ten years after *Dreams from My Father* and expressing a more mature outlook, Obama explores more explicitly the potential of double-consciousness as a collective adaptation. He explains that he is a "prisoner of my own biography" and that he "can't help but view the American experience through the lens of a black man of mixed heritage, forever mindful of how generations of people who looked like me were subjugated and stigmatized, and the subtle and not so subtle ways that race and class continue to shape our lives."[57] In this later portrayal, Obama is no longer just a lost and lonely teenager but a racially marked and representative citizen. The biracial confusion of his youth has now been translated into an ability "to stand in somebody else's shoes and see through their eyes."[58] Obama describes his youthful disagreements with the white grandfather who raised him, for example, as presenting an opportunity for him to learn to become more attentive to opposing points of view and to realize "that in insisting on getting my own way all the time, without regard to his feelings or needs, I was in some way diminishing myself."[59] He explicitly connects this insight to his realization that he is "obligated to see the world through George Bush's eyes, no matter how much I may disagree with him."[60] Though he dismisses this "awakening" as "nothing extraordinary," in Obama's case the ability to slip back and forth between his own point of view and his grandfather's—or his own politics and Bush's—is presented as rooted in and to some degree a product of his mixed-race heritage. His mature public persona, as presented in *The Audacity of Hope,* acknowledges the doubled effects of double-consciousness; Obama is both alienated from white America by virtue of the fact that he looks like those who have suffered and do suffer racial oppression, and he recognizes that he has gained from that alienation an appreciation and perhaps an aptitude for the essential political and citizenly skill of seeing the world from another's perspective.[61]

The evolution presented in Obama's memoirs is of double-consciousness from a literary trope to a useful civic skill, from a concept that he found useful while crafting his personal identity to a potentially valuable mode of public and political engagement. It is this second mode of double-consciousness that is of particular interest to this book. Though its political capacity can never be fully dissociated from the deeply personal experiences that led initially to its formation—and, indeed, as generations of feminist theorists have reminded us, to achieve such a dissociation between the personal and the political would be catastrophic to both—the focus of this book remains the political, civic, and democratic potentials of double-consciousness. Double-consciousness, as Lawrie Balfour puts it, would not only "allow us to 'see in the dark' but to assist us in 'seeing the darkness,'" so that we, as democratic citizens, may simultaneously clear our vision without abandoning the critical ability to discern the obstacles that cloud our vision.[62] As citizens, even as we continue to strive to erase the exclusionary components of our civic culture, we must never succumb to the temptation to pretend that their influence does not continue to be felt. In order to see past the obstacles, we also have to see the obstacles; the new modes of inclusive citizenly engagement that we seek to invent must always retain something of the alienation that prompted their formulation. Double-consciousness, thus, should be recognized as an endemic and permanent feature of democratic citizenship.

Democratic Double-Consciousness

I use the term *democratic double-consciousness* to refer to the mode of citizenly engagement that may be invented through a critical engagement with Barack Obama's public address. In doing so, I intend to signal both an investment in Du Bois's thought and a distinction from it. While both Du Bois and Obama are addressing a U.S. civic culture that is informed by the long-standing implication of race in the definitions and practices of citizenship, they do so from different positions, in different eras, with access to different forms of power, and are addressing different audiences and with different purposes. As a result, a double-consciousness invented through engagement with Obama's discourse would differ from one invented through engagement with Du Bois's discourse—Obama's discourse of duality, crafted by a public orator trying to gain and then hold the highest U.S. elected office, arguably would lend itself more directly to the invention of a politically and publicly engaged form of double-consciousness.[63] Obama's public discourse provides an opportunity to observe a mode of address that brings into a contemporary milieu some perspectives and sensibilities that are continuous with Du Bois's thought, but with several key shifts in emphasis. These shifts do not present a wholesale split with Du Bois but rather constitute a form of what Kenneth Burke might term "casuistic stretching," an extension of double-consciousness toward new horizons of meaning while yet remaining faithful to the original principles.[64] The object is to extend some of Du Bois's original insights and formulations so that they are more useful in describing the inventional resources that can be made available through Obama's public discourse.

I want to emphasize three specific extensions of Du Bois's thought. First, as the resources of democratic double-consciousness are articulated in the public discourse of Barack Obama, their manifestation as a public or collective practice is emphasized over their expression as a private or individual experience. Obama often speaks overtly about citizenship, so much so that many portions of his public addresses take the form of lessons in civics. While, as I have argued, Du Bois's formulation is implicitly connected to African American experiences of U.S. citizenship, in Obama's discourse the inventional resources most relevant to imagining double-consciousness are more explicitly linked to citizenship. Second, in Obama's public discourse double-consciousness is manifest as a mode of address. This follows the connection between double-consciousness and citizenship but extends it to account for the emphasis in this project on citizenship as a discursive act. Double-consciousness, in this context, is seen more broadly as a way of performing citizenship, in addition to being a psychic state imposed through the frustrations and exclusions of citizenship. To this extent, democratic double-consciousness visualizes an active and agentive role for citizens as they address power, justice, and one another. Finally, in referring to "doubleness" and "duality" I intend to designate not a final rigid polarity but rather an initial bifurcation. As Obama addresses widely diverse audiences, presentations of duality compound upon one another in a paratactic logic that opens the possibility for a proliferation of voices and perspectives. Democratic double-consciousness engenders a critique of a monovocal public sphere that may eventuate in practices of citizenship that far exceed the apparent limitations of doubleness.

These three key extensions of Du Bois's conception of double-consciousness—an emphasis on its value as a resource for public citizenship, its manifestation in a mode of address among citizens, and its potential to serve as an entering wedge for the proliferation of multiple points of view—characterize democratic double-consciousness as it is invented through an engagement with Obama's discourse. They mark out the key principles or axioms of democratic double-consciousness. Naturally, as the analysis proceeds, these three components may at times shade into one another and, more important, may participate in the invention of other expressions of duality, but they will serve as the guiding analytical *topoi*.

The remainder of this chapter is devoted to developing these *topoi*. I begin by situating the discussion within the context of the long-standing articulation of race and citizenship in the United States, to support the assertion that it is both appropriate and productive to draw upon concepts that arise out of that troubled racial history, like double-consciousness, as sources of a contemporary theory and critique of citizenship. Then the first two components of democratic double-consciousness are developed in detail. Its value as a resource for citizenship is developed by drawing upon the work of political theorists and others who have described citizenship practices in terms that resemble or suggest forms of double-consciousness, as well as on work in this vein that draws explicitly from Du Bois. Its manifestation as a mode of address is then developed by drawing on work that has emphasized Du Bois's own meticulous attention to matters of rhetorical style. The third component of democratic double-consciousness, its capacity for opening up possibilities for multiple voices and perspectives, is not treated separately in this chapter because it is best understood as a consequence or effect of the other two and thus is developed throughout the remainder of this book in conjunction with explorations of double-consciousness as a resource for citizenship and as a mode of address.

Of course, in generalizing double-consciousness from a particular effect of oppression into a concept with broader reach, we must not forget the specific forms of physical and psychic torture that drove Du Bois to formulate the concept in the first place. And we must not assume that Du Bois's personal experience can be made to stand in for the experience of all African Americans or even for all twentieth-century African American male geniuses.

This is a note of caution frequently recommended by scholars. Reed, for example, acknowledges that the "'double-consciousness' or 'two-ness' image has been a remarkably, but variously, evocative characterization of the black American condition for several generations of observers identified with widely different intellectual and political projects."[65] But such appropriations may be, Reed continues, "naïve or inattentive with respect to matters of history and context" and "presume an unchanging black essence" rather than "the possibility that Du Bois's construction bears the marks of historically specific discursive patterns, debates, and objectives."[66] C. Eric Lincoln, as well, notes that while it may not be surprising "that Du Bois's personal apperceptions would be seized on and universalized because of his stature as a scholar and intellectual," nonetheless we must remember that Du Bois "if objectively evaluated would have been exceptional in any company irrespective of race" and that therefore his ideas should not be understood as "the archetype to an alleged psychosis which disparaged an entire subculture."[67] And while Shamoon Zamir realizes that the "frequency with which Du Bois's description is used suggests that it is commonly accepted as a universally and transhistorically true analysis of a tragic aspect of African-American self-consciousness," he also reminds us that

"Du Bois's dramatization of 'double-consciousness' is a historically specific and class-specific psychology."[68]

I do not wish to argue that Du Bois's ideas either do or do not present an accurate or universal account of African American experience. I can discern no consensus in the scholarly literature on this point, I would not want to posit any universal experience in any case, and as a white person I am in no position to offer an otherwise informed opinion. Certainly we should move forward cautiously and avoid overgeneralizations. But this reasonable forbearance should not in turn cause us to limit preemptively the reach of Du Bois's ideas. When Du Bois wrote in *The Souls of Black Folk* that "the problem of the twentieth century is the problem of the color line," Carole Lynn Stewart suggests, he "meant that all those who had undergone oppression because of modern imperialism shared a kind of 'family resemblance,' and thus they might be looked on as harbingers of new possibilities for democracy and freedom."[69] While it will not do to stretch Du Bois's ideas unrecognizably and then still call them Du Bois's, an equal and perhaps greater sin would be to neglect the inventional potential of his ideas out of a reluctance to make use of them in ways that he may not have intended. Our public culture has been immeasurably diminished through the neglect of such resources as may be provided through the public discourse of women, persons of color, individuals who identify as LGBTQ, and others who have been and are excluded from full U.S. citizenship. Double-consciousness was formulated within a particular context, of course, as all ideas must be, but this is no reason to dismiss its value as the basis for observing and theorizing practices that are well suited to contemporary democratic culture in the United States.

It also is valuable to remember that Du Bois's ideas did not spring from his forehead fully formed, based only on his own personal experiences; an important aspect of the context within which he developed the concept of double-consciousness is its intellectual genealogy. Reed points out that at the time that Du Bois was writing and ever since, cultural theory of all types described an alienated and divided self, and the self imagined by such theory "was by no means restricted to representatives of marginalized and subordinate groups like blacks or women."[70] Double-consciousness, from its inception, was an intellectual project as much as a political one and indeed presents an exemplary moment when those two motives cannot productively be separated. Du Bois's ideas are valuable as a starting place and as a goad for thinking about how public discourse that has been shaped by the racial inequity inherent in conceptions of U.S. citizenship can be drawn upon as a resource for addressing and ameliorating those same inequities.

As McPhail reminds us, double-consciousness invites us to "address the material realities of difference without losing sight of the possibilities of identification."[71] The democratic double-consciousness that I am describing invites us toward a conceptual and politically engaged space where our identities are neither lost through accommodation and assimilation nor imagined as isolated or fragmented, where our obligations to our fellow citizens limit the range of our possibility while at the same time opening up the very possibility of citizenship. Characterized as a mode of civic engagement, it is a middle space without the connotations of political inaction and isolation that sometimes accrue to such positions. Even as democratic citizenship carries both a price and a promise, so too does democratic double-consciousness present both a burden and a benefit.

Citizenship and Race

If we fail to acknowledge the "mixed inheritance" that characterizes our political and civic practice, Balfour argues, then "we limit our capacity to see the contours of the present. And we handicap efforts to construct a democratic theory that is itself broadly democratic."[72] Democratic double-consciousness stimulates a form of citizenly discourse that draws upon our mixed inheritance with regard to race and citizenship and is informed by the problematics of racial exclusion that have characterized the history of U.S. citizenship, and as such it presents an especially rich resource for the invention of speech well suited to addressing the contours of the present. This echoes Danielle Allen's statement that "interracial distrust in the United States serves as a case study for thinking about the modes of citizenship that are generally needed to deal with congealed distrust."[73] Without trust and inclusion our politics are stillborn, and it is in the spaces where the trust between citizens has been most sorely tested that the resources for its revival most likely will be found.

The implication of race and citizenship is not new, of course, and is not limited to the United States. Susan Lape argues, indeed, that citizenship was understood through racial parameters even in ancient Athens, which of course is at least the implicit exemplar of all contemporary democracies.[74] Helen Heran Jun, similarly, defines "the institution of citizenship" in general as "a narrow discursive field in which differentially racialized groups are forced to negotiate their exclusion in relation to others."[75] This may be the "dark little secret" of democratic citizenship, kept from view in order to foster the mythologies of unity upon which many contemporary notions of citizenly practice depend: "the largely unexplored fact that the citizenship construct, although widely accepted as requiring equality among those with the status, also contains a lesser-known aspect that accepts and, arguably fosters differences in the treatment of individuals living in a society."[76] As citizens are defined, categorized, included, and excluded according to race, citizenship is premised upon and defined in relation to race.

Rogers Smith has reminded us that U.S. citizenship "has always been an intellectually puzzling, legally confused, and politically charged and contested status."[77] The links between race and citizenship are especially vivid in the United States because of the pox of slavery in our collective past. Judith Shklar reminds us that the harsh fact of "black chattel slavery stood at the opposite social pole from full citizenship and so defined it" and that slavery's legacy, including the fear of being reduced to something like slavery and thus to something less than a citizen, has been a presence in every subsequent discussion or redefinition of American citizenship.[78] Our collective conversations about citizenship have taken place within this context. "Much of the history of race relations in our country is a story of pain and inhumanity and guilt," Kenneth L. Karst points out, yet "that very history has served as the crucible for the American ideal of equal citizenship."[79] The continuing attempt to strive toward this ideal is responsible for many of the redefinitions of citizenship status and practice, so that race is baked deeply into even our most progressive revisions of citizenship.

Given an imbrication of race and citizenship that is both fundamental and pervasive, a thorough review is well beyond the scope of this book. But its significance and prevalence can at least be hinted at by a brief summary of a handful of some of the more consequential legal decisions and legislative acts through which U.S. citizenship has been defined in racial terms. Again, the concept and enactment of citizenship that inform this book exceed its legal status, but, as Rogers Smith reminds us, laws such as these not only reflect the motives and prejudices of a culture but also "literally constitute—they create with legal words—a collective civic identity."[80] The legal status of citizenship has a profound influence on the discursive articulation of citizenship. The racial context for U.S. civic identity is established early on, indeed at the same moment as the nation itself. One of the most prominent places that the United States Constitution defines citizenship also is one of its few oblique references to slavery —the clause of Article 1, Section 2, that determined that representatives to Congress would be apportioned among the states "according to their respective Numbers, which shall be determined by adding to the whole Number of free Persons, including those bound to Service for a Term of Years, and excluding Indians not taxed, three fifths of all other Persons." Many of the legislative and legal attempts to expand the scope of citizenship in the United States or to normalize its practices have been attempts to address the deficiencies of citizenship experienced by these "other Persons."

One prominent event would be the Dred Scott decision of 1857, which Karst marks as "surely the most infamous decision in the the Supreme Court's history" and as the "dismal starting point" in the long march within the United States toward the ideal of equal citizenship, a goal that sometimes has seemed to retreat into the distance as quickly as it is approached.[81] Dred Scott was a slave in Missouri who had resided with his owner in states where slavery did not exist; he sued for his freedom on the grounds that his residence in these "free" states, where he could not have been held legally as a slave, had rendered him free. Chief Justice Roger B. Taney, in the 7–2 majority opinion, determined that Scott could not bring suit in court because he was not a citizen, and he was not a citizen because he was of African descent. He found that "the enslaved African race were not intended to be included" in the words of the Declaration of Independence and that the Constitution refers "directly and specifically to the negro race as a separate class of persons" who "were not regarded as a portion of the people or citizens of the Government then formed."[82] This decision thus rendered not only slaves but also the sizeable population of free African Americans quite literally beyond the pale, marking them as so far differentiated from whites that they were to partake in neither the privileges nor the burdens of citizenship. Eventually, the Fourteenth Amendment negated Taney's ruling and introduced into the Constitution an explicit definition of citizenship: "All persons born or naturalized in the United States, and subject to the jurisdiction thereof, are citizens of the United States and of the State wherein they reside." Notably, the text of the Fourteenth Amendment makes no explicit mention of race in relation to citizenship.[83] Though the Amendment was a direct response to Taney's language in the Dred Scott case, which defined citizenship explicitly in racial terms, it does not explicitly acknowledge the extent to which citizenship has been implicated with race—together with sex, marital status, and other matters—throughout U.S. history.

In 1896, the Supreme Court relied on the Fourteenth Amendment in *Plessy v. Ferguson*. Homer Plessy had been recruited by the Citizens' Committee of New Orleans to challenge Louisiana's law requiring persons of African descent to ride in segregated railroad cars. The majority opinion, against Plessy and written by Justice Henry Billings Brown, argued that states were free to enact laws that construed citizenship as a narrow legal or political status while restricting various rights deemed merely "social." In the dissenting opinion Justice John Marshall Harlan argued that "In respect of civil rights, common to all citizens, the constitution of the United States does not, I think, permit any public authority to know the race of those entitled to be protected in the enjoyment of such rights." He even went so far as to predict that this decision will "prove to be quite as pernicious as the decision made by this tribunal in the

Dred Scott Case." But though Harlan's dissent praised the Thirteenth, Four-teenth, and Fifteenth Amendments for having "removed the race line from our governmental systems," it also predicted that "the principles of constitutional liberty" would enable whites to remain "the dominant race in this country . . . for all time."[84] Harlan's eloquent and forceful dissent illustrates Smith's obser-vation that "Americans have mixed inconsistent views, expressing both inclusive and exclusionary motives, in their most basic legal definitions of citizenship."[85]

The same passage in the U.S. Constitution that determined that an Afri-can American slave should be counted as three-fifths of a citizen also excluded "Indians not taxed." This meant that Native Americans who identified as mem-bers of tribes were not to be considered among the citizens counted in order to determine representation in the House of Representatives. Technically, Native Americans who were fully assimilated into the dominant white culture would be so counted, but, though Native Americans occupied land over which the U.S. government claimed authority, they were not considered citizens. This status enabled the Indian Removal Act of 1830, which authorized the forced removal of Native Americans residing in the southeastern United States to areas west of the Mississippi River.[86] The Civil Rights Act of 1866 asserted that "all persons born in the United States and not subject to any foreign power . . . of every race and color, without regard to any previous condition of slavery or involuntary servitude" were citizens—but still excluded "Indians not taxed."[87] Of course, the Fourteenth Amendment, passed two years later, famously declared: "All per-sons born or naturalized in the United States, and subject to the jurisdiction thereof, are citizens of the United States and of the State wherein they reside." However, a Senate Judiciary Committee four years after that determined that this definition did not apply to Native Americans and in fact that "the four-teenth amendment to the Constitution has no effect whatever upon the status of the Indian tribes within the limits of the United States."[88] It was not until the Indian Citizenship Act of 1924 that Native American citizenship was codified.[89]

Laws regarding immigration and naturalization are especially instructive regarding the ways that citizenship has been marked by race. As Smith reminds us, "for over 80 percent of U.S. history, American laws declared most people in the world legally ineligible to become full U.S. citizens solely because of their race, original nationality, or gender."[90] Justice Harlan's dissent from the Dred Scott decision, for example, acknowledged that "the Chinese race" was "so dif-ferent from our own that we do not permit those belonging to it to become citizens of the United States. Persons belonging to it are, with few exceptions, absolutely excluded from our country."[91] The Chinese Exclusion Act of 1882 banned Chinese immigration for ten years, required identification certificates for Chinese laborers already in the United States, and declared that "hereafter no State court or court of the United States shall admit Chinese to citizenship; and all laws in conflict with this act are hereby repealed."[92] The Chinese Exclusion Act was extended and amplified in 1892 by the Geary Act, which required Chinese immigrants in the United States to obtain and carry a "certificate of residence," under penalty of deportation.[93] Such legislation follows in the tradition of one of the earliest laws passed by the U.S. Congress, the Naturalization Act of 1790, which created a path toward U.S. citizenship available only to immigrants who were "free white person[s]" (this is why even Native Americans who were willing to break all ties with their tribes still could not enjoy full U.S. citizenship), and the subsequent Naturalization Acts of 1795 and 1798 lengthened the residency requirements but retained the racial qualifications. The Naturalization Act of 1870 amended these laws to offer a path toward citizenship "to aliens of African nativity and to persons of African descent."[94] The Chinese Exclusion Act remained in effect, in one form or another, until the passage of the Chinese Exclusion Repeal Act of 1943.[95]

Not all implications of citizenship and race had the status of legal statutes. In the so-called Gentlemen's Agreement of 1907, the Empire of Japan agreed not to allow its citizens to emigrate to the United States; in exchange, the United States agreed not to impose restrictions on immigration from Japan. This did not explicitly restrict citizenship and was largely ineffective in any case, as Japan continued to issue passports for emigration to Hawaii.[96] But in 1944, in *Korematsu v. United States,* the Supreme Court upheld Franklin Roosevelt's wartime removal of American citizens of Japanese ancestry to relocation camps, again policing the limits of citizenship along racial lines.[97]

The 1923 Supreme Court ruling regarding Bhagat Singh Thind, a native of India, reveals the convoluted logic that often follows upon racialized conceptions of citizenship. Thind argued that he was Caucasian and thus "white," but the Court determined that the framers "intended to include only the type of man whom they knew as white," a category that "does not include the body of people to whom the appellee belongs."[98] Consequently, natives of India living in the United States were stripped of their citizenship; they could not become citizens until the passage of the Luce-Celler Act of 1946. The 1923 decision had the consequence of stripping citizenship from U.S. women who had married men who were natives of India, because the status of a woman's citizenship was tied to that of her husband.[99]

Of course, that was not the only circumstance in which U.S. citizenship was policed by sex and marital status. The U.S. Constitution of 1787 did not mention women specifically and, through this silence, left intact the state and local laws restricting women's access to full citizenship.[100] Unlike nineteenth-century Native Americans, women legally were citizens but possessed what

Nancy F. Cott describes as "less-than-participatory citizenship," meaning that they could not participate in all of the privileges of white male citizens—including the ownership of property and the right to vote.[101] It was more than 130 years of struggle by activists and orators, including many who understood the goal of women's suffrage as intimately connected to the abolition of slavery and full citizenship rights for African Americans, that eventuated in the passage of the Nineteenth Amendment, in 1920. Even then, the citizenship status of married women remained tied to the citizenship status of their husbands until Franklin D. Roosevelt signed the equal-nationality treaty in 1934. It was not until 1952 that the McCarran-Walter Act specifically asserted that the "right of a person to become a naturalized citizen of the United States shall not be denied or abridged because of race or sex or because such person is married."[102]

I cannot begin to give adequate attention here to perhaps the most visible and divisive present-day issue regarding the relationship between race and citizenship—and one in which a rhetoric of double-consciousness resonates around the metaphor of the *border*—U.S.-Mexico immigration reform.[103] Barack Obama has supported strengthening border security and providing a pathway to citizenship for undocumented immigrants, including in his 2013 State of the Union Address, but as I write this there has been no significant reform legislation. Other contemporary issues that point to the continually shifting boundaries of full U.S. citizenship include access to birth control and abortion, marriage equality, LGBTQ rights, statehood for the District of Columbia and Puerto Rico, the PATRIOT Act and other post-9/11 legislation that restricts or redefines civil liberties, whether access to adequate health care is a right of citizenship, the efforts to remake or to defund public education, and myriad other issues too numerous to list.[104]

Still, it was African American access to full citizenship that was most central to Du Bois's thinking in 1903, when he wrote *The Souls of Black Folk,* just a few years after *Plessy v. Ferguson,* and that is most relevant as a context for exploring the inventional resources provided by the public discourse of Barack Obama. Du Bois wrote that there are "no truer exponents of the pure human spirit of the Declaration of Independence than the American Negroes" and that "the Negro Problem" is "a concrete test of the underlying principles of the great republic."[105] The second sight inculcated by African American second-class citizenship may provide a resource through which the values expressed in the founding documents might be made manifest. The centrality of black-white race relations to redefinitions of U.S. citizenship is further emphasized by Danielle Allen, who begins *Talking to Strangers* in Little Rock, Arkansas, with the implications of the 1954 Supreme Court decision in *Brown v. Board of Education of Topeka, Kansas* that "separate educational facilities are inherently unequal."[106] Allen argues that the widely circulated pictures of that day in Little Rock that depicted Elizabeth Eckford as a lone black figure at the center of a white mob showed that the "democracy of the United States in 1957 was made up of not one but at least two, and maybe three, four, or more, peoples, all living in the same polity but under different laws, with differential rights and powers, and with different habitual practices of citizenship." It was through this display of doubled and multiplied citizenship, she suggests, that "U.S. democracy was reconstituted."[107]

Citizenship and Duality

My purpose in this section is to show that approaches to citizenship across a range of different disciplines and schools of thought have employed terms and concepts that resemble ideas associated with Du Boisian double-consciousness. To put it another way, I mean to suggest here that double-consciousness, as it was described by Du Bois, is a deeply generative notion that finds analogues and parallels in many different approaches to citizenship. This may not be surprising and indeed may be seen as a confirmation of Du Bois's assertion that double-consciousness offers a particularly rich resource for thinking about citizenship.

There is wide agreement, for example, that in order to function together as citizens we must be able to imagine the world, however temporarily, from another's point of view—not a hypothetical point of view only but the point of view of another actual, embodied individual or group of individuals with whom or against whom or for whom we are attempting to engage as citizens. To be an effective citizen, Ronald Beiner reminds us, "I must project myself, imaginatively, into a position I do not actually occupy, in order to enlarge my perspective and thereby open up an awareness of new possibilities, to broaden the range of alternatives from which my judgment then makes its selection."[108] Note that Beiner's description begins with a dual perspective, one's own perspective and another's, as the enabling move that opens up additional possibilities, broadening as a consequence of bifurcating. Citizenship, in this view, is a mode of engagement through which an individual both relinquishes the limitations inherent in perceiving the world from a single perspective and yet retains her or his awareness of those limitations; the more limited perspective is not transcended, relinquished, or forgotten but is taken up with others within a broadened range.

The dual commitment to the individual self and to the (potentially) shared culture that is captured in Du Bois's understanding of double-consciousness, in which a citizen seeks not to lose her or his identity within in the larger collectivity while still becoming a full participant within that collectivity, is suggested by Jason A. Scorza, who notes "the intrinsic value of the practice of civic friendship, which contributes both to the development of the individual and to the shared democratic culture."[109] Ruth Lister further articulates this notion from a feminist perspective, calling for "a universalism that stands in creative tension to diversity and difference and that challenges the divisions and exclusionary inequalities which can stem from diversity." Using a paradoxical term, Lister suggests that the "underlying principle that can guide us is that of a *differentiated universalism,* which embodies the creative tension between universalism and particularity or difference."[110] Democratic double-consciousness, as I am defining it, speaks directly to this creative tension, to the divided obligation to the particular and to the universal that Lister describes. Catriona McKinnon writes that "the two key skills of civility" are the paradoxical pair "acknowledgement of difference, and empathy," skills that would enable both the recognition that lines of demarcation exist and an effort to reach across those lines, skills that would both result from and foster double-consciousness. This framework can be said to embrace the value of "wholeness," in Danielle Allen's terms, rather than "oneness," as the paradigm trope of American civic culture, as wholeness can encompass a recognition of diversity and heterogeneity that often is elided when conceiving of contemporary American political culture as homogeneous and coherent.[111]

George Kateb has contributed substantially to this line of thought, conceiving of the practices of citizenship in ways that both comport productively with democratic double-consciousness and thicken its conceptualization. He proposes both "detached attachment" and "democratic individualism" as paradoxical and multivalent attitudes that are required for effective citizenship. He describes a sort of alienation, as well, as essential to citizenship when he argues that citizenship requires that "one must first learn some detachment from oneself, from one's familiar attachments, without, of course, pretending to be able or wanting to abandon them."[112] Such a citizen would necessarily be doubled, dual, at once both detached from oneself and connected with others in a way that mitigates that detachment. The ideal citizen that Kateb is describing would be able "to play many roles" and also "to reverse roles" and through this role-playing foster the facility for perspective-taking that is fundamental to citizenly engagement. If an individual is inflexibly bound to the expression of a single authentic self—to true self-consciousness—then she or he will find it extraordinarily difficult to accept another's perspective as legitimate or to occupy that perspective as valid. Citizens well adjusted to the demands of contemporary democratic practice, in this view, must always stand slightly off to one side when contemplating their relationship to the collective, observing themselves as they are observed by others, semidetached, as Obama often is said to be, from both themselves and their culture.

This stance may recall the "moral hesitancy" that Du Bois describes as characteristic of someone who is denied a unitary consciousness; rendered unable to perceive an issue or opportunity only from her or his own point of view, an individual possessing double-consciousness would be incapable of acting without self-reflection and thus would be subject to a form of hesitation endemic to a lack of moral certainty. On the one hand, this sort of ethos might be something of a disadvantage, as it would allow others to make points on issues or gain access to resources more decisively and rapidly; on the other hand, it also is a deeply democratic form of restraint that allows time for the apprehension of complexity and the consideration of input from and effects on others besides oneself.[113] "One must remain somewhat strange to oneself and respect the strangeness of other individuals," Kateb explains. "Only then is there honesty in the face of human complexity. One must welcome the dialectic in one's soul of resistance and acceptance."[114] A moral hesitancy allows time for this dialectic and removes perhaps some of the pressure and expectation for its transcendence.

Democratic double-consciousness entails a recognition that the duality of the productively engaged citizen is both a part of the price of citizenship and a part of the promise. The adaptive ability to walk a mile in the other person's shoes, as the old saying has it, to see the world from another's perspective, doesn't come free. The potential benefits of this perspective-shifting—empathy, inclusion, reciprocity—are essential ingredients of a productive mode of contemporary citizenship, but they also are a result of or an effect of the burden of acknowledging oneself as a member of a civic culture. Alex Zakaras reminds us that "it is crucially important that we recognize democratic citizenship not only as a status that confers rights and other benefits but also as a role that involves substantial responsibilities."[115] Zakaras's phrasing suggests that this mutually dependent quality of democratic citizenship is especially emphasized when citizenship is understood as a role performed rather than a status conferred, because it is through interaction with others that one's obligation to them becomes a "sensation," in Du Bois's words, a felt experience. It is one thing to theorize about the necessity of mutual recognition and quite another to acknowledge the experience of feeling obligated to one's fellow citizens.

Many theorists and critics have drawn upon the metaphor of "friendship" and especially on Aristotle's notion of "civic friendship" to capture this ethic of obligation. Danielle Allen reminds us that "Aristotle argued that good citizenship amounted to interacting with strangers in ways that look like friendship even if, since they lack the emotional charge, they don't feel like friendship."[116] The emphasis on sight and on appearances is characteristic of Aristotle but also echoes Du Bois's understanding of the power inherent in the gaze that citizens direct at one another.[117] When "Aristotle explains . . . that friends are 'second selves' to each other," he means that civic friendship is characterized by an ability to recognize one's self in others, to see one's self as not only interacting with others but as being in others; the result is an "equitable self-interest," Allen explains, in which we experience duality through the practice of acting in the self-interest of ourselves and of our civic friends, simultaneously.[118]

It follows, then, that a productive notion of citizenship necessarily entails a rejection of what Michael Sandel describes and critiques as the ubiquity of the ideal of the "unencumbered self," unbound by political commitment. Because the unencumbered self seeks to avoid defining itself within a civic context, it seeks also to avoid the dualism that inevitably would result; the unencumbered self is unitary and undivided because it also is isolated and unburdened. Such an individual would bear a strong resemblance to the "sincere" speaker that Elizabeth Markovits critiques, an individual who is dedicated to the maintenance of "an authentic, unitary self" and thus is wildly unsuited to democratic citizenship.[119] Persons who imagine themselves to be unencumbered, in other words, retain the privilege of being entirely sincere—of retaining a "true self-consciousness" in Du Bois's terms—for they can express precisely what they mean, can make use of their interactions with others as opportunities to deliver an unmodulated reflection of their inner commitments without regard for the commitments and biases of their audience; such persons need not stand to one side to observe themselves acting in response to the encumbrances represented by others because they do not imagine themselves to affected by such encumbrances. As Markovits puts it, for such persons "there is no split self . . . that would allow the speaker to manipulate her own words for greatest effect."[120] Such a unified self might be free from the taint of alienation that Kateb and Du Bois describe but also would be "inadequate to the liberty it promises."[121]

The resonance between these understandings of the performance of democratic citizenship and Du Bois's thought can be made more explicit; in fact, as Balfour puts it, "the American democratic experiment" may be viewed "through the writing of W. E. B. Du Bois." "Du Bois's work is rightly celebrated for the living force of its metaphors," she continues, drawing attention especially to "double-consciousness, the Veil, the color-line—perhaps the best-known images of his best-loved book."[122] These concepts, associated as they are with the most painful chapters of U.S. history, disallow the impulse to construct a sanitized version of that history and, to the extent that they may be incorporated into contemporary theory and critique, disallow also the possibility of engaging in theoretical and critical projects that might also contribute to that sanitizing impulse. Correspondingly, they allow the possibility that the pain associated with that history may be the source of ameliorative modes of engagement, because no such amelioration can be imagined that does not draw for inspiration upon the racial traumas that continue to inform contemporary civic culture. Du Bois's thought, and particularly the cluster of metaphors that orbits around the central concept of double-consciousness, offers "badly needed guidance" for a critique of contemporary democratic culture that would be accomplished within the full view of this mixed heritage.[123]

Du Bois understood that the alienation from the practice of democratic citizenship experienced by African Americans could be a source of double-consciousness and that double-consciousness was a source of insight about U.S. citizenship. This may be, in part, what he means when he writes that "Negro blood has a message for the world."[124] Certainly, it is what Meira Levinson argues when she writes that in order make possible a culture in which "'American' will no longer be taken as synonymous with 'White,'" members of the dominant culture must "become conscious of their own limitations of perspective, and their own subjection to the gaze and judgment of others."[125] What Levinson argues, in other words, is that a more widespread experience of double-consciousness could be a potent force for change, altering perceptions and, as a result, modes of interaction. Those who bear double-consciousness are open to the probability that their own position is invented through interactions with others rather than a result of some form of pure expression. Here again is the sense of "moral hesitancy" fostered by double-consciousness, a sort of provisional detachment that heightens observational capacity and opens space for self-reflection, here connected explicitly to the potential for the duality characteristic of double-consciousness to open out into a multiplicity of perspectives. Such multiplication requires time and attention, resources that can be depleted in an environment characterized by a commitment to sincerity, unity, and moral certitude.

When Du Bois writes that he would not "Africanize" America, he means that he would not do so *thoroughly;* a thoroughly Africanized America would be just as dysfunctional as a thoroughly white America, to the extent that it would be just as unable to cultivate and appreciate the gifts of double-consciousness. The key is to cultivate and sustain what Stewart calls the "racial ambiguity" of U.S. citizenship, the not-quite-thorough alienation felt by all citizens in a democratic culture that is characterized by inequity, a feeling that can be drawn upon by those same citizens as a way of repairing that alienation.[126] A productive understanding of double-consciousness includes acknowledging that "it becomes a prison house only if it is understood to signify just racial difference. When it is understood to signify plurality and ambiguity, humankind's 'variety,' then it should not be overcome—it represents both hope and tragedy."[127] If the self-conscious duality and perspective taking suggested by double-consciousness were to become more widely experienced and enacted as practices of citizenship, even and especially among members of the dominant culture, then the burden of double-consciousness would fall less tragically on the marginalized. This again is the hope and tragedy, the promise and price, of citizenship. Democratic double-consciousness, as I am defining it, can be understood as an essential component of a robust democratic citizenship, because a democratic culture would become more robust as more citizens, not only the marginalized ones, cultivate at least a doubled perspective. In this view, double-consciousness is both inherent in a pluralistic culture and a resource that can be drawn upon for the correction and improvement of that culture.

The litany of exclusionary legal statutes through which U.S. citizenship has been policed and defined can be understood as an extended effort to retain a culture characterized by the valorization of a singular, monovocal, unitary perspective. As Justice Harlan reveals in his *Dred Scott* dissent and as is evident throughout this long and shameful history, most of those laws and statutes were enacted for the purpose of retaining a relatively homogeneous conception of citizenship. This would aspire to be a culture untroubled by double-consciousness; at the same time, of course, it is the effort to invent and sustain such a culture that fosters double-consciousness in the first place, at least among those who are excluded yet long to participate. Such laws contribute to the constitution of a civic identity that would remain willfully ignorant of its own heritage, its ability to address the divisive issues at its core gravely diminished through its refusal to embrace the experiences of those who are the targets of that division.

Individuals subject to the shrunken form of civic identity constituted through such monocular discourse cannot adequately account for their own participation in a civic collectivity and thus cannot adequately know themselves. Inclined to imagine themselves as unencumbered, they cannot recognize themselves as "members of this family or city or nation or people, as bearers of that history, as citizens of this republic."[128] The ubiquitous responsibilities we have to our fellow citizens always impinge upon the expression of our individual identities; we express our individuality by addressing both "our personal and cultural inheritance," the mixed inheritance through which we recognize that our personal identity depends upon the simultaneous presence of others. We cannot imagine ourselves as democratic citizens and yet also imagine ourselves as unitary, unencumbered selves relieved of the burdens of double-consciousness. We must learn to acknowledge, as Du Bois puts it, the peculiar sensation of "looking at one's self through the eyes of others" if we are to come to know ourselves as citizens. And, in particular, because public discourse is the medium of citizenship, we must learn to address one another in an idiom that is inflected by a self-reflective duality.

Doubled Speech

In order for democratic double-consciousness to provide an inventional resource for citizenly communication, it must be understood as a mode of address. It cannot be merely a way of seeing or knowing or being but must also be a way of speaking. It is a consciousness manifest in language and cultivated through language, and it is this quality that makes it available as a mode of civic interaction. This connection, too, is rooted in Du Bois's thought; Du Bois was a writer, after all, an extraordinarily prolific one, and a notable rhetorical stylist in his own right who, at least in his early work, seemed to place great faith, not unlike Obama, in the power of a well-crafted public statement. As Zamir points out, "Du Bois's foregrounding of listening, speech, and writing ties consciousness to the production of language and to the relationship of self to others."[129] Double-consciousness is an effect of the experience of communicating with others within a civic context; an individual "feels his [or her] two-ness" as a result of attempting to engage with others as a citizen while being rejected by others as a noncitizen. This political quality of double-consciousness marks Du Bois's thought as inherently more engaged than that of the philosophers with whom he often is considered: "Du Bois is able to *locate* the subject in relation to the world, particularly the political and social realms,"[130] as Zamir puts it, and as a result his notion of double-consciousness is both "social" and "creative."[131] Du Bois's double-consciousness is not merely a philosophical hypothesis but a mode of embodied performance, "social" because it is not manifest merely within a soul or within individual consciousness and creative because it encourages the invention of discourse through a critical response to the discourse of others.

Democratic double-consciousness, as I am defining it, emphasizes this facet of Du Boisian double-consciousness as a way of talking to strangers, a way of speaking that acknowledges that one's self always is defined in part through engagement with others and that is characterized by an effort to perceive one's self from the perspectives of strangers. Democratic double-consciousness, in other words, is manifest in a mode of discourse through which citizens address one another as citizens. Figuring double-consciousness as an inventional resource for the discursive enactment of democratic citizenship draws our attention to its rhetorical qualities. The verbal figures associated with democratic double-consciousness both express the dual perspectives that characterize it as a mode of engagement and invite others to share these doubled points of view. Acknowledging that democratic double-consciousness is associated with specific formal characteristics is in keeping with Du Bois's own predilections; as Arnold Rampersad points out, a "notion of duality is central to Du Bois'

46

perception," the "most important concept" in *The Souls of Black Folk* "reflects Du Bois' sense of dualism," and Du Bois's thinking and writing exhibits a tendency "to reduce apparent chaos or flux to duality, dilemma, or paradox." "Du Bois' concern with form is constant," Rampersad continues, "reflecting the influence of his training in the classical tradition of rhetoric and oratory taught to him at Fisk and Harvard."[132] The manner of expression associated with double-consciousness is not incidental but fundamental, as is evidenced by the fact that throughout *Souls* Du Bois describes double-consciousness in an idiom replete with balanced phrases and doubled figures.

The significance of doubled tropes in African American literature has prompted Henry Louis Gates Jr. to declare that the "black tradition is double-voiced."[133] He argues that "figures of the double"—doubled figures of speech as well as double-voiced mythical figures, such as Esu Elegbara—figure prominently in the search for a voice that is depicted in so very many black texts, both providing an opportunity to develop a voice out of a position of marginality and enabling that voice to attain legibility beyond those margins. Du Bois's articulation of double-consciousness participates in this tradition, so that the experience of reading his prose may foster or suggest the feeling of two-ness that he ascribes to the African American experience.

The doubled tropes that I have mentioned would fall into this category— parallelism, paradox, isocolon, metaphor, parataxis—and Gates specifically mentions *chiasmus,* the doubled figure through which ideas are repeated in an inverted order, as "perhaps the most commonly used rhetorical figure in the slave narratives and throughout the subsequent black literature," one that "is figured in the black vernacular tradition by tropes of the crossroads, that liminal space where Esu resides."[134] Through the recursive metabolism of such doubled figures, the duality *imposed* upon African Americans as a result of oppression and marginalization is then *expressed* as an adaptive invitation toward the inventiveness and flexibility necessary for effectively making their way in the world with themselves and with others. Du Boisian double-consciousness is both an effect of the ways that African Americans are figured in language and a mode of expressing or critiquing that figuration. Democratic double-consciousness, in drawing upon Du Bois, who in turn is participating in a long African American literary tradition, is deeply rooted in African American experience. In adapting double-consciousness to describe a mode of democratic citizenship, the "second sight" these traditions and experiences bring to the study and enactment of citizenship is broadened in its application.

While double-consciousness might be invented through engagement with almost any type of discourse, including theory and literature, it is most properly extended into a democratic context through the engagement with public discourse. Public discourse is the vehicle of citizenly enactment and circulation and is distinguished by its express purpose of locating its subjects politically and socially. When Barack Obama's public discourse provides the inventional resources for democratic double-consciousness, it becomes a resource upon which his audiences may draw when they are seeking ways to speak and think in public, as citizens. Rather than hearing Obama's speech as an outward effect of an inner psyche, inventional criticism enables his public address to be heard as a performed resource for the further performance of citizenship. Obama's discourse, in this view, encourages and perhaps to some extent even authorizes citizens to perform a citizenship inflected by double-consciousness.

Conclusion

Obama is something of an icon of duality, as both his critics and his supporters seem compelled to note in their assessments of him. Many observers discern a transcendent or dialectical quality in Obama or in his public discourse, but actually the most prominent feature of his speech is a resistance to the centripetal force of dialectic. His public discourse, whether his speeches or his memoirs, presents a tendency to hold two (or more) perspectives in balance rather than a desire to synthesize a new whole out of the fragments. This paratactic logic presents any number of political liabilities, not the least of which is a recurrent assertion that Obama lacks backbone or mettle or even identifiable positions. But it also presents particularly rich resources for the invention of discourse fostering citizenly engagement, in the form of attitudes, motives, and their attendant rhetorical forms. These resources are suggestive of double-consciousness, as originally conceived by W. E. B. Du Bois in *The Souls of Black Folk*. Like Obama's presentation of duality, Du Bois's formulation carries both negative and positive valences. The tendency always to see oneself through the eyes of another, for example, is the result of repeated attempts to be accepted by a culture that is committed to sustaining its homogeneity, a cultural alienation that contributes to a self-alienation that deprives the subject of a true self-consciousness. On the other hand, Du Bois notes that this self-reflective stance and heightened attunement to the impositions of other points of view, born of the struggle to hold "two souls, two thoughts, two unreconciled strivings" together through the force of will, can be the source of a "second-sight in this American world," a perspective on U.S. citizenship that is denied to those privileged enough to enjoy a unitary consciousness.

The resources of double-consciousness that are manifest in Obama's public discourse are not mere copies of Du Boisian concepts, time ported from the early twentieth century into the early twenty-first; because Obama's discourse is directed toward contemporary audiences in a plural culture in an effort to bring individuals together as a public poised for political engagement, it necessarily emphasizes particular facets of double-consciousness. The three most important of these facets for the purpose of this book are the assertion, implicit in Du Bois, that double-consciousness is a productive mode of citizenship; the manifestation of double-consciousness as addressed through a recognizable and reproducible language of duplex figures, tropes, and schemes; and the potentiality for double-consciousness, when manifest as a mode of discourse, to foster the invention of multiple voices and perspectives.

The remainder of this book explores the possibilities and limitations of democratic double-consciousness as a resource for rhetorical invention through the analysis of case studies consisting of speeches delivered by Barack Obama. The particular mode of inventional criticism through which the resources of democratic double-consciousness are made available takes the form of a close reading that focuses on the inventional potentialities of this public discourse. The next chapter focuses on Obama's most thorough articulation of democratic double-consciousness, his well-known "race speech" delivered in Philadelphia on March 18, 2008. Here Obama addresses explicitly the racialized problematics of American citizenship, working firmly within the literary and theoretical traditions evoked by Du Bois to formulate not only a way of speaking about race but also a way for citizens to speak to one another. The text presents racial division as representative of and analogous to broader divisions within the contemporary public and political sphere, and in this way it serves as a paradigm statement of democratic double-consciousness and will inform the remainder of the analyses in this book.

CHAPTER 3

A More Perfect Union

B arack Obama was not the presumptive candidate.[1] In the 2008 Democratic primary, that was Hillary Rodham Clinton, New York senator and
former U.S. First Lady. She was well known and well respected and was backed
by the formidable Clinton political machine, well oiled from several decades
of almost continuous campaigning. When Obama won the Iowa caucuses on
January 3, 2008, it "in itself was not an earthquake," as Obama's campaign
manager, David Plouffe, put it, and did not by itself establish Obama as the
front-runner, but it did mean that Obama's campaign "would be riding the
crest of a wave of media coverage about everything we had done right while
Clinton was eviscerated for what she had done wrong."[2] The win in Iowa gave
the Obama campaign a stamp of legitimacy. This was a moment, as Obama put
it in his victory speech, "when the improbable beat what Washington always
said was inevitable."[3] But he still was far from gaining the nomination and in
fact lost to Clinton five days later in New Hampshire. He then eked out a partial victory in Nevada, where he lost the popular vote but gained more pledged
delegates than Clinton.[4] His campaign picked up endorsements from Caroline
Kennedy and Ted Kennedy and put in an impressive performance on "Super
Tuesday," February 5, when twenty-two states held simultaneous primaries. In
these contests, Obama won fourteen states, matched Clinton in the popular
vote, and earned fifteen delegates more than Clinton did.[5] Over the next two
weeks, Obama won decisive victories in a series of states, including Louisiana,
Maine, Maryland, Virginia, and Wisconsin.[6] Obama's lead in the delegate
count was large and growing, and, despite Clinton's wins in Ohio and Texas on
March 4, she began receiving some pressure from within the Democratic Party
to pull out of the race.

Then, on March 13, a controversy emerged that threatened the emerging
Obama juggernaut. In a report on *Good Morning America,* Brian Ross told
viewers that "Senator Obama has been a member of the same church in Chicago for twenty years, where his pastor has been the Reverend Jeremiah Wright,
the man who performed the Obamas' marriage ceremony, and the man Obama

credits for the title of his book, *The Audacity of Hope*." Over video of an African American church choir clapping and singing, Ross continued: "Reverend Wright has built a large and loyal following at his church, the Trinity United Church of Christ, on Chicago's South Side. With a powerful voice, and his strong words, Reverend Wright can be a mesmerizing presence. And he often uses the Gospel to affirm his strong political views. As in this 2003 sermon, damning the United States for its treatment of blacks." Wright is shown standing in his pulpit and shouting into a microphone: "The government gives them the drugs, builds bigger prisons, passes a three-strike law, and then wants us to sing *God Bless America*? No, no, no. Not *God Bless America*—God damn America! That's in the Bible, for killing innocent people. God damn America for treating its citizens as less than human!"[7] Other video clips shown in the report feature Wright referring to "white America" as the "U.S. of KKK-A" and castigating African Americans affiliated with the Republican Party as living "below the 'C' level—they live below the level of Clarence [Thomas], Colin [Powell], and Cond-amnesia [Condoleezza Rice]." A particularly controversial excerpt showed Wright, worked up into a righteous lather, reminding his congregation that "We bombed Hiroshima! We bombed Nagasaki, and we nuked far more than the thousands in New York and the Pentagon, and we never batted an eye!" "We have supported state terrorism against the Palestinians and black South Africans," he continues, "and now we are indignant? Because the stuff we have done overseas is now brought right back into our own front yards! America's chickens are coming home to roost!"

Any incipient notion that Barack Obama was a postracial candidate—or that his campaign successes proved that "Race doesn't matter!," as the crowd had chanted in January during his victory speech in South Carolina[8]—was rather stiffly rebuked by Ross's report. The images and the commentary placed Obama squarely into a black religious tradition about which most whites knew little or nothing and that some were sure to find disquieting. No matter that Ross and his team had combed through some twenty-nine hours of Wright's sermons that they had purchased on DVD from the Trinity website in order to locate these few fiery moments—the report dominated the news for the next few days.[9] Public reaction was forceful: Wright was referred to as "'anti-American,' 'ranting,' 'crazy,' 'divisive,' 'a self-centered jerk,' 'militant,' 'a hate-filled prophet,'" and "a racist."[10]

In this chapter, I focus on the speech that Obama gave in response to the controversy stirred up by the circulation of Reverend Wright's statements. That speech, which Obama titled "A More Perfect Union," is his most clarion call to democratic double-consciousness, an extended invitation to his audience to develop its own doubled vision; the balanced phrases and dual perspectives that characterize this text provide a lexicon through which a doubled consciousness might be provoked and expressed. Obama invites his audience not merely to observe the world as doubled selves but also to speak and act in it in accordance with this doubled perspective; he not only invites audience members to divide themselves but also models for them a manner of speaking and acting that perpetuates and deploys that division. In this speech, then, Obama gives voice to double-consciousness, translating it from sensation or perspective into a mode of address.

Because Obama's speech is a direct response to the circulation of snippets of Reverend Wright's sermons, I begin there, with Wright and his preaching. Then, I turn to Obama's speech text itself, to track the translation of double-consciousness from sensation to style. Its disposition, for example, outlines a process through which this translation can occur. Obama begins by presenting himself as an embodiment of double-consciousness, so that his own biracial body is an icon of potential racial reconciliation. Obama seems able to transcend the color line, absorbing into himself all the various fragmented identities divellicated by America's racial frictions. But though Obama may apparently seem poised then to position himself as a savior whose election would initiate a postracial millennium, this is not what he does. Instead, it becomes clear that presenting an embodied model of a doubled perspective is only the first step in mobilizing a way of speaking—the next step is to enlist the members of his audience as active participants. If this perspective is to contribute to citizenship as a practice, then a passive witnessing of double-consciousness is insufficient; citizens themselves must be invited to experience and enact doubled consciousness. Thus, in this speech Obama invites his audience to share the doubled perspective that is afforded by his own bifurcated body, making clear that racial reconciliation cannot be had by proxy; while he might embody double-consciousness himself, the key to a more perfect union is for his audience to become doubled. The disposition of this speech provides a process through which the Du Boisian double-consciousness that Obama portrays himself as possessing is translated into the democratic double-consciousness he asks his audience to cultivate. This speech offers the fundamental components of democratic double-consciousness: it is explicitly concerned with citizenship, it illustrates the way in which a fundamental duality might proliferate through parataxis into multiplicity, and it presents duality as a mode of address.

Blood in the Water

Adolph Reed has dismissed Obama's affiliation with Wright's church as "quite likely part of establishing a South Side bourgeois nationalist street cred because his political base was with Hyde Park/University of Chicago liberals and the foundation world."[11] Indeed Obama was and remains an irregular churchgoer; his grandparents, with whom he lived in Hawaii throughout his teen years, were largely secular; his mother, in Obama's words, "had a healthy skepticism of religion as an institution."[12] And it cannot be denied that Obama is preternaturally strategic. Mike Kruglik, who worked with Obama on the South Side, suggests that Obama saw Wright's church as "a power base" and that "you can't interpret what Obama does without thinking of the power factor."[13] But at the same time, the African American church continues to be one of the most enduring and influential institutions in black communities, so it is not surprising that much of Obama's work as a community organizer in Chicago was either church based or church supported. And if Obama actually were to choose a church through the cold calculations of a man positioning himself for political ascension, one wonders if he might have selected one with a less controversial pastor.

In any case, when Obama began to feel some pressure to join a church—a pressure felt, as he describes it, both externally, because so many of the community leaders he worked with expected it, and internally, because of an awaking religious consciousness—he found himself drawn to Wright's Trinity United Church of Christ. Obama developed a relationship with the Reverend Jeremiah Wright that, while perhaps not as close as some of his political opponents would have preferred to portray it, still was substantive. As Brian Ross's report pointed out, for two decades Obama counted himself a member of Wright's congregation, Wright officiated at Obama's wedding, and it was from one of Wright's sermons that Obama borrowed the title of his second book, *The Audacity of Hope*. It also was Wright who baptized Obama's two daughters, Malia and Sasha.

However, March 2008 was not the first time that Obama's long association with Wright had emerged as a potential political liability. Obama initially had invited Wright to deliver the invocation when he announced his run for the presidency in Springfield, Illinois, on February 10, 2007, but then rescinded the offer. In an interview published on February 6 in the *Chicago Tribune*, Obama evidently had sensed trouble, as he defended Wright and Trinity United against conservative critics. He enumerated the tenets of Reverend Wright's church— "commitment to God, black community, commitment to the black family, the black work ethic, self-discipline and self-respect"—and noted that because "those are values that the conservative movement in particular has suggested are necessary for black advancement" he would be "puzzled" that his critics "would object or quibble with the bulk of a document that basically espouses profoundly conservative values of self-reliance and self-help."[14] This preemptive rhetorical strike evidently had little effect, and, after much debate among Obama's campaign staff, Obama called Wright and told him that he did not want him to deliver the invocation because he "can kind of go over the top at times" and his campaign thought it would be better not to have him "out in the spotlight."[15] He still asked Wright to fly to Springfield, however, to pray with the Obamas privately, off stage.

A few weeks later, a widely circulated profile of Obama in the February 22 issue of *Rolling Stone* presented Wright precisely as over the top. The article, by Ben Wallace-Wells, described Trinity United as "a leftover vision from the Sixties of what a black nationalist future might look like" and emphasized Wright's potential influence on Obama: "This is as openly radical a background as any significant American figure has ever emerged from, as much Malcolm X as Martin Luther King Jr." The article also quoted the evangelical leader Jim Wallis as saying that "if you want to understand where Barack gets his feeling and rhetoric from . . . just look at Jeremiah Wright." And then a few weeks after that, perhaps as a consequence of the *Rolling Stone* article, Wright was invited to appear on the then-popular Fox News TV talk show *Hannity and Colmes*. Host Sean Hannity opened the segment by noting that a previous guest had described Trinity as a "separatist movement" similar to the Branch Davidians, who were besieged by the ATF, the FBI, and the Texas National Guard near Waco, Texas, in 1993. Hannity then suggested that the "Black Value System" described on Trinity's website is "racist," to which Wright responded by pointing out that this doctrine should be understood within the context of the writings by James Cone and others on Black Liberation Theology.[16] The exchange quickly deteriorated into incoherence as neither man would acknowledge the questions or statements of the other.

The *Rolling Stone* essay and the exchange with Hannity highlight the central problem raised by Wright and his sermons. It is true that some would understand them as being anti-American and as raising questions about Obama's faith. But, above all, they were a problem because they raised the specter of race. As T. Denean Sharpley-Whiting puts it, "Wright's homiletics had the effect of coloring Obama in a bit too darkly," threatening to tip the delicate racial balancing act that had so far characterized Obama's campaign.[17] Several white ministers from the United Church of Christ even traveled to Chicago and spoke at Wright's church in support of the embattled preacher, but that mattered little.[18] The fact was that Wright was simply "too identifiably black" for a "postracial" culture that had convinced itself that colorblindness was ideal, and certainly too race-conscious for a presidential campaign that had thus far studiously avoided the topic of race. The excerpts from Wright's sermons reminded many whites, as the *Economist* observed, "of everything they find alarming about black Americans."[19] Wright's comments also presented many white Americans with the potentially alarming possibility that persons of color might be saying things behind closed doors that they don't say in public, which meshed well with the suspicion felt by some that Obama was hiding something racially sinister behind a postracial façade. Wright's comments disturbed the placid surface of race relations that so many white Americans prefer to imagine.

When Wright became pastor at Trinity United, he determined to build a church in the tradition of Martin Luther King's Ebenezer Baptist, committed to addressing civil rights and social ills. Wright did built the church, from eighty-seven active members in 1972 into a congregation of more than eight thousand by the time he retired from the pulpit, in early 2008. He also initiated a number of social-outreach ministries, including HIV/AIDS care, hospice care, child care, and a reading program for the poor. The United Church of Christ, with which Trinity is affiliated, is a predominantly white denomination that describes itself, on its website, as open to all, "notwithstanding race, gender, sexual orientation, class or creed"; as "in the tradition of the prophets and apostles," the church believes that "God calls the church to speak truth to power, liberate the oppressed, care for the poor and comfort the afflicted." The denomination traces its history and its spiritual tradition, in part, to New England Puritanism.[20]

Of particular importance in understanding the context of the sermons that ignited the controversy that threatened to derail Obama's presidential bid is Wright's use of the *jeremiad,* a well-established pattern of preaching that originated with the Puritans and that has a long tradition within the African American church. Following a form established by some of the Old Testament prophets, such as Jeremiah, a jeremiad may begin with a reminder of the values of the community and of the great promise that follows from being true to those values before descending, like Jonathan Edwards's "Sinners in the Hands of an Angry God," into a vivid exploration of the degree to which the community has forsaken those values and of the resulting depths of depravity and unholiness into which it has fallen. Often, like Martin Luther King Jr.'s, well-known "I Have a Dream" speech, a jeremiadic sermon closes with a rousing call for a return to the neglected virtues and a stirring reiteration of the boon that would follow upon such a return.[21] This is a homiletic structure that itself participates in some aspects of the fundamental dualities that lie at the heart of African American culture specifically and U.S. citizenship more broadly. It allows a preacher simultaneously to praise and to blame the congregation, denouncing members' current behavior without ever losing sight of their ultimate capacity for redemption, castigating the current state of their culture while also affirming the foundational virtues upon which that culture rests. The jeremiad, in other words, is a part of a long tradition wherein "both black and white ministers damned America for its failings," within a form that at the same time "was filled with underlying optimism about America's fate and mission"; the jeremiad's "dark portrayal of current society never questioned America's prom-ise and destiny."[22]

The sermons referred to in Brian Ross's report on Reverend Wright are jeremiads, and the excerpts catch Wright just at the nadir of the form, in the midst of a full-throated condemnation of the contemporary falling away from righteousness. The sermon that contained the reference to America's chickens coming home to roost is representative and as such warrants close attention. It was delivered on September 16, 2001, and titled "The Day of Jerusalem's Fall." This was, as Ross points out, Wright's first sermon after the 9/11 terrorist at-tacks. It begins with a reference to the biblical prophet Jeremiah and to Psalm 137, which describes the Jews' poignant and poetic yearning for Zion, including memories of hanging their harps upon the willows, and concludes with striking images of violent revenge against the Babylonians who exiled the Jews from their homeland, including dashing the heads of their children upon the rocks. Wright takes this psalm as a something of a condensed jeremiad and focuses on those final verses as a cautionary tale about the dangers of allowing a thirst for vengeance to give rise to blood lust. He draws a number of associations be-tween acts of senseless violence portrayed in the Bible and the terrorist attacks of 9/11, "killing thousands for no reason other than hatred," and then between the desire for revenge felt by the Jews and those felt by Americans in the wake of the attacks. The psalm, Wright argues, "spotlights the insanity of the cycle of violence and the cycle of hatred," which "is a dangerous place to be."

At this point in the sermon, in what he calls a "faith footnote," Wright tells a story about seeing Edward Peck, a former U.S. ambassador to Iraq, on Fox News. In that broadcast, Peck had advised that "in the midst of all this horror, one of the things that seems to be largely ignored is the question of people look-ing carefully into the question of, why do they hate us this much?" "You don't have to apologize for a policy or alter it," he goes on. "But you ought to look at what your policies are being perceived as, by the other side, because that's what controls how they react."[23] Wright seizes upon these comments from Edward Peck, elaborating and embellishing them in a way that itself augments their invitation to the dualism of seeing things from the point of view of others. He sums up Peck's statement by asserting that it amounted to endorsing what "Malcolm X said when he got silenced by Elijah Mohammad . . . America's chickens are coming home to roost!"

It is at this point that the jeremiadic form expects a litany of depravity, and Wright fulfills this expectation with the gusto of an extraordinarily gifted preacher determined to bring before the eyes of his congregation verbal im-ages to rival anything found in the Old Testament. From the taking of North America from the Native Americans to the bombing of civilians in Grenada and Iraq and then on to Hiroshima, Palestine, and South Africa, he delivers a panoply of the ways that the United States has fallen away from its promise. His point, as he clarifies, is that "hatred begets hatred and terrorism begets terrorism," and as a result the United States should resist responding to violence with violence. He rounds out his jeremiad by offering three responses to his own prayerful question: "What should our response be right now in light of such an unthinkable act?" His first recommendation is a "self-examination" of our relationship to God and family, and he asks his congregation to turn "to the person sitting next to you, worshipping next to you," and say, "I love you." The second response is a call for "social transformation," for example through a re-evaluation of "the way we have been doing things as an arrogant, racist, military superpower," or by declaring a "war on greed," or by resolving to change "the mishandled educational system and provide quality education for everybody, every citizen, based on their ability to learn, not their ability to pay." And, finally, he asks his congregation to recognize that this "is the day that the Lord has made" and thus to "rejoice and be glad in it."[24]

Despite the fact that Wright's sermons trod a well-worn homiletic path with roots extending back to the Puritans as well as within the African American Christian tradition and despite the fact that much of the radicalism of Wright's comments was a result of their being taken out of context, still those snippets from his sermons quickly became a crisis too big to ignore. Years before, when the previous reports first introduced the Reverend Jeremiah Wright to a national and world stage, Barack Obama was merely the junior senator from Illinois and a long-shot presidential candidate. In March 2008, when Ross's exposé appeared, the situation was very different: Obama was a household name, and he was emerging as a front-runner for the Democratic nomination. The effect was further exacerbated because, even after the reservations about Wright in 2007, no one in the Obama campaign had bothered to read or listen to Wright's sermons, despite the fact that they were readily available. "We failed the candidate in that regard," Remnick quotes Plouffe as saying.[25] As a result, when the clips from Wright's sermons began to saturate the media, Obama had no prepared response. Jon Favreau, Obama's chief speechwriter on the campaign, watched some of the coverage on TV and felt sick. The Clinton campaign "sensed blood in the water."[26]

Obama tried to dampen the controversy with a series of short statements, such as the one posted at the widely read "Huffington Post" blog on March 14, which read, in part: "I vehemently disagree and strongly condemn the statements that have been the subject of this controversy. I categorically denounce any statement that disparages our great country or serves to divide us from our allies. I also believe that words that degrade individuals have no place in our public dialogue, whether it's on the campaign stump or in the pulpit. In sum, I reject outright the statements by Rev. Wright that are at issue."[27] Obama also posted a video on YouTube, in which he repeated this statement almost verbatim and ended by asking his supporters to "please forward this video on and get this message out to everyone you can."[28] In an interview with Keith Olbermann on MSNBC, Obama noted that he "wasn't in church during the time when these statements were made" and that if he had been he would have "expressed [his] concern directly to Reverend Wright." He also described Wright as being "like an uncle" with whom he talked not so much about politics as about family and faith.[29] The campaign removed Wright from its "African American Leadership Committee" so quickly that Wright heard about this from the news rather than directly from Obama.[30] But the controversy continued to build until it became clear that a more dramatic response was required.

Race Speech

Obama told his staffers that he wanted to give a speech on race. But any such speech would have to be written and delivered almost immediately, and his campaign schedule was tight, with Obama's days booked solidly from early in the mornings until late into the evenings. He insisted that none of his commitments over the next few days should be canceled and that he'd work on the speech "during downtime" in his hotel room at night. He told Plouffe: "I already know what I want to say in this speech. I've been thinking about it for almost thirty years."[31] He called Favreau and related some of his ideas in "stream of consciousness" fashion. "Well," remembers Favreau, "his stream of consciousness was pretty much a first draft." Favreau worked Obama's monologue into a basic structure on Sunday, March 16, and then e-mailed it to Obama that evening. Obama helped put his girls to bed and then settled down to work on the speech in earnest. At two or three in the morning, he sent a revised draft back to Favreau and others with a note saying that he needed one more night to work on it but that "This is what I want."[32] Obama didn't send staffers a completed draft of the speech until early in the morning of Tuesday, March 18, the day the speech was scheduled to be delivered.

The campaign selected the second floor of the National Constitution Center in Philadelphia as the venue; it was the first day of spring, the vernal equinox. The immediate audience was small, as the room could accommodate only about a hundred people besides members of the press, but the speech was broadcast live and distributed on the Internet.[33] It has been viewed and downloaded millions of times. It has been subjected to countless analyses from pundits and academics and has been the subject of several books. The analysis I offer here differs from these others because it seeks specifically to caste this speech as an inventional resource for citizenship. By attending closely to this text, and in particular to interactions between its stylistic and its ideational elements, I understand this speech as an archive of tropes associated with double-consciousness and as providing a mechanism through which that double-consciousness can be translated into a democratic double-consciousness that fosters the invention of discourse about race and, in turn, the invention of talk among citizens.

Embodiment

In thinking of this speech as an inventional resource for citizenly discourse, it is useful to understand it as an extended critique of the trope of "oneness" that Danielle Allen describes as dominating and constraining our current ways of addressing one another as citizens. This trope invites citizens to imagine themselves as "one people" with "shared dreams" residing in "one America" and "is generally inadequate to describe the proper aspirations of a democratic people to solidarity and community" because it cannot account for difference in the ways that individuals within the United States experience citizenship.[34] Obama's critique of this trope is evident as he reveals that he "chose to run for President at this moment in history" because he believes that we must "perfect our union by understanding that we may have different stories, but we hold common hopes that we may not look the same and may not have come from the same place, but we all want to move in the same direction." In this vision of the United States as consisting of diverse bodies moving together toward a common goal, Obama begins to articulate a mode of citizenship that would account for difference while retaining the notion of a single polity, a notion that would allow us a sense of U.S. identity that would not require us to imagine ourselves as identical. In Allen's terms, this might be expressed as a trope of "wholeness" that would describe "a people that is not one or homogeneous but, despite its diversity, a coherent, integrated body to which citizens willingly give their allegiance."[35]

Obama develops this critique of oneness, in part, from his "own story." Obama presents his own biracial body as a material manifestation of a duality that stands in stark contrast to the homogenous singularity that so often is held up as an ideal in the United States. In a series of carefully balanced phrases, he describes himself as "the son of a black man from Kenya and a white woman from Kansas," recalling that he has "gone to some of the best schools in America and . . . lived in one of the world's poorest nations" and that he is "married to a black American who carries within her the blood of slaves and slave owners."[36] As the paired terms accumulate—black man and white woman, Kenya and Kansas, best schools and poorest nations, slaves and slave owners—Obama's story presses against the confines of oneness. If the naïve tropes of oneness are inadequate to describe Obama, then certainly they are not up to the task of describing the United States. Yet Obama reiterates that this more capacious story, one that begins to divide our attention among different bodies and differing points of view, is no less quintessentially American than more familiar stories involving melting pots and homogeneity. In a rhetorical move that he repeats in many of his addresses, as we will see in subsequent chapters, he frames his discourse of duality as residing within U.S. political traditions and thus his own discourse as one of recovery rather than radical change. He promises that he "will never forget that in no other country on Earth is my story even possible"; while he admits that it is "a story that hasn't made me the most conventional of candidates," he also affirms that it is a story that nonetheless has fused man and country, as it "has seared into my genetic makeup the idea that this nation is more than the sum of its parts—that out of many, we are truly one."

The "one" that Obama is describing here, a single entity composed of distinct and differentiated parts, is a critique of the cultural norms of unity and commonality. Obama acknowledges this when he describes a "temptation to view my candidacy through a purely racial lens," a one-sided tactic that would fragment his doubled image into separate racial halves: "some commentators have deemed me either 'too black' or 'not black enough,'" and "the press has scoured every single exit poll for the latest evidence of racial polarization, not just in terms of white and black, but black and brown as well." It is in this context, highlighted by the Wright controversy and by subsequent attempts to fit Obama and his campaign into the racialized categories familiar in U.S. politics, that he broaches the central subject of his speech: the "recent firestorm" created by the wide circulation of excerpts of Wright's sermons, which has caused "the discussion of race in this campaign" to take "a particularly divisive turn."

Obama provides a two-part analysis of the controversy, with both parts describing the limitations of the one-sided discourse produced by others, which will contrast with the two-sided discourse that Obama himself introduces. He begins by again distancing himself from Wright, condemning his comments as not "simply controversial" but as presenting a "profoundly distorted view of this country—a view that sees white racism as endemic, and that elevates what is wrong with America above all that we know is right with America." Wright's comments present a perspective that distorts, a point of view that is "not only wrong but divisive . . . racially charged at a time when we need to come together to solve a set of monumental problems . . . problems that are neither black or white or Latino or Asian, but rather problems that confront us all." Wright's comments, Obama explains, are wrong because they are one-sided, a monocular discourse that distorts the panorama of American diversity, cleaves the public sphere into separate and unequal halves, and makes it impossible to incorporate multiple experiences of citizenship into a cohesive public. The second part of Obama's analysis returns to his critique of the press and of the racialized categories that it seems intent on promoting. He notes that "if all that I knew of Reverend Wright were the snippets of those sermons that have run in an endless loop on the television sets and YouTube . . . there is no doubt that I would react in much the same way." In other words, were Obama himself informed by only a single perspective such as that supplied by the decontextualized remarks circulated by the media, then only a single and predictable reaction would be available to him. "But the truth is," he points out, "that isn't all that I know of the man."

Against both of these one-sided perspectives—that evident in Wright's own comments as well as that "being peddled by some commentators"—Obama proposes a second perspective. He does not directly refute those more one-sided portrayals but instead addresses them by setting another portrayal alongside, complicating the picture through parallelism and parataxis without making an effort to resolve the two into one. Obama begins to shape this more complex portrait by describing the congregation at Trinity United in a series of balanced pairs that echo those he used to describe himself: "Like other predominantly black churches across the country, Trinity embodies the black community in its entirety—the doctor and the welfare mom, the model student and the former gang-banger. . . . The church contains in full the kindness and cruelty, the fierce intelligence and the shocking ignorance, the struggles and successes, the love and, yes, the bitterness and biases that make up the black experience in America." Reverend Wright seems to have absorbed and embodied this doubled collective, for he "contains within him the contradictions—the good and the bad—of the community that he has served diligently for so many years." Obama is not refuting the claim that Wright is a bad man but instead is refuting the claim that a one-sided view of Wright enables an adequate appraisal. Yes, what Wright said was wrong; yes, Wright is a good man. There is no contradiction, substitution, or transcendence implied, but merely the presentation of the man and his congregation as a doubled amalgam.[37]

In this passage of Obama's race speech, a metonymic logic is introduced through which Wright represents the complex dualities of Trinity United, which itself represents the dualities of "the black experience in America." None of the complexity is lost in these reductions; rather, if we look upon Wright as Obama has, then we are invited to see him as a doubled figure and in fact to see him as a figure of multiple binaries, as his dualities and those of his congregation and those of African American culture compound upon one another. In this way, Obama has begun to model for his audience a flexible and capacious doubled perspective that is a productive model of citizenship. He is able to see two sides of Wright and, by extension, two sides of the congregation at Trinity, which makes it more difficult to dismiss either as being beyond the pale of citizenship. He also begins to model a manner of addressing those inherent manifestations of division within individuals and by extension, because like Obama himself Wright is an embodiment of those whom he is addressing, the divisions inherent within the body politic.

This metonymic progression continues as Obama further opens up his biracial body to encompass not only Kansas and Kenya, Punahou and the projects, but also the multiple dualities represented by Wright, Trinity, and the black experience in America. During his delivery, at this point in his speech Obama looks down from the teleprompter to read a passage from his book, *Dreams from My Father*, that describes his experience attending his first service at Trinity United:

> People began to shout, to rise from their seats and clap and cry out, a forceful wind carrying the reverend's voice up into the rafters. . . . And in that single note—hope!—I heard something else; at the foot of that cross, inside the thousands of churches across the city, I imagined the stories of ordinary black people merging with the stories of David and Goliath, Moses and Pharaoh, the Christians in the lion's den, Ezekiel's field of dry bones. Those stories—of survival, and freedom, and hope— became our stories, my story; the blood that spilled was our blood, the tears our tears; until this black church, on this bright day, seemed once more a vessel carrying the story of a people into future generations and into a larger world. Our trials and triumphs became at once unique and universal, black and more than black; in chronicling our journey, the stories and songs gave us a means to reclaim memories that we didn't need to feel shame about . . . memories that all people might study and cherish—and with which we could start to rebuild.[38]

In this passage Obama himself seems to soak up the entire scene—the shouting, the singing, the wet tears and the dry bones—into his own capacious persona. Implied here as well is the idea that this experience is both "black and more than black," addressed both inward to the immediate audience and outward to the world, presenting something very like the "gift" of which Du Bois wrote, an understanding that is available to those whose experience includes exclusion but that also is valuable to a broader civic culture.

This scene sets up what probably is the most often-cited passage in the speech. Specifically referring to Wright, Obama says that "I can no more disown him than I can disown the black community." And then, making his own biracial identity explicit and aligning it with the dualities he is absorbing, he continues:

"I can no more disown him than I can disown my white grandmother." His grandmother, as well, cannot be reduced to a unidimensional figure, for though she "loves me as much as she loves anything in this world," she also "on more than one occasion has uttered racial or ethnic stereotypes that made me cringe." This passage—which recalls a similar passage from his memoir, cited earlier—often was taken up, mainly by Obama's critics and opponents, as evidence that Obama was willing to do or say anything, even sacrifice his own beloved grandmother, to win the election.[39] But his grandmother is not being "thrown under the bus," as so many pundits put it; both the black-pride preacher and the white maternal grandmother are doubled figures, and both are intrinsic parts of Obama. As identities have multiplied geometrically through this section of the speech, they present an extended antidote to the limitations of one-sided portrayals. Neither Wright, nor Obama's grandmother, nor Obama himself can be properly understood through a monocular perspective. Also, none of these identities can be reconciled into homogeneity. As Wright absorbs the contradictions of his congregation, they retain their distinction; similarly, Obama absorbs all of them into himself without resolving their contradictions, presenting his own doubled body as a metonymy for the divided, yet whole, body politic: "These people are part of me. And they are part of America, this country that I love."

To this point, then, Obama has not only encouraged a form of identification that does not require sameness and has not only modeled a mode of understanding that embraces difference but also has displayed his own biracial body as the material manifestation of racial reconciliation. G. Reginald Daniel points out what many have observed, that Obama's multiracial heritage "enhances his image as the physical embodiment of the principles of inclusiveness and equity."[40] But in this speech Obama has entextualized his biracial body so that he becomes racial reconciliation in a sort of epiphany, bearing witness to the potential of the American mythos to accommodate difference. His audience is invited to see him as the literal and figurative embodiment of accommodation and reconciliation. His audience, however, if confined merely to witnessing this revelation, would remain relatively passive, having not yet been invited to take an active role in making manifest its promise.

Doubled Gaze

Racial salvation cannot be had on the cheap. Obama's audience cannot be saved through sharing in his double-consciousness, however striking or well articulated it may be. Obama's best friend, the Chicago business executive Marty Nesbitt, told him that the Jeremiah Wright controversy might be "a blessing in disguise" because "circumstances have created a hurdle that only you can clear."[41] But Obama will not be satisfied if he's the only one going over the hurdle. He wants his audience to clear it as well, and to do so his listeners must learn to cultivate their own double-consciousness. This section of the speech provides a procedure through which the double-consciousness as described by Du Bois is refigured as a democratic double-consciousness that is cultivated among citizens and manifest in their discourse.

First, reflecting the required shift in agency, the speech changes suddenly from the active voice that has characterized the first section to a passive voice that contributes to a detached and somewhat academic or disembodied tone. In this way, Obama's text seems to withhold his body, with its fabulous redemptive powers, and redirects his audience's gaze away from himself and toward one another. This redirection is essential: if contemporary citizens must develop a capacity to speak in a doubled style, they must first cultivate the ability to see each other in a doubled way. He would have his audience avoid making "the same mistake that Reverend Wright made in his offending sermons about America—to simplify and stereotype and amplify the negative to the point that it distorts reality." Wright's error was that he saw things from only a single perspective, resulting in monocular distortion rather than stereoscopic clarity. What is called for, instead, is a willingness to address "the complexities of race in this country that we've never really worked through—a part of our union that we have not yet made perfect."

Assuming a professorial voice perhaps honed during his days as a senior lecturer in constitutional law at the University of Chicago, Obama explains that "understanding this reality requires a reminder of how we arrived at this point." Citing William Faulkner—"The past isn't dead and buried. In fact, it isn't even past"—sustains the lecture mode, as does a rather affected professorial "we," as in: "We do not need to recite here the history of racial injustice in this country. But we do need to remind ourselves that so many of the disparities that exist between the African American community and the larger American community today can be traced directly to inequalities passed on from an earlier generation that suffered under the brutal legacy of slavery and Jim Crow."[42] As an antidote to the overheated denigration that characterized much reaction to Reverend Wright, Obama guides his listeners through a clinical historical assessment of twentieth-century inequity.[43]

In stark contrast to the tone of personal revelation that characterizes the first part of the speech, here we have a distanced and objective voice that renders Obama's own body and voice conspicuously absent. Observations of the racial realities of America's past and present are ticked off in phrases that, at least grammatically, would not be out of place in a school textbook (albeit an erudite and progressive one): "Segregated schools were, and are, inferior schools," he reminds us, and this "helps explain the pervasive achievement gap between today's black and white students"; "Legalized discrimination . . . helps explain the wealth and income gap between blacks and whites"; "A lack of economic opportunity among black men, and the shame and frustration that came from not being able to provide for one's family, contributed to the erosion of black families," and "the lack of basic services in so many urban black neighborhoods . . . helped create a cycle of violence, blight and neglect that continues to haunt us."

This detached historical survey establishes the tone for a peculiarly dispassionate analysis of passion. This tendency toward dispassionate analysis is related to and in some ways a manifestation of the "moral hesitancy" that Du Bois associates with double-consciousness. When persons are placed into the role of observer, rather than of active participant, alienated from the action, they have more space and time to reason and weigh and as a result may become less inclined to the headlong certainty of a true believer. It is worthwhile to pause here to note that many observers have commented in other circumstances on Obama's performance of detached observation. David Maraniss, for example, notes that Obama is the son of an anthropologist and may have inherited an anthropologist's mindset; he approaches situations as "a participant observer, sitting on the edge of a culture and learning it well enough to understand it from the inside, yet never feeling fully part of it."[44] In an interview with George Stephanopoulos, Obama himself acknowledged that some people might see "remoteness and detachment" as a part of his character.[45] In a perceptive op-ed piece in the *New York Times,* David Brooks describes Obama as a "sojourner," being continually "in, but not of" the institutions and organizations with which he is associated. Brooks goes on to suggest that this "ability to stand apart accounts for his [Obama's] fantastic powers of observation and his skills as a writer and thinker. It means that people on almost all sides of any issue can see parts of themselves reflected in Obama's eyes. But it does make him hard to place."[46]

Double-consciousness points exactly to this feeling of problematic emplacement, drawing upon systematic exclusion as an interpretive resource of significant potential, the denial of the authenticity of a single perspective that is granted to those with "true self-consciousness," in Du Bois's words. Obama discusses each side of the color line, without critique; the two points of view are allowed to exist side by side, without conjunction, each offering a view of the world that is comparable to but not reducible to the other. This is a moral hesitancy used to great effect, as he speaks to first his white and then his black audiences, withholding judgment, inducing each of his audiences to view themselves through the eyes of the other and thus inviting them toward double-consciousness.

Speaking to his white audience, Obama reveals that "for the men and women of Reverend Wright's generation, the memories of humiliation and doubt and fear have not gone away; nor has the anger and the bitterness of those years." He acknowledges that this anger "may not get expressed in public in front of white co-workers or white friends. But it does find voice in the barbershop or the beauty shop or around the kitchen table."[47] "And," he admits, "occasionally it finds voice in the church on Sunday morning, in the pulpit and in the pews." The black church often serves as what Vorris L. Nunley and others have termed a "hush harbor," a place in which African Americans are "free to engage in and deploy otherwise heavily monitored practices, knowledges, and rhetorics disallowed in the public sphere under the disciplining gaze of Whites and Whiteness."[48] The Wright controversy had been, in part, precipitated by the spectacle of a discourse of difference drifting out of the hush harbor.

The anger that is sometimes voiced in these hush harbors, Obama acknowledges, is not always productive, because it can keep us from "facing our own complicity within the African-American community in our condition."[49] But it is "real" and "powerful," and "to simply wish it away, to condemn it without understanding its roots, only serves to widen the chasm of misunderstanding that exists between the races." Obama invites his white audience to view their own reaction to Reverend Wright through a black lens—that so many (white) Americans were surprised to hear this anger in Wright's sermons, Obama notes, "simply reminds us of the old truism that the most segregated hour of American life occurs on Sunday morning." This is a representative instance wherein whites are insulated from the color line, blissfully unaware of the degree to which it impacts the lives of many of their fellow citizens. For whites, the opacity of the color line precludes double-consciousness, making it impossible for them to see as the other does; in drawing their attention to the color line, then, Obama opens for his white listeners an opportunity for double-consciousness.

The speech next guides the African American audience, noting that "similar anger exists within segments of the white community," because "most working- and middle-class white Americans don't feel that they have been particularly privileged by their race." They have "worked hard all their lives," and "when they are told to bus their children to a school across town; when they hear an African American is getting an advantage in landing a good job or a spot in a good college because of an injustice that they themselves never committed; when they're told that their fears about crime in urban neighborhoods are somehow prejudiced, resentment builds over time." The veil falls across white America as well as black, for, "like the anger within the black community, these resentments aren't always expressed in polite company." And just as it would be counterproductive to wish away genuine black anger, so also "to wish away the resentments of white Americans, to label them as misguided or even racist, without recognizing they are grounded in legitimate concerns—this too widens the racial divide, and blocks the path to understanding."

Some observers think that Obama is equating these two quite dissimilar varieties of frustration. They understand him as saying, for example, that the frustration felt by white citizens who are told their children must attend a school across town is the same as the frustration felt by African Americans whose children are denied access to a good education or that the anger felt by whites who perceive themselves to be slighted by affirmative action is somehow equal to the anger felt by African Americans after generations of racist hiring practices.[50] But that is a misreading, as David Frank notes.[51] If Obama were equating these different varieties of anger, that would entail an evaluative judgment that would be at odds with the objective and uninterested persona that he has adopted in this section of the speech.[52] This is, again, a paratactic logic: because he merely presents the fact that there is racial anger and frustration on each side of the color line, he is able to preserve their distinctiveness. The point is not to bring the two perspectives into a harmonic equilibrium but to recognize that both perspectives exist. This is a radical revisioning of the color line, neither a dismissal nor an elision but an instruction in viewing it differently—and for some, perhaps, it is an instruction in how to see it for the very first time. Obama's speech has invited his audience on each side of the color line to view themselves with others' eyes, and these doubled perspectives present a potentially powerful critique of the unitary, monoscopic tropes that dominate contemporary public discourse.

But still, Obama describes "where we are right now" as "a racial stalemate we've been stuck in for years." If progress is to be made toward a more perfect union, it will be neither through dismissing the doubled perspectives that Obama has just opened up through his discussion of anger nor, as he makes explicit, through the deus ex machina of his ideologically commodious and racially bifurcated body. "Contrary to the claims of some of my critics, black and white," he explains, "I have never been so naïve as to believe that we can get beyond our racial divisions in a single election cycle, or with a single candidate—particularly a candidacy as imperfect as my own."[53] To this point in his speech, his listeners have been asked first to view Obama's doubled body as a physical embodiment of racial atonement and then to imitate Obama's doubled perspective as they view one another, but they remain relatively passive. They have been invited to alter their gaze but have not yet been asked to speak in accordance with their altered perspective. To perfect the union, a doubled gaze is necessary but insufficient, unable by itself to sustain either more productive race relations or a more effective democratic culture. Obama's audiences must be provided with the inventional resources that will enable them to address one another.

Doubled Discourse

The first section of the speech is marked by an active voice in the first person, directing Obama's audience to attend to Obama; the second section, marked by the passive voice, directs the audience to consider, dispassionately, the passion present on either side of the color line. The third section is characterized by a more richly elevated style, through which Obama models an attitude of constructive critique, progressive remembrance, and doubled address. Cultivating in the members of his audience a facility for speaking in a doubled style requires that Obama first urge them to accept a doubled consciousness as a legitimate perspective and then invite them to experience a doubled consciousness of their own before providing a repertoire of doubled tropes through which such a consciousness might be enacted. Obama now revisits the two sides of the color line, providing first his African American audience and then his white audience with an appropriately doubled mode of address. Articulated within the components of democratic double-consciousness outlined in the previous chapter, up to this point the speech has focused primarily on the value of double-consciousness as a citizenly resource and on its capacity for geometric progression toward a multiplicity of perspectives; in this section of the speech, Obama specifically emphasizes the need to see this as a form of *addressed* discourse, as a way of speaking to and for one another as citizens.

"For the African-American community," Obama explains, the path toward a more perfect union "means embracing the burdens of our past without becoming victims of our past." Here is the appreciation of the burden of citizenship as presenting not merely an encumbrance but also an opportunity, the twofold price and promise of citizenship characteristic of democratic double-consciousness. We are to understand not only that we cannot escape the past but that it would be a mistake to do so, for the past provides valuable resources through which the present and the future might be addressed. The parallelism and near-alliteration enhance the twofold nature of this attitude, setting "embracing" and "becoming" in apposition so that their distinction is emphasized; while *becoming* entails conversion, *embracing* suggests simultaneous closeness and differentiation. *Becoming* is totalizing, while *embracing* is additive. To become a victim is to undergo a complete change in identity, in other words, while to embrace a burden individuals must both retain their identity and supplement it. The phrase not only endorses a doubled attitude, then, but also provides a linguistic form through which that attitude might be expressed.

This two-ness similarly is evident in Obama's argument that perfecting the union "means continuing to insist on a full measure of justice in every aspect of American life" while at the same time "binding our particular grievances . . . to the larger aspirations of all Americans." The phrasing suggests a balanced narrowing and then expanding of scope—from the expansiveness of a "full measure" to the specificity of "every aspect" and then from "particular grievances" to "larger aspirations"—that models the doubled attitude required to maintain a balance between individual aspiration and community norms.[54]

The shifting or oscillating of perspectives is evident as Obama argues that African Americans must learn to see themselves as comparable to "the white woman struggling to break the glass ceiling, the white man who's been laid off, the immigrant trying to feed his family" but must also learn to take "full responsibility for their own lives—by demanding more from our fathers, and spending more time with our children, and reading to them, and teaching them that while they may face challenges and discrimination in their own lives, they must never succumb to despair or cynicism." And though he acknowledges that limitations are imposed by the dominant culture upon African Americans, black children "must always believe that they can write their own destiny."

"Now in the white community," Obama continues, "the path to a more perfect union means acknowledging that what ails the African-American community does not just exist in the minds of black people; that the legacy of discrimination—and current incidents of discrimination, while less overt than in the past—that these things are real and must be addressed." Again, parallelism brings phrases into apposition, in this case aligning the ailments of the African American community with the legacy of discrimination. This would be in contrast to those who might instead assert that the problems are caused by the inherent failings of persons of color, including an imagined tendency to perceive affronts where actually there are none. It is not necessary for whites to share completely the perspective of African Americans for them to recognize that racial injustice is not a mere specter. Significantly, then, Obama's listeners are asked here not merely to acknowledge the visibility of the color line and not merely to look at themselves in two ways at once; rather, his audience is urged to speak and act in doubled ways as an appropriate response to a divided culture—to *address* the ailments of the African American community that have been revealed through this doubled gaze. Wright's "profound mistake," as Obama sees it, is "that he spoke as if our society was static; as if no progress had been made; as if this country . . . is still irrevocably bound to a tragic past." The problem is not merely that Wright was mistaken but that he spoke inappropriately, voicing a unidirectional orientation and a rigid perspective that did not embrace the past as a source of productive invention but instead remained entrapped by it. In contrast, the doubled address that Obama is modeling is directed toward both the past and the future, appreciating the continued influence of history without becoming immobilized by it and encouraging a flexibility without which the union can never be perfected. Wright's discursive style, in this way, is presented as emblematic of the ways of speaking that must be exposed and replaced if the stalemate is to be resolved and if Obama's doubled discourse is to gain cultural traction.

In this speech, this attitude is captioned with the so-called Golden Rule. In many circumstances, relying on this old chestnut to summarize a central argument would risk reducing the speech to schmaltz. But in this context the maxim is thickened considerably by emphasizing the doubled entailments of doing unto others: "In the end, then, what is called for is nothing more, and nothing less, than what all the world's great religions demand—that we do unto others as we would have them do unto us. Let us be our brother's keeper, Scripture tells us. Let us be our sister's keeper. Let us find that common stake we all have in one another, and let our politics reflect that spirit as well." Not only does this provide an opportunity to reassert Obama's religious convictions in a thoroughly unobjectionable way, but the Golden Rule also provides a thumbnail sketch of the ethic of reciprocity, and, as Allen reminds us, "democratic citizenship consists primarily of reciprocity."[55] The Golden Rule evokes Aristotle's dictum to treat a friend as "a second self," and that a friend ought "to share his friend's consciousness." The foundation of political friendship, what Aristotle refers to as "concord," depends upon reciprocity that is enacted through this ability to treat the other as the self, to see oneself from the other's point of view.[56] To the extent to which we find ourselves incapable of standing in another's shoes, we find our efforts to perform citizenship crippled.

Stylistically, the Golden Rule usually is phrased, as Obama phrases it here, in the form of a chiasmus; as Henry Louis Gates reminded us in the previous chapter, chiasmus is a foundational trope in African American literature.[57] When reciprocity is animated in this form of verbal performance, it cannot be reduced to a simple mimetic mirroring, in which one gives to another precisely what has been given, for chiasmus, like all tropes, but perhaps particularly, *turns.*[58] As the "we" who are agents become the "us" who are objects, the Golden Rule requires us to see ourselves as the potential recipients of our own potential actions. Like Du Bois a century before, Obama does not advise us to *become* our brother or sister or even to become *like* them; he urges us to recognize our "common stake" in one another and to experience the sometimes uncomfortable sensation of seeing ourselves through their eyes. The Golden Rule as Obama deploys it presents in compressed form the relationship between doubled consciousness and doubled agency that is demonstrated in this speech; it is a way of phrasing our relationship to others that in turn asks us to act in accordance with that phrasing. To move toward a more perfect union, we must then incorporate this interstitial perspective into our speech, addressing one another as citizens in ways that constitute and sustain this "whole" public culture. To "find that common stake we all have in one another" requires a doubled consciousness; to "let our politics reflect that spirit" requires a doubled address.[59]

Conclusion

As is perhaps to be expected with regard to a discourse of duality on a sensitive subject, the speech provoked wildly disparate reactions. Some keyed on the detached tone of much of the analysis, noting that it resembled a "thoughtful history and sociology lesson,"[60] or appreciated it as masterful political strategy, the work of "a politically astute man who had been placed in the unenviable position of contributing to the ruination of the reputation of a man he deeply admired."[61] While Andrew Sullivan, writing in his blog for the *Atlantic,* called the speech "deeply Christian" and "the most honest speech on race in America in my adult lifetime,"[62] Adolph Reed Jr. described it as the "Philadelphia compromise speech—a string of well-crafted and coordinated platitudes and hollow images worthy of an SUV commercial," grounded with the reassuring "acknowledgment" of blacks' "behavioral inadequacies" of the sort that "has appealed to centrist liberals ever since Booker T. Washington's comparably eloquent 1895 accommodation to Southern white supremacy."[63]

These observations are not wrong but fragmented. Like the old story about the blind men and the elephant, each one points out one or two of the qualities of the speech without taking into account its composition as a whole. But much of the potential for this particular speech to serve as a resource of citizenly invention is revealed most clearly when its contrast, detachment, political mastery, and pervasive religious imagery are placed in the context of its disposition. It might be argued that a contemporary conception of productive citizenly discourse requires a certain sort of facility with sound bites, but certainly it also requires more than that; it takes time and space to engage one another effectively as democratic citizens, and a sustained discourse can model relationships among various positions, histories, and experiences that cannot be accounted for in shorter forms. Somewhat paradoxically, perhaps, it is important to account for this speech as a whole because it is through the interaction of its various parts that it produces its vibrant critique of unity.

An insistence on unity, especially when manifest as a predilection for homogeneity, either ignores or rejects the diversity that actually describes contemporary U.S. civic culture and thus renders it impossible for marginalized individuals and groups to participate in the mainstream without relinquishing the heritage, culture, and identity that make them distinctive. An insistence on this form of unity thus contributes to the disarray and dysfunction that characterize contemporary practices of U.S. citizenship.

The antidote presented by Obama in this speech is most clearly illustrated through an implied contrast between the singular figure of Reverend Wright and a doubled figure introduced in an anecdote near the end of the speech. Obama rejects one-sided characterizations of Wright, and he rejects Wright's own comments that present a too one-sided characterization of race relations in the United States. What Obama is rejecting, then, is a discursive style, specifically a single-minded, single-voiced style that would be anathema to the doubled style that Obama is modeling for his audience and that would not provide the resources that encourage productive reciprocal relations among citizens.[64] Wright's doubled persona—the version of Wright that Obama says that he cannot disown, the one who "contains within him the contradictions" of his varied congregation—may present a productive way to perceive one's fellow citizens. As in Obama's own doubled persona, which in fact seems here to enfold within it his white grandmother's dual reactions to difference as well as Wright's doubled persona, this fundamental duality is not as exceptional as it is typical. As citizens, we must be able to see the ways that our fellow citizens, like ourselves, are not unified or homogeneous.

More important, we also have to learn how to talk with one another. As I have noted, citizenship is a practice that is enacted through discourse as much as it is a status that is conferred. In his peroration, Obama presents a particularly productive model of citizenly discourse. He tells the story of "a young, twenty-three year old woman, a white woman, named Ashley Baia," who worked for Obama's campaign in Florence, South Carolina. When Baia was young, Obama recalls, her mother was diagnosed with cancer and then lost her job and then, with it, lost her health insurance. Money was tight, and to stretch their savings Ashley told her mother that she wanted to eat only "mustard and relish sandwiches." Her mother got better, and Ashley later shared this story at a roundtable with other volunteers working for Obama's campaign. When it came time for an "elderly black man" in the room to tell why he had volunteered, he said, according to Obama, "I am here because of Ashley." This story asks the listeners to divide their attention so that they might identify with both the black man and the white girl—if they're unable to do so, then the impact of the story largely is lost. The story also asks the audience to witness the mutual recognition of these two characters, who seem to understand that they are "comparable" without being compelled to imagine that their experiences are interchangeable or are reducible to one another. The story depends upon and illustrates democratic double-consciousness as a mode of discourse; it shows two people who have found a way of speaking to and about each other that recognizes their commonality while still sustaining their difference. Obama recognizes that "by itself, that single moment of recognition between that young white girl and that old black man is not enough," but he concludes that "it is where we start," that it is "where our union grows stronger," and that "that is where the perfection begins."[65]

This was and remains Obama's most fully developed statement on U.S. race relations, as well as being his most fully realized articulation of a doubled verbal style. In his analysis of this speech, George Lakoff suggests that it is not a speech on race but "a speech on what America *is* about, on what American values are, on what patriotism is, on who the real culprits are, and on the kind of new politics needed if we are to make progress in transcending those flaws that are still very much with us."[66] But of course this *is* a speech on race, because race is so much of what America is about. I don't mean for this distinction to be exclusive; this is a speech that is about race and also is about broader practices of citizenship, because the two cannot easily be distinguished. As I noted in the previous chapter, citizenship as a concept and as a practice in the United States historically has been closely associated with race, and W. E. B. Du Bois articulated double-consciousness as an effect of and a response to the racial problematics of U.S. citizenship. In the context of the United States, racial division is a representative anecdote for political division more generally and as such presents an opportunity for the invention of discursive practices ameliorative to the fragmentation that characterizes contemporary civic culture.[67] Discursive practices that model ways of speaking that encourage and sustain the sort of productive division that is fundamental to addressing the color line might be deployed in addressing the multiple divisions and stalemates that characterize democratic citizenship in the United States.

I have argued that Obama's articulation of democratic double-consciousness draws upon and addresses the long and fundamental interconnection between race and citizenship in the United States. This speech is animated by all three topics that characterize democratic double-consciousness. It is explicitly a discourse on *citizenship,* exploring its problematics through a doubled perspective presented not only as an effect of racial division but also as a fitting response to it. It shows also, through its disposition, that any ameliorative potential that may inhere in this discourse cannot be accessed passively. Citizens must cultivate modes of *address* through which to recognize one another and themselves as imbricated in a complex web of reciprocity and interdependency. A way of seeing is necessary but not sufficient; a way of speaking is fundamental. And, finally, through the layering of doubled perspectives that characterizes the middle part of the speech, as Obama's bifurcated body comes to represent the dualities of his pastor, his grandmother, and the entirety of his white and black heritage, this speech demonstrates the potential for double-consciousness to provide an initial critique of homogeneity that can proliferate into *multiplicity*.

This speech, then, provides an extraordinarily rich resource for the invention of democratic double-consciousness. It treats racial division as representative of broader forms of division and references the Golden Rule as a mode of address not only between races but among citizens. This might seem to suggest that the mode of speech that I am describing is an inevitable product or quality of public discourse about race; it might seem reasonable to conclude, in other words, that the discursive phenomenon I am describing can be counted upon to emerge in any public discourse that addresses the divisions and problematics of race in the United States. In the next chapter, I focus on Obama's other public discourse about race, both during the 2008 campaign and during his first term in office; this discourse illustrates, instead, that actually "A More Perfect Union" was designed to address an exceedingly rare rhetorical opportunity in U.S. public culture, a moment in which the rather severe strictures that police the boundaries of race talk only momentarily were softened.

— CHAPTER 4 —

The Confines of Race

The speech on race that Barack Obama gave in Philadelphia was an anomaly. It drew upon the problematics of American racial politics to present a productively doubled rhetorical style that is an especially rich inventional resource for American citizenship, but it was not typical of the discourse on race that Obama delivered throughout his campaign and into his presidency.[1] The rhetorical situation that produced that address was rare and possibly unique. It was a moment when the topic of race had broken into public consciousness, puncturing the veil of ignorance and apathy and worse through which we typically view racial difference. This situation had to be addressed quickly and effectively if Obama's campaign to become the first African American president was to survive; it was an exigency characterized by "an imperfection marked by urgency," in Lloyd Bitzer's classic formulation.[2] More typically, when Obama's speeches did focus on race, it was to associate himself with the 1960s U.S. African American civil rights movement and to position his campaign as an extension of that movement. It may seem obvious that cultivating that association can be an especially potent rhetorical strategy for an African American candidate, but it does pose something of a dilemma that in turn contributes to our understanding of some of the limitations of democratic double-consciousness when it is articulated within talk about race.

In this chapter, I analyze public discourse produced by Barack Obama that demonstrates the restrictions that this dilemma places upon the circulation of double-consciousness in contemporary civic culture. These limitations follow from the nature of double-consciousness, in W. E. B. Du Bois's formulation, as a response to African American exclusion from full U.S. citizenship. Democratic double-consciousness, as I am describing it in this book, is an extension of Du Bois's notions but still sustains its roots in racial frictions. When double-consciousness is made available as a resource for the invention of rhetorical citizenship broadly, in other words, it retains its inflection as an aspect of African American discursive culture. Democratic double-consciousness is an agency through which habits of thought and speech associated with African

American culture are amplified and circulated. This is not abstract or uninterested theory but a discursive practice tied to racial experience, and as such it is to be expected that its circulation is affected by the contours of civic discourse. Specifically, where race talk is severely restricted, so too is the scope of double-consciousness that is articulated within such talk.[3]

Rather than focus on a single speech, in this chapter I explore these restrictions by examining a series of addresses that Obama gave mostly to African American audiences during the 2008 presidential campaign and after his election. Where in the previous chapter I was concerned with establishing an exemplar of democratic double-consciousness that would provide a touchstone for the remaining analyses in this book, here I am concerned with describing the extent to which other public texts might be framed as resources for the invention of democratic double-consciousness in the vein of the exemplar. I am interested, in other words, in the way that this discourse contributes to our understanding of the impact that the limitations placed on race talk in our culture has on the articulation of double-consciousness as an inventional resource for democratic citizenship. Inventional criticism, again, is defined not by any particular object or method but by purpose, and throughout this chapter the purpose remains firmly the exploration of the potential for these discourses to serve as resources for the invention of democratic citizenship.

Each of the addresses examined here reiterates a basic narrative that places Obama and his campaign as an episode in a continuing civil rights movement. It is a narrative that allows public talk about race without breaching social norms that generally restrict such talk, thus avoiding the traps that ensnared the Reverend Jeremiah Wright. Two episodes during the first year of Obama's presidency in which Obama strayed from this relatively safe and sanctioned script also are discussed because the reaction to these instances illustrates the power of racial norms to police public discourse. Obama's remarks at the 2011 dedication of the Martin Luther King Jr. memorial on the National Mall in Washington, D.C., show that a moment marked out specifically as an opportunity to talk about race to a diverse audience can foster the invention of democratic double-consciousness, though even then only in a relatively restricted register. The chapter concludes with a discussion of the implications of these analyses for our understanding of double-consciousness as an explicitly rhetorical form of discourse, one addressed to particular audiences in particular circumstances and for particular purposes.

Finishing the Story

Obama was born in 1961, nearly six years after Rosa Parks refused to give up her seat on that bus in Montgomery, Alabama; he was only a toddler when

Martin Luther King Jr. described his dream during the March on Washington for Jobs and Freedom; and he was a young boy in Hawaii, Seattle, and Indonesia during years most closely associated with the U.S. civil rights movement. Obama, as a result, had no direct experience of the movement; neither he nor his parents or grandparents were actively involved. Nevertheless, almost from the moment of his appearance on the national stage, the civil rights movement has been evoked as a framework for understanding the man and his promise. A short poem that was widespread on the Internet and elsewhere during the 2008 presidential campaign goes as follows: "Rosa sat so Martin could walk, / Martin walked so Obama could run, / Obama is running so our children can fly!"[4] Remnick opened his book *The Bridge* with an epigraph attributed to John Lewis: "Barack Obama is what comes at the end of that bridge in Selma." For many of Obama's admirers, his candidacy was "the first time since the civil rights movement of the 1960s" that they "had real hope for change."[5] Henry Louis Gates Jr. called Obama's election "the symbolic culmination of the black freedom struggle, the grand achievement of a great collective dream."[6] *Time* magazine suggested that Obama's election meant that Martin Luther King's dream "is being fulfilled sooner than anyone imagined."[7] Sasha Abramsky noted that "President Obama is, in many ways, a successor figure to Martin Luther King Jr. and his vision of a beloved community moving America away from its divided, segregated past."[8] In the *Chicago Tribune,* James Oliphant wrote that Obama has "essentially brought the civil rights movement almost full circle."[9]

Obama actively cultivates these associations. As John Lewis puts it, Obama "was born long after he could experience or understand the movement. . . . He had to move toward it in his own time."[10] He did move toward it, not only in his youthful efforts to explore his biracial identity through reading books that he checked out of the library but also as a canny adult crafting a public persona. Remnick relates this anecdote: at the luncheon following Obama's swearing in as the forty-fourth president of the United States of America, Congressman John Lewis, a true hero of the civil rights movement, "approached Obama with a commemorative photograph and asked him to sign it. The President wrote, 'Because of you, John. Barack Obama.'"[11] There also is the often-repeated story that after reading *Parting the Waters,* the Pulitzer Prize–winning first volume of Taylor Branch's trilogy on King and the civil rights movement, Obama reportedly told a friend that "this is my story."[12]

For the purposes of my argument, these ubiquitous associations are of interest not because they indicate something—sinister, noble, or otherwise—within the psyche of Barack Obama but because they indicate Obama's method of managing a dilemma that likely confronts almost any African American public figure and thus outline the limits on race talk in the United States.

On the one hand, he "needed to persuade whites that he was different from the black public officials and spokespeople who had dominated the airwaves for decades."[13] Obama had to distance himself from "the black politicians who had paved his way," especially from many of those whose perspectives were developed through and whose political coalitions were modeled upon their involvement in the civil rights movement.[14] He couldn't risk seeming too deeply implicated in that fractious time, and as a result he had partially to distance himself from the very narrative that he was cultivating. As Remnick puts it, "Obama's manner, his accent, his pedigree, his broad approach to the issues, told white voters, among other things: *I am not Jesse Jackson*."[15]

On the other hand, probably it was impossible for Obama to avoid some sort of association between himself and the African American civil rights movement, because that movement, those figures, and those issues have become so much the lens through which race is viewed in America. The civil rights movement has become the dominant frame within which race is understood, perhaps particularly for public figures, so that Obama becomes legible as an African American to the extent that he is identified with that movement. While many of Obama's critics and supporters recognized that he was a viable candidate because he was not directly linked to the civil rights movement, they also "resented it, and they resented Obama for his willingness to distance himself from the symbolic issues that had historically defined Black political activism."[16] Indeed, the possibility of a black major-party candidate at the top of the ticket for president roused mixed reactions. Many, like John Lewis, initially were committed to supporting Hillary Rodham Clinton, continuing a long history of support among African Americans for the Clintons and in particular for Bill Clinton, whom Toni Morrison had famously declared "our first black President."[17] Many others were reluctant to support Obama because they did not believe that he or any African American could win. As Jesse Jackson himself explained, in supporting Clinton these people "thought they were betting on a winning horse."[18] Some, like Princeton professor Cornel West, questioned the degree to which Obama identified as black: "My criteria is [sic] fundamental," he told Tavis Smiley, the PBS talk show host. "I want to know how deep is your love for the people?"[19] Many thought that it was either too soon for the United States to support a black candidate for president or too early in Obama's political career. And others were reluctant to support Obama for more unsettling but no less understandable reasons—as Obama himself put it, as he was beginning to consider running for president: "The white folks want me to run. And the black folks think I'm going to get killed."[20]

Thus, Obama had to distance himself from some the perceived political liabilities of an association with the civil rights movement at the same time that he had to embrace, at least to some extent, the association between himself and that movement that so many necessarily would make. This dilemma is amplified by the effect of what David Leo Goldberg has termed "racial neoliberalism," the tendency in contemporary public culture to equate the mere mention of race with an expression of racism. As a corollary of color blindness being posited as a cultural ideal, a widespread belief has emerged that race "once marked individuals, to be sure, but now it has (and should have) no reference point, no measure, no determination"; as a result, Goldberg argues, "racism is redirected to malign those who invoke race, implicitly or explicitly," so that "racism is reduced in its supposed singularity to invoking race, not to its debilitating structural effects or the legacy of its ongoing unfair impacts."[21] In a culture characterized by racial neoliberalism, the mere mention of race is equated with racism; where race is supposed to be invisible, a tendency to see it is suspect. Darrel Wanzer, drawing on Goldberg, notes that "Obama is in a bit of a double-bind and he probably knows it. On the one hand, failure to acknowledge race leaves him open to critiques . . . for failing to be proactive on policy issues relevant to racial minorities. On the other hand, if he acknowledges race or claims racism, he (a) risks the charge of racism by violating the rhetorical norms of neoliberalism and (b) risks marking himself further as 'different' in the eyes of many voters."[22]

Obama approaches this dilemma in his public address through a carefully calibrated maneuver, an attempt to thread the needle, seeking to avoid appearing either too black or not black enough by associating himself with the African American civil rights movement, but only with its most purified version. Thomas J. Sugrue has pointed out that Obama "embraced a particular version" of the civil rights movement, one that avoided "association with either its most principled or its most problematic practitioners, for even though whites professed color blindness, they remained skeptical of politicians whose rhetoric or style appeared 'too black.'" In this rather severely edited version of the movement, the "freedom struggle, once divisive, had become domesticated, transformed into a narrative of unity."[23]

The version of the civil rights movement that is invoked in most of Obama's race talk centers specifically on Martin Luther King Jr. as he has been canonized among the icons of American civil religion. As Thomas Dumm reminds us, "to cite King on just about anything now is to gird oneself with a powerful shield that makes criticism of your position into a criticism of the most sainted American since Abraham Lincoln."[24] When Obama cites King—not only referencing him but cultivating a particularly intimate relationship with him—he is invoking a protective incantation that shields his race talk from criticism. On the one hand, this makes even more remarkable an address as poignant and textured as

"A More Perfect Union," a text that mentions King exactly once. On the other, however, it renders sharply ironic the fact that Obama employs and embraces this narrow, linear, and monovocal narrative that so powerfully illustrates precisely the forms of discourse he so eloquently countered in "A More Perfect Union."

For the most part, only those events and persons that have been granted inclusion within the official canon of mainstream American history are recalled in Obama's oratory. The Montgomery bus boycott, the Freedom Rides, the March on Washington, and the Selma-to-Montgomery marches all make this list, as do Martin Luther King Jr., Rosa Parks, and John Lewis; Malcolm X, Stokely Carmichael, Julian Bond, Ella Baker, Angela Davis, and Fannie Lou Hamer do not. Interestingly, Jesse Jackson also doesn't make the cut, even though he is among the contemporary public figures most closely associated with King and his legacy. This illustrates the fine edge of the blade Obama is walking—he can't identify himself with Jackson because Jackson too closely epitomizes a recognizable form of contemporary African American leadership that is grounded in the 1960s U.S. civil rights movement. For one thing, like the Reverend Jeremiah Wright, Jesse Jackson's preacherly public persona might threaten to color Obama "a bit too darkly."[25] Also, if Obama is to be the heir of the civil rights movement, then he really can't brook other living contenders to the throne.

The movement with which Obama associates himself must be idealized in the misty past, forgotten just well enough so that it can be productively partially remembered. The narrative that Obama invites us to remember is remarkable in its singleness and monovocality, centered almost exclusively on King; the events he recalls in the most detail are those that directly involved King, and most of the people who earn more than the briefest possible mention are those who were close associates of King. And even within this narrow focus on King, Obama rarely mentions in public any events from before 1955 or after 1963. In his later years, King said many things that might be considered radical today and certainly were then, among them a devastating critique of the Vietnam War that contained passages very nearly as inflammatory as anything contained in Reverend Wright's sermons; it probably would be impossible for any American politician to gain wide acceptance by invoking that version of King, and this is perhaps especially true for someone like Barack Obama.[26]

Some might insist that an ability to speak about race in public at all points to the progress made during the past half-century. But the narrow confines of this accepted narrative also should be understood as a grave disservice to the women and men who put their lives on the line in the effort to achieve some modicum of political and social equality in the United States. The ubiquity in contemporary public culture of this sanctioned narrative, which presents as homogeneous a movement that actually was wonderfully diverse, is a stunning indication of the absence of the sort of multivoiced, multiperspectival discourse that I have been describing as a resource for democratic double-consciousness. The civil rights movement itself could be more accurately described not as a single movement at all but as a complex and loosely organized phenomenon that encompassed but never unified a wide range of voices, personalities, ideologies, goals, and tactics—but portraying this reality in public would entail an extended critique of collective public memory and the ideology of unity that would risk alienating a significant portion of the electorate.

While Obama was not, during his campaign, interested in alienating the electorate, at the same time he was, as Shelby Steele puts it, "a man nothing less than driven by a determination to be black."[27] This point is reiterated by many Obama observers, both supporters and critics. Remnick, for example, recalls Obama's portrayal of himself in his memoirs as "touchingly, awkwardly . . . giving himself instruction on how to be black."[28] The awkwardness is even mocked by Bobby Rush—who has the distinction of being the only politician ever to defeat Obama, when in 2000 Obama challenged him in the Democratic primary for his long-held seat in the U.S. House of Representatives—who describes even Obama's way of walking as "an adaptation of a strut that comes from the street" that has been acquired by Obama artificially, through observation and mimicry, rather than naturally, as a consequence of a more authentic immersion in an African American experience.[29] But Steele concludes that, as a result of his efforts to paint himself black, Obama is a "bound man who cannot serve the aspirations of one race without betraying those of the other."[30] This is a misreading of the delicate racial dance that informed Obama's 2008 campaign and has impacted his presidency. It also is representative of an ironic error made by many of Obama's critics who do not attend carefully to his public address. When they try to make Obama seem more like a radical by pointing out his efforts to associate himself with a specifically African American experience, they miss the fact that the particular African American experience with which Obama most often chooses to associate himself is perhaps the most banal available. While many of even his staunchest critics praised "A More Perfect Union," the doubled tropes, dual perspectives, and multivocalic critique of homogeneous unity that characterize that speech are infinitely more radical than the sanctified version of African American activism with which he explicitly aligns himself.

In this way, Obama's close identification with the sanctioned civil rights movement attenuates much of the alienation that prompts double-consciousness, in Du Bois's original formulation. King, at least in this purified and tightly constrained form, has been fully integrated into mainstream public culture, his status as a citizen firmly cemented. As a result, addresses on race produced from within the confines of the sanctioned King-centered civil rights narrative are not rich resources for democratic double-consciousness. The persona portrayed in these addresses does not seem to present "two warring ideals in one dark body, whose dogged strength alone keeps it from being torn asunder" but rather one single unified body, as Obama and King, the civil rights movement and his campaign, meld into a seamless whole. Obama also does not ask his audiences in these addresses to cultivate a detached, observational perspective, as he did in "A More Perfect Union," but instead presents and invites his hearers to share a full engagement and dedication to a particular memory of King and the civil rights movement.

With regard specifically to the tenets of democratic double-consciousness, these are not addresses about citizenship, broadly conceived, but rather are powerful speeches of identity and identification in which Obama asks his hearers to commit themselves to him, to his campaign, and, after the election, to his administration. Though the campaign speeches in particular can be understood as invitations to participate in a democratic process, they do not specifically model ways of addressing one another as citizens more broadly within a democratic culture. And as a result of the narrow channel generally allowed racial discourse in contemporary U.S. public culture, the various forms of discursive duality through which double-consciousness is manifest are severely restricted, so that the proliferation of multiple perspectives that characterizes democratic double-consciousness does not have an opportunity to develop.

The Joshua Generation

On March 4, 2007, both Hillary Rodham Clinton and Barack Obama visited Selma, Alabama, to mark the forty-second anniversary of Bloody Sunday. On March 7, 1965, John Lewis, the Reverend Hosea Williams, and hundreds of other civil rights marchers were beaten violently as they attempted to cross the Edmund Pettus Bridge out of Selma to begin a march to Montgomery, the state capital, to protest the killing of Jimmie Lee Jackson and to agitate for voting rights. Clinton and Obama both participated in a reenactment of the crossing of the bridge as a part of their visit in 2007, and they both delivered addresses in churches. The two speeches show some remarkable and perhaps unsurprising similarities, but their differences are of particular interest.

In her speech, at the First Baptist Church (located at the corner of Martin Luther King Boulevard and Jefferson Davis Street), Clinton reminded a crowd of about 750 that the milestones of the civil rights movement, "like the creation of SCLC and the integration of Central High and that fateful Sunday with that march across the Pettus Bridge . . . do not mark the end of the journey." "Yes," she continued, "that long march to freedom that began here has carried us a mighty long way. But we all know we have to finish the march . . . toward one America."[31] Clinton particularly drew attention to the Voting Rights Act of 1965, which "gave more Americans from every corner of our nation the chance to live out their dreams. Today it is giving Senator Obama the chance to run for president of the United States. And by its logic and spirit, it is giving the same chance to Governor Bill Richardson, an Hispanic, and yes, it is giving me that chance, too. . . . I know where my chance came from, and I am grateful to all of you, who gave it to me." This is all fairly standard stuff—almost any presidential candidate addressing a predominantly African American audience in Selma, Alabama, on the anniversary of Bloody Sunday would be expected to recognize the sacrifices made by the previous generation and to note that the journey continues into the present.

Obama said all this, too, when he addressed some 450 people—including John Lewis—about three blocks away, at Brown Chapel. Brown Chapel was the key rallying point in 1965, and it was from Brown Chapel that King led two subsequent marches, the last one actually successful in reaching Montgomery.[32] Obama acknowledges this legacy in a series of repeated phrases: "it's because they marched that the next generation hasn't been bloodied so much. It's because they marched that we elected councilmen, congressmen. It is because they marched that we have Artur Davis and Keith Ellison. It is because they marched that I got the kind of education I got, a law degree, a seat in the Illinois senate and ultimately in the United States senate. It is because they marched that I stand before you here today."[33]

The repetition of the phrase "it's because" groups these milestones together under a single heading, but this is not a paratactic logic that asks us to survey distinct or even opposite images simultaneously. Rather, these examples are all of a piece, so that their effect is to situate Obama within the "next generation," underlining his affiliation with the others, minimizing distinction rather than emphasizing it. The repetition may give Obama's address a tincture of African American oratorical tradition, and indeed this speech was sometimes used by his critics as an example of Obama's alleged tendency to adopt some features of a stereotypical black dialect when it suits him politically and thus as evidence of his inauthenticity. Otherwise, these phrases could have been inserted into Clinton's speech with little modification.[34]

Obama did two things in his address, however, that Hillary did not and could not. The first is to extend the "journey" metaphor through which, as James Darsey has pointed out, Obama "places his personal trajectory along the long, hard path that Americans and African Americans have followed en route to the promised land."[35] As John Murphy has pointed out in detail, Obama embellishes this metaphor by establishing himself as Joshua to the "Moseses" of the civil rights generation, in this way asserting a relationship to the civil rights movement while avoiding any appearance of attempting to usurp the mantle of King. This appropriation also makes it possible for Obama "to craft a strong version of American exceptionalism" because white, black, moderate, and even conservative Americans might respond to the image of the United States as a "chosen nation."[36] Obama has exploited the double bind in which his race deposits him to both align himself with the narrative of the civil rights movement and articulate an entirely unobjectionable version of that narrative.[37]

It is the emotional climax of Obama's address, however, that presents the most telling difference between him and Clinton. It would not be too much to say that Brown Chapel is one of the most sacred places of the civil rights movement, and in his address there Obama articulates an almost divine connection to those events. Not only "is my career the result of the work of the men and women who we honor here today," Obama insists, but indeed he owes his "very existence" to the movement. After acknowledging that some people might question whether he has had "the same experience" as African Americans who participated in the movement itself or lived during its immediate aftermath, he narrates an origin story that gives him access to its very fount. It begins when "a bunch of women decided they were going to walk instead of ride the bus after a long day of doing somebody else's laundry, looking after somebody else's children. When men who had PhDs—were working as Pullman porters—decided that's enough and we're going to stand up, despite the risks, for our dignity and our respect. That . . . sent a shout across oceans so that my grandfather began to imagine something different for his son." He notes that the Kennedys became inspired "to do an air lift" to bring "young Africans over to this country" and that his father, "this young man named Barack Obama[,] got one of those tickets." Obama continues: "And he met this woman whose great-great-great-great-grandfather had owned slaves; but she had a good idea—there was some good craziness going on because they looked at each other and they decided that we know that in the world as it has been it might not be possible for us to get together and have a child. There was something stirring across the country because of what happened in Selma, Alabama, because some folks are willing to march across a bridge. So they got together and Barack Obama Jr. was born." The crowd responds in a crescendo, building slowly from relatively muted affirmations and responses, in a pattern common in African American church services, to clapping and laughter when he refers to the "good craziness" responsible for his conception, and then by the end of the speech people are standing and Obama is shouting over their ovation: "So don't tell me I don't have a claim on Selma, Alabama. Don't tell me I'm not coming home to Selma, Alabama."

As several critics pointed out, Obama was taking some poetic license. The Selma marches actually took place four years after he was born. The Kennedys did not become involved in the educational program for young Kenyans until 1960, though Barack Obama Sr. arrived in Honolulu in September 1959.[38] The significance of the tale, however, is not its historical accuracy but its mythic impact.[39] In Obama's version, the airlift that brought his father to Hawaii, the meeting of his parents, and even Obama's birth itself are attributed to the civil rights movement, and specifically to the Selma to Montgomery march. Obama is thus an effect of the movement, a result of it, a Joshua sprung if not quite from the loins of the movement itself then—perhaps even more appropriately—from a "shout," as he puts it, roused by the movement, like the shout that felled the walls of Jericho at Joshua's command.

A comparison with the presentation of Obama's embodiment in "A More Perfect Union" is instructive. In that speech, he presents his commodious biracial body as capable of enveloping multiple perspectives, traditions, and experiences without resolving them into a homogeneous unity. That was not a transcendent or synthetic embodiment but instead a bringing together that preserved the distinctions of a multifaceted whole. In this speech at Selma, however, the civil rights movement is presented as a linear narrative with Obama as its endpoint, so that he appears to gather up the threads and weave them together into a single cloth. This is very much a sort of transcendence, a bringing together that is intended to dissolve differences and promote unity of identification and action.

While the specific narrative of miraculous birth seems unique to the address at Brown Chapel, Obama did develop similar themes throughout his campaign. In a speech he delivered at the annual Howard University Convocation, on September 28 of that same year, Obama promises that "If I have the opportunity to lead this nation, I will always be a President who hears your voice and understands your concerns; a President whose story is like so many of your own, whose life's work has been the unfinished work of our long march towards justice." As he draws his talk to a conclusion, he asks that his audience "remember the story of Moses and Joshua." The short narrative that follows begins the work of conflating the story of King and Obama with story of Moses and Joshua. He reminds them, for example, that "Moses was called by God to lead his people to the Promised Land" and that he led those people "across an unforgiving desert and along the walls of an angry sea" but that "it was not in God's plan to have Moses cross the river. Instead He would call on Joshua to finish the work that Moses began. He would ask Joshua to take his people that final distance."

The strongest association between Obama and Joshua occurs later in the speech, when Obama cues his audience to fill in the connections and in this way to participate in an *enthymeme,* a mode of persuasion in which an audience is invited to contribute elements of reasoning that have been implied but not explicitly supplied. "When Joshua discovered the challenge he faced," Obama continues, "he had his doubts and his worries. He told God, 'Don't choose me, I'm not strong enough, I . . . I'm not wise enough, I don't have the training, I don't have enough experience. . . . But the Lord told Joshua not to fear. He said, 'Be strong and have courage, for I am with you wherever you go.'" As there was at Brown Chapel, there is a palpable reaction from the audience, suggesting the rhetorical power unleashed as the two stories, Obama's and Joshua's, fuse in their minds. Obama's performance encourages this synergy, as he takes on the role of Joshua, performing his stuttering self-doubt with knowing glances over the top of the lectern. Richard Wolffe suggests that Obama "was drawing a line between King and himself, between the civil rights movement and his campaign, between African Americans and other minorities, between blacks and whites." But actually Obama does not need to spell out for this audience that King is Moses and that Obama is Joshua; Obama merely pauses for a moment, and there is an almost electric charge as his listeners assemble Obama, Joshua, Moses, Exodus, Selma, and King all together into a single garment of historical and biblical allusion.[40]

Obama does remind his audience that "one man cannot make a movement," that it "will take a movement to finish what began in Topeka, Kansas, and Little Rock, Arkansas," and that as "members of the Joshua generation . . . it is now up to you to finish the work that they began. It is up to you to cross the river." But while there may be many members of the Joshua generation, there is only one Joshua. While it may take a movement to complete the work of the Moses generation, the movement appears to have only one leader. Only one person can stand before them and promise to complete the "long march towards justice" begun decades ago. In 2007, no other candidate could have positioned himself as Obama did; perhaps no other candidate will be able to do so again. But the contrast is clear between these speeches and "A More Perfect Union," which was to come almost exactly a year later. In that later speech, Obama's does not ask his audience to follow him as his deploys his own biracial body to encompass dualities and negotiate divides but instead sets before them the task of developing this faculty in themselves. It is not enough for them to witness Obama's epiphany; they must turn to one another, address one another as fellow citizens, draw from his experiences and discursive model. In Selma, on the other hand, witnessing appears to be enough or at least nearly enough—these folks are expected to perform the citizenly obligation of going to the polls to express their allegiance to the new Joshua, it is true, but there is no expectation that witnessing this speech may embellish their ability to address one another as citizens or may foster the proliferation of additional perspectives. Not only is the historic civil rights movement portrayed here by reference to a single leader, King, but its continuation into the present is associated also with a single candidate, Obama.

A few months after the Howard speech, on January 20, 2008, Obama spoke in the new sanctuary of the famed Ebenezer Baptist in Atlanta, where King, with his father, was copastor from 1959 until his assassination. This speech bears some superficial resemblance to "A More Perfect Union." Much of it is devoted to describing an "empathy deficit," which he defines as "the inability to recognize ourselves in one another, to understand that we are our brother's keeper and our sister's keeper."[41] He explains that "racial reconciliation" cannot be "purchased on the cheap" and that it is "not easy to stand in somebody else's shoes." But while his address a few months later, in Philadelphia, would explore the trope of "wholeness," in Danielle Allen's terms, promoting cohesion while recognizing diversity, this speech at Ebenezer remains focused on a more homogeneous conception of unity.

The opening figure of the speech at Ebenezer relies on a misdirection; it at first seems that Obama will take as his text the story of Joshua and Jericho, when "at the chosen hour when the horn sounded and a chorus of voices cried out together, the mighty walls of Jericho came tumbling down." But he immediately funnels the scope of our attention through a progressive narrowing from the broad recognition that there are "many lessons to take from this passage, just as there are many lessons to take from this day, just as there are many memories that fill the space of this church," to the question of "which ones we needed to remember at this hour," and finally to a focus on "King the young preacher and a people who found themselves suffering under the yoke of oppression." Obama directs his audience away from the example of multiple voices shouting as one and toward attending only to one voice that spoke on behalf of the multitude. Indeed, Obama takes as his text at Ebenezer a quotation from Dr. King: "Unity is the great need of the hour."[42] It is through unity, Obama assures the audience, that "we shall overcome," recalling of course a hymn closely associated with King and with the sanctioned narrative of the civil rights movement.

This basic structure is reiterated throughout the speech at Ebenezer, as apparent calls for something like the more radically self-aware appreciation of plurality as articulated in "A More Perfect Union" are immediate attenuated or disciplined by a more traditional call for unity. Repeatedly, a potential for double-consciousness begins to emerge and then is quashed by the limitations that mark the boundaries of race talk in the United States. It is as though Obama repeatedly seeks out the broader vistas afforded by democratic double-consciousness, only to be rebuffed by the intractable confines of the racial narrative he is inhabiting. His audience is given fleeting glimpses of the possibility of a perspective-changing wholeness but is never allowed to pause to enjoy the view. Obama reminds his listeners, for example, that King believed that "if enough Americans were awakened to injustice, if they joined together North and South, rich and poor, Jew and Gentile, then perhaps that wall would come tumbling down, and justice would flow like waters of righteousness, like a mighty stream," but the apparent recognition of diversity is undermined when Obama urges his audience to "see past our own differences" rather than hold them before our eyes and appreciate them. When Obama asks his audience "to acknowledge the deep-seated violence that still resides in our own communities, in too many of the hearts of our young people," he seems to be inviting a communal self-reflection that can be an important component of double-consciousness. But as he continues, it becomes evident that he actually is urging each member of his audience to look at his or her community in the same way, to see the same problems, and to agree together on a single mode of action intended to address those problems. While Obama does suggest that achieving these goals will require some degree of "sacrifice" and "responsibility," this is not the broadly democratic public sacrifice that Allen and Du Bois describe but instead a circumscribed, private, and individualized responsibility to "be better parents, and turn off the television set, and put away the video game, and our men have to be home with our children."

It is in this address at Ebenezer that Obama first uses the story about Ashley Baia, the young campaign volunteer who as a child subsisted on relish sandwiches to save money while her mother battled cancer. The basic outline of the story remains the same as it will appear later in "A More Perfect Union," and it has the same denouement: when the older black man is asked why he has chosen to work on the Obama campaign, he says that he is there because of Ashley. But the story accomplishes markedly different ends in the two addresses. In "A More Perfect Union," as I have argued, the story of Ashley Baia and the elderly black volunteer models the ethic of reciprocity, as Ashley and the man seem able, at least in that moment, to address each other in a way that recognizes their differences and yet renders them comparable and retains their distinction without demanding that they remain entirely separate. At Ebenezer, however, the Ashley story is presented as a part of a form of a fortiori argument; that is, it is framed as describing an instance of unity where it might not have been expected, in order to advocate for some form of unity where it might be more expected. If it is possible for "that young white girl and that old black man" to recognize a common cause in each other, then certainly the African American community he is addressing, which he clearly is framing as more comparatively homogeneous, can recall how to "pray together . . . work together, and . . . march together."

This argumentative form appears elsewhere in the speech. If "Dr. King could love his jailer," Obama observes, for example, "if he could call on the faithful, who once sat where you do, to forgive those who had set dogs and fire hoses upon them, then surely we can look past what divides us in our time and bind up our wounds and erase the sympathy deficit that exists in our hearts." And really it is the primary trope that motivates the address as a whole: if the founders, and the abolitionists, and Lincoln, like King, were able to craft unity in their times and places, which were more complex and dangerous even than our own, then surely we shall be able to do so. In "A More Perfect Union" the Ashley story suggests the generative possibilities inherent in adopting a mode of address that encourages dual perspectives and thus the potential for a proliferation of speech acts to follow, ensuring that this single anecdote is not the single path to a more perfect union but only a place "where the perfection begins." At Ebenezer, the function of the Ashley story, amplified through the repetition of form, is very nearly the inverse, as it tamps down a proliferation of possibilities and instead direct its hearers toward a single action, a coming together as one.

These are campaign speeches, after all; they bear many markers of epideictic or ceremonial address, but ultimately Obama is asking for us to vote for him. Like the inaugural address discussed briefly in the first chapter, a campaign speech carries certain expectations, and these speeches meet those. The goal is to win an election, and it is advantageous for many potential voters to imagine that election as a continuation and perhaps as a potential culmination of a long historic narrative through which American ideals may be manifest at long last. These are not values from which Obama and his African American audience are alienated but rather are values that they already possess, and their manifestation does not require a multiplicity of voices and perspectives cultivated through a discourse of duality; double-consciousness plays little role here, and the tropes and figures through which it is fostered are either entirely missing or so tightly restrained that their transformative potential is blunted. The explicit goal of these speeches is to cultivate unity through the transcendence of difference.

The conflation of Obama's campaign with the African American civil rights movement is a potent rhetorical strategy, despite the limitations it presents to the invention of double-consciousness. But while it is possible to imagine a presidency that sustained this trope, transforming the constant campaign of the modern presidency into something more like a perpetual movement—indeed, it may be that this is what at least some of his supporters were hoping for when they elected him to office—in Obama's case this immensely powerful analogy is dropped almost entirely after the election. The result is that in his addresses the civil rights movement recedes into the distance, presented no longer as an ongoing event extending unbroken from the past and into the present with Obama's election as the culmination of the narrative but instead as a historical exemplar.

This is illustrated in Obama's address to the NAACP Centennial Convention, delivered on July 17, 2009, about seven months after his inauguration. The disjuncture with the past is clear, for though he begins by acknowledging that he stands "on the shoulders of giants," he also acknowledges that "the barriers of our time" are "very different from the barriers faced by earlier generations. They're very different from the ones faced when fire hoses and dogs were being turned on young marchers."[43] His use of pronouns is instructive. At Selma and Ebenezer, when he says "we" he generally is referring to his listeners as though they were members of this collective and continuing movement, but in this postelection address to the NAACP "we" refers unambiguously to him and to his administration: "we, all of us in government, have to work to do our part by not only offering more resources, but also demanding more reform," "when it comes to higher education we're making college and advanced training more affordable," "we're creating a Race to the Top fund," "these are some of the laws we're passing. These are some of the policies we are enacting. We are busy in Washington." "We" are not a transhistorical collective united in its efforts to continue the civil rights movement and not even a coalition of Obama and his audience; there is no productive ambiguity deployed here, no divine mythical synecdoche wherein Obama stands in for Joshua and King. This is the royal "we" of the modern bureaucrat describing and defending his agenda.

The few moments in which something like the expansiveness of "A More Perfect Union" begins to emerge are quickly disciplined through an attenuation similar to what we saw in the address at Ebenezer. Obama reminds his audience, for example, that "government programs alone won't get our children to the Promised Land," recollecting the movement-inflected "we" and opening the possibility for ground-level citizen engagement. It quickly becomes clear, however, that the mode of engagement suggested in this address to the NAACP is characterized by individual initiative rather than collective action. When he encourages young people and parents to "accept our responsibility," the pronoun includes him, personally, as a part of the group but does not present any sense of shared or communal responsibility. Though he says, with unintended irony, that this individualized sense of responsibility is "the meaning of community," there is no sense of double-consciousness here, no effort to cultivate the perspective of others, no obligation to recognize the burdens of citizenship. Obama makes it plain: "Your destiny is in your hands."

After Race

When Obama spoke about race during the 2008 presidential campaign, with the exception of "A More Perfect Union," he elicited a narrowly defined yet widely sanctioned version of the civil rights movement and placed himself and his campaign within its context, inviting his audiences to imagine his campaign as a continuation of that struggle and their vote for him as a means of participating in that movement. After he was elected, both the collective "journey" motifs and the Moses-Joshua story line dropped away and the civil rights movement receded into the past, but otherwise his public discourse when discussing race, even when addressing an explicitly activist organization such as the NAACP, remained fundamentally consistent with that from his campaign. This suggests that the limitations of race talk in the United States are unusually persistent. Obama's public address is confined by the same narrow channel of sanctified U.S. race talk regardless of his status as candidate or incumbent. It also indicates that these strictures are exceptionally powerful, capable of policing the public discourse even of the elected official often styled the leader of the free world. Of course, there are additional obstacles faced by an African American who would engage in public speech in the United States about race; the boundaries that confine the race talk of all citizens are particularly stringent for citizens of color. Many of Obama's supporters and even some of his critics have been disappointed that he has not spoken on race more often and more forcefully as president, but in actuality the wonder is that the myriad elements of the rhetorical situation aligned as they did in March 2008.

It should also be noted, of course, that the addresses examined thus far in this chapter were delivered before predominantly African American audiences. Further, the audiences in Selma or at Ebenezer and the NAACP were gathered because they wanted to imagine themselves to be unified, to share in a common collective memory, and to come together in a common cause. It may be, then, that the presentation of doubled tropes would have been inappropriate or even redundant in such venues. Du Bois's point, after all, was that double-consciousness was an inevitable effect of being black in America, a phenomenon with which African Americans necessarily would be familiar and thus a feeling that Obama would not need to reiterate when addressing such audiences. This also illustrates that democratic double-consciousness requires the conceptual space of a larger stage. It is a discourse of citizenship and perhaps as such requires

an audience that is imagined to be or that is addressed as though it were representative of the citizenry writ large, in all of its diversity and incipient duality;
it may also require a rhetorical situation that invites an explicit contemplation
of citizenship as a mode of address, rather than as some more instrumental act,
such as voting or supporting a campaign.

It is often by looking at the moments when social norms are breached that
they are brought to our attention most vividly, and two incidents that occurred
during Obama's first term in office serve that function here. The arrest of Henry
Louis Gates Jr.—the same theorist whose work has been cited several times in
this book—early in Obama's first term in office and the shooting of Trayvon
Martin late in that same term produced rhetorical situations that were not conducive to breaching the norms governing race talk in the United States and yet
invited Obama to comment on race.[44] In both cases, his comments were brief,
but their perceived transgression of these norms evoked an outsized response.

On July 22, 2009, just a few days after Obama's speech to the NAACP, at
the end of a press conference on health care reform, Lynn Sweet, of the Chicago *Sun-Times,* was given the opportunity to ask the president about Gates's
recent arrest. Gates had returned from the airport to find the front door of his
home jammed and asked his cab driver to help force it open. A passerby called
911, and a police sergeant, James Crowley, soon arrived and asked Gates for
identification. Accounts vary as to what happened next, but the upshot was that
Gates was arrested for disorderly conduct. The charges were quickly dropped,
and the entire incident likely would have gone largely unnoticed had it not been
for Obama's response to Sweet's question: "What does that incident say to you
and what does it say about race relations in America?" After acknowledging
that Gates "is a friend" and that "I don't know all the facts," Obama stated
that "the Cambridge Police acted stupidly in arresting somebody when there
was already proof that they were in their own home" and reminded the press
corps that "that there is a long history in this country of African Americans and
Latinos being stopped by law enforcement disproportionately."[45] Public outcry
was immediate and unrelenting, echoing in many ways the outcry that had met
Reverend Wright's sermons, suggesting that this was a similar breach of racial
decorum; the radio and television talk show host Glenn Beck, for example, declared that Obama was a "racist" with a "deep-seated hatred for white people
or the white culture."[46]

A few days later, Obama made an unannounced appearance in the White
House briefing room to clarify his remarks. In his statement, he notes that
"race is still a troubling aspect of our society" and that "whether I were black
or white, I think that me commenting on this and hopefully contributing to

constructive—as opposed to negative—understandings about the issue, is part of my portfolio." He believes, in other words, that commenting on situations like this is a part of his obligation as president, signaling that from his point of view this was a rhetorical situation that called for his response. But he also acknowledges that his particular response had "obviously helped to contribute [to the] ratcheting . . . up" of media attention to the incident and says that he "could have calibrated those words differently." Those differently calibrated words evidently would have been in a more doubled idiom, as suggested by Obama's observation that "there was an overreaction in pulling Professor Gates out of his home" but that also "Professor Gates probably overreacted as well." "My sense," he continued, "is you've got two good people in a circumstance in which neither of them were able to resolve the incident in the way that it should have been resolved and the way they would have liked it to be resolved."[47] He recommends that "instead of pumping up the volume" we should "spend a little more time listening to each other."

These comments seem aligned with the sentiments of the Philadelphia address in that they encourage his listeners to view the issue from dual perspectives and present an obligation to address issues like this both as a part of his burden as president and as a part of his listeners' burden as citizens. At the same time, however, the stated goal of these brief remarks to the press is not to cultivate a constructive public conversation on race or to model a more productive public dialogue but to walk back his previous comments and to close down further discussion. He comes close to apologizing for bringing up the issue in the first place—"to the extent that my choice of words didn't illuminate, but rather contributed to more media frenzy, I think that was unfortunate"—and even closer to dismissing the entire affair because it is a distraction and "nobody has been paying much attention to health care." The speech in Philadelphia was prepared and delivered in response to the Reverend Wright crisis and presents an unusually rich resource that can be drawn on in the invention of ways to address one another as citizens. In contrast, the rhetorical end point of the Henry Louis Gates kerfuffle consisted of Obama inviting Gates and police sergeant Crowley to the White House to have a beer.

This was to be a "teachable moment," as Obama put it, but it was a peculiarly quiet lesson.[48] The three principals in the matter (and Vice President Joe Biden) sat around a table at the edge of the Rose Garden, well out of earshot of the gathered press, and they drank their beers. What they said or how they said it was not reported; no ways of speaking in public were modeled. The implied message was that discussions about race, even and perhaps especially in highly visible public spaces, should be entirely private affairs. As a lesson in how democratic citizens should talk to one another—about race, about other controversial issues, or indeed about anything at all—the beer summit was a particularly chilling exercise.

On February 26, 2012, Trayvon Martin was shot and killed in Sanford, Florida. Martin was seventeen years old and was walking from a convenience store to his father's fiancé's home in a gated community, carrying candy and a drink. George Zimmerman, a neighborhood watch volunteer, saw Martin and called 911 to report his suspicions about him. The operator asked Zimmerman not to pursue Martin, but he did so anyway. Exactly what happened next remains unclear and in fact was a central issue in the subsequent trial, but in the end Zimmerman shot Martin once in the chest at close range. The incident drew national attention, in part because Zimmerman initially invoked Florida's controversial "Stand Your Ground" law, which sanctions the use of deadly force when a threat is perceived, and in part because Zimmerman initially was released by police after the shooting—but mostly the matter drew attention because of its racial dynamics: Martin was black, and Zimmerman was of a white and Hispanic mixed background. Obama was just beginning his reelection campaign and at first remained silent about the case despite the fact that many urged him to weigh in on the matter. Then, on March 23, at the end of a press conference announcing Jim Yong Kim as his choice to be president of the World Bank, Obama took a question on the Trayvon Martin case. Obama called the incident a "tragedy" and continued: "I can only imagine what these parents are going through. And when I think about this boy, I think about my own kids." His "main message," he continued, "is to the parents of Trayvon Martin. You know, if I had a son he'd look like Trayvon."[49]

It was this last comment that elicited vigorous rebukes from some of Obama's political opponents. On Sean Hannity's radio show, Newt Gingrich called the comment "disgraceful" and went on to note that it should not matter whether Martin "had been Puerto Rican or Cuban or if he had been white or if he had been Asian American or if he'd been a Native American." "Trying to turn it into a racial issue is fundamentally wrong," Gingrich concludes. "I really find it appalling."[50] Rick Santorum, on other talk radio programs, observed that "the president has been not a uniting figure on an issue that I think many Americans thought he would be" and that bringing up "very sensitive issues" such as race "is out of line for this president."[51] Michelle Malkin argued that "Obama is all too willing to pour gas on the fire" of race relations and that Martin's "race and looks" had nothing to do with the matter.[52] Even Abigail Thernstrom, vice chair of the U.S. Commission on Civil Rights, in phrasing that recalls much of the criticism that was leveled at Obama after his comments about the arrest of Henry Louis Gates Jr., wrote that "President Obama's interference in a local law enforcement matter was unprecedented and inappropriate, and he comes away from the case looking badly tarnished by his poor judgment." In particular, she accuses Obama of playing the tragedy for political gain, for although if Martin had been Obama's son "he would have been born to extraordinary privilege and raised with all the advantages of two very affluent and highly educated parents," Obama "wants disadvantaged Americans to believe that he and his family are one of them."[53]

Such criticisms, however, again miss that the real significance of Obama's comments is not that he brings race into the issue but rather that he does so in such a restrained and confined manner. He does not place the incident in any historical context, does not bring to bear the collective obligations of citizenship, certainly does not invite dual perspectives or multivocal flexibility, and does not either explicitly or implicitly invite or model further public address. Instead he suggests that we all should turn inward and "do some soul searching to find out why something like this happened," and he frames his statement as a personal message to Martin's parents. Yet still he was criticized because his comments strayed from the sanctioned racial narrative that he more safely evoked at Brown Chapel and Ebenezer Baptist. If the "beer summit" following the Gates incident was notable as a peculiarly quiet teachable moment about how U.S. citizens might best address one another, Obama's comments on Trayvon Martin were barely audible—and even then, too loud for some.

Dedicated to King

A productive contrast to the other addresses analyzed in this chapter is Obama's brief statement at the dedication of the Martin Luther King Jr. memorial in Washington, D.C. The memorial, located at the edge of the Tidal Basin, just south of the reflecting pool on the National Mall, was supposed to be dedicated on August 28, 2011, the forty-eighth anniversary of the March on Washington for Jobs and Freedom and of course the anniversary also of King's most famous address. But then an earthquake on August 23 damaged the Washington National Cathedral, where one of the prededication events was scheduled, and Hurricane Irene made landfall in North Carolina, Virginia, and New Jersey on August 27–28, pushing the dedication ceremony to October 16, 2011.[54] Obama's brief address bears a similarity to "A More Perfect Union," delivered about three and a half years earlier, demonstrating that this mode of discourse has not entirely vacated Obama's public statements on racial issues. At the same time, however, this example of democratic double-consciousness is domesticated by the occasion; at the dedication of a memorial portraying King, it is not surprising that the discourse that governs the contemporary portrayal of King would exert an unusual influence. While the broad reach of a dedication of a new monument on the National Mall affords Obama an opportunity to evoke democratic double-consciousness, still the narrow confines of the safe and sanctioned civil rights movement narrative blunts its transformative potential.

This speech begins by positioning King as one voice among many, suggesting that King would agree that the "movement of which he was a part depended on an entire generation of leaders" as well as "the multitudes of men and women whose names never appear in the history books" but to whom we owe "our everlasting gratitude." We also are instructed to "draw strength from those earlier struggles" and to display the same "persistence" and "determination" that King and others have shown in the past when confronting outrages and inequalities in the present. When "we think about all the work that we must do" we must recall the sacrifice that has been made and be willing to reciprocate through sacrifices of our own. This is neither a detached professorial "we" nor an agenda-defending bureaucratic "we" but a collective "we" that includes himself, the civil rights movement veterans gathered with him, African Americans, and U.S. citizens in general, brought together in an interdependent web of sacrifice and reciprocity.

The portrait of King that Obama presents here stands in contrast to the single-dimensional figure presented in his campaign speeches, including those at King's own churches, Brown Chapel and Ebenezer Baptist. In a series of balanced parallel phrases of the sort almost entirely missing from those addresses, Obama reminds his audience that although "it is right for us to celebrate today Dr. King's dream and his vision of unity . . . it is also important on this day to remind ourselves that such progress did not come easily" and that while it is "right for us to celebrate Dr. King's marvelous oratory, . . . it is worth remembering that progress did not come from words alone." In describing what he hopes his own daughters will take away from this monument, he wonders what King's advice might be, and he phrases that advice in couplets: he imagines that King would "want them to know that he had setbacks, because they will have setbacks. He would want them to know that he had doubts, because they will have doubts. He would want them to know that he was flawed, because all of us have flaws." This is not merely a portrayal of a complex and ultimately human King—"a man of flesh and blood and not a figure of stone," as Obama puts it—but also a way to talk about King. King is not here merely standing in for Moses as an icon of heroic leadership and martyrdom but is presented as an exemplar of human-scale action. This way of speaking about King also is a way of speaking about each of us as citizens, as people who sometimes are right, sometimes wrong, sometimes sure, sometimes not, and perhaps sometimes eloquent but always and inevitably flawed.

The emotional climax of this speech comes when Obama summarizes King's teachings, engaging in a form of *prosopopoeia,* or speaking in the voice of another, the rhetorical effect perhaps amplified in the moment, as Obama and his audience stand before the giant statue of King and partially enclosed by walls inscribed with King's words. "He calls on us," Obama says, "to stand in the other person's shoes; to see through their eyes; to understand their pain. He tells us that we have a duty to fight against poverty, even if we are well off; to care about the child in the decrepit school even if our own children are doing fine; to show compassion toward the immigrant family, with the knowledge that most of us are only a few generations removed from similar hardships." These are not King's words and are not attributed to him by Obama as quotations but are presented as a distillation of King's political and moral philosophy —though the emphasis on sight, mutual recognition, and the cultivation of a duality of perspectives perhaps recalls more strongly Du Bois's pragmatism than King's sometimes more ethereal vision. The sacrifice of previous generations recalls both the 2009 inaugural and "A More Perfect Union," as does a critique of a homogeneous unity even more explicit than in those addresses: "To say that we are bound together as one people, and must constantly strive to see ourselves in one another, is not to argue for a false unity that papers over our differences and ratifies an unjust status quo."

With reference to the tenets of democratic double-consciousness, this clearly is a speech about citizenship, citizenship not as legal status but rather as a mode of address, not merely a recognition of one's self in another but also a way of speaking to one another in manner that articulates that recognition with a democratic political culture. "If he were alive today," Obama continues, now more explicitly presenting his own discourse as an interpretation of King, "I believe he would remind us that the unemployed worker can rightly challenge the excesses of Wall Street without demonizing all who work there; that the businessman can enter tough negotiations with his company's union without vilifying the right to collectively bargain. He would want us to know we can argue fiercely about the proper size and role of government without questioning each other's love for this country." Challenging, demonizing, negotiating, vilifying, arguing, questioning: these are all modes of address, presented here in pairs that themselves suggest the agonistic character of the dialogic civic culture that Obama is imagining. Again, the dream here arguably owes at least as much to Du Bois as to King, recalling Du Bois's "foregrounding of listening, speech, and writing [that] ties consciousness to the production of language and to the relationship of self to others."[55] But in Obama's articulation, the relationship between address and duality bears a distinctly and explicitly democratic inflection: the passage concludes with his admonition that "in this democracy, government is no distant object but is rather an expression of our common commitments to one another."

And yet, this expression of democratic double-consciousness is constrained by the sanctioned King-centered narrative. Though Obama acknowledges that others contributed to the civil rights movement and that King "would be the first to remind us that this memorial is not for him alone," none of the specific contributions of these others is mentioned. While Obama does acknowledge that King was a complex person, none of King's more radical statements, especially those from later in his career, are recalled. This speech flows comfortably within the channel of the accepted King narrative, and the banks of this channel limit its possibilities. The third inventional resource associated with a discourse of democratic double-consciousness is unrealized here; a proliferation of voices and perspectives cannot be accommodated within a sanctioned King narrative that has been crafted specifically through an effort to edit out multiple voices and perspectives. Though Obama does present King as advocating a form of democratic dialogue, there is little suggestion that this dialogue might expand into a more multivalent conversation. This rhetorical situation offers an opportunity to speak about race to a diverse audience and thus to enact some tenets of democratic double-consciousness; but still the strictures on race talk in the contemporary U.S. public culture prevail, attenuating its potential.

Conclusion

Obama's dedication of the King memorial displays the inventional resources of democratic double-consciousness far more richly than the other addresses analyzed in this chapter. One factor that contributes to this difference is audience. When he is dedicating the memorial, the speech is imagined to be addressed to the entire nation, in all of its diversity, about a subject that is potentially divisive.[56] This is a situation that calls for the broadened scope fostered through doubled tropes and dual perspectives; in a speech delivered on the National Mall and nationally televised, addressing the whole polity and multiple perspectives on King and the civil rights movement, the evocation of double-consciousness provides an unusually productive and flexible rhetorical adaptation. Though this emphasizes the extent to which Obama was addressing his African American audiences as though they were homogeneous, it also suggests that a democratic discourse is perhaps best imagined as addressing a diverse plurality. It should invite an acknowledgment of the various points of view that characterize the public and model a way of speaking through which those points of view can be acknowledged without becoming obstacles to further discourse. While this speech does not do all of those things as copiously as "A More Perfect

Union," it does do some of them, and the particular rhetorical situation it was crafted to address accounts, in part, for that.

These analyses, then, emphasize the nature of democratic double-consciousness as *addressed;* it is a *rhetoric,* a verbal performance drawing upon the inventional resources available in specific situations and directed to specific audiences, with the purpose of equipping citizens for productive public engagement. Obama, like Du Bois, is describing not a state of being but a mode of action, and particularly a mode of speech. The self-consciousness that characterizes this mode of speech becomes most salient when it is practiced within a public addressed as diverse, when the "second persona" of citizenly address, the imagined or implied audience, is representative of the entire polity. It is then that the gaze of multiple others is most intense, and it is then that the motive to acknowledge division without calling for homogeneity is most appropriate. Where the resources of democratic double-consciousness are most fully manifest, as in "A More Perfect Union," they provide an unusually powerful store of deeply democratic rhetorical possibility, animated by an obligation to shuck off the limitations of an unencumbered self and instead to view oneself from the point of view of another, not only to appreciate but also to participate in a networked ethic of reciprocity and sacrifice, to become *engaged* in the most radical and transformative sense.

These analyses also illustrate both the severe limitations on race talk in contemporary U.S. culture and the effects of those constraints on the articulation of democratic double-consciousness. All of these discourses address U.S. race relations, but with the exception of the remarks at the dedication of the King memorial they are almost completely devoid of inventional resources that might foster double-consciousness, and even the articulation of double-consciousness in the dedicatory remarks is incomplete. These limitations can be drawn into relief when considering Obama's avowed interest in and admiration for Malcolm X. In *Dreams from My Father,* Obama declares that Malcolm's "repeated acts of self-creation spoke to me" and that "the blunt poetry of his words, his unadorned insistence on respect, promised a new and uncompromising order, martial in discipline, forged"—like Du Bois's conception of African American character—"through sheer force of will."[57] Obama also acknowledges that Malcolm's autobiography was useful to him as he "tried to untangle the twin strands of black nationalism, arguing that nationalism's affirming message—of solidarity and self-reliance, discipline and communal responsibility—need not depend on hatred of whites any more than it depended on white munificence."[58] David Remnick suggests that "it is not impossible to figure out why Obama is so taken with Malcolm. Malcolm's is a narrative of mixed race, a missing father, and self-invention." Remnick also suggests that Obama admired Malcolm's ability to embrace opposing ideas, "the self-confident, charismatic, eloquent leader who comes to see his faith in a broader, more humanist light, the militant who begins to see the value of a broader embrace."[59]

Malcolm X, however, is completely absent from Obama's oratory. The public memory of Malcolm X never underwent the transformation, sanitization, and domestication that King's did; there is not, nor shall there ever be, a U.S. federal holiday in honor of Malcolm X. Unlike King, Malcolm X is remembered with much of his complexity and imperfection—and his blackness—intact. His absence from Obama's version of racial reconciliation is only the most obvious sign that this is a story of the civil rights movement as a rather one-sided affair, characterized by a heroic and monovocalic narrative rather than by vibrant dis-agreement among diverse people with varied histories, concerns, and goals. So while it certainly would be possible to tell a story that portrayed the civil rights movement as microcosm of democratic practice, as characterized not by homog-eneous unity but by often-vehement argument among individuals representing a vast array of perspectives who nonetheless, collectively, were able to move the public culture of the United States toward a more perfect union—Taylor Branch's trilogy, with which Obama has said that he identifies, is one way such a story might be told—close attention to Obama's public discourse reminds us that even when the strictures on race talk are temporarily suspended, however incompletely, this is not a story one can easily tell.[60] Though it is possible to treat memoir as a form of public discourse, as I have been throughout this book with regard to Obama's *Dreams from My Father,* in doing so we must remain cognizant of the rhetorical specificities of its audience, purpose, and context. Apparently, there are things that Obama might say in a memoir, particularly in one written before he was a national public figure, that he cannot say in a public speech. Only in truly exceptional circumstances, such as those afforded Obama by the emergence of the Reverend Wright sermons at the precise moment in his campaign when he was poised to take control of the Democratic primaries, can democratic double-consciousness be voiced in discourses that address racial matters outside of the sanctioned civil rights movement narrative.

Though the concept of double-consciousness is rooted in American race relations, race as a topic of public discourse presents rather severe limitations for the development of the tropes of duality through which double-conscious-ness may be cultivated or sustained. In the next chapter, I turn my attention to some of Obama's public address that is not explicitly about race, to explore the potential for such discourse to present inventional resources that foster demo-cratic double-consciousness. To the extent that they do so, they present not a break with race but rather a continuation and expansion, as they show Obama drawing a mode of address that is deeply implicated in U.S. race relations into public discourse that is not explicitly about U.S. race relations. These addresses illustrate the way that a form of double-consciousness, though associated with the work of an African American cultural theorist who described an African American experience of citizenship more than a hundred years ago, might be brought to bear upon issues that exceed questions of race in the present. The speeches analyzed in the next chapter, in other words, show Obama bringing a deeply raced discursive sensibility into a contemporary public sphere character-ized by a pervasive allergy to discourses on race.

— CHAPTER 5 —

Beyond the Veil

W. E. B. Du Bois describes *The Souls of Black Folk* as inviting his readers to cross between the "two worlds within and without the Veil." The veil is a central motif in the book, portrayed as an "awful shadow" that falls between him and the opportunities that are afforded those in the white world, though also, in a flight of fancy, Du Bois imagines that he might "dwell above the Veil," however temporarily. The veil, as Du Bois portrays it, is a multifaceted and semipermeable membrane that both marks division and conceals it, drawing our attention to racial difference while also obscuring its significance. It settles on us all, but of course it is more visible to some than to others and is more easily lifted in some circumstances than in others. The "second sight" that Du Bois describes makes the veil not only more clearly visible but also more permeable. The veil is a portal between worlds, as described by Du Bois, through which insights native to one world might be made available to the other.[1]

This chapter focuses on three speeches that Barack Obama delivered during his first term in office that traverse the veil, bringing the transformative potentials of democratic double-consciousness out of the narrow strictures imposed upon race talk. They present some of the ways that a discursive practice firmly rooted in African American experience and rhetorical culture might be brought out onto a wider stage; they present instances in which the "mixed inheritance" of U.S. civic culture is drawn upon as a heuristic designed to map "the contours of the present" and, through this process, to contribute to the construction of "a democratic theory that is itself broadly democratic."[2] Any theory of discursive citizenship that is especially well suited to contemporary U.S. civic culture would incorporate and bring into the present the rhetorical resources made available through the problematics of race and citizenship; to ignore such resources would be to severely limit such conceptions. The speeches that are focused on in this chapter—Obama's address to Congress on health care reform, delivered September 9, 2009; his Nobel Prize Lecture, delivered December 10, 2009; and his address on the economy at Osawatomie, Kansas, on December 6, 2011—are rich resources of duality as a discourse of citizenship that also demonstrate some of the variation and limitation that accrue to democratic double-consciousness within contexts that exceed the confines of race.

In "A More Perfect Union," the rhetorical situation presented an opportunity to address the significance of race in U.S. civic culture and, in the process, present an unusually rich resource for the invention of citizenly discourse. That speech models a manner not only of talking about race but also of talking to one another as citizens. It presents a full enactment of democratic double-consciousness as it offers a dual perspective as a productive mode of citizenship, transforms this duality into an active mode of address, and suggests that an initial duality that is enacted in this way might foster a proliferation of multiple voices and points of view. That speech was an anomaly, however, as illustrated in the previous chapter. Even for someone with the prodigious rhetorical prowess of Barack Obama and even after he had gained a political office of immense power, the boundaries imposed upon race talk in the United States prove to be formidable. The rhetorical situation that made possible the rich articulation of democratic double-consciousness in "A More Perfect Union" is difficult to replicate. Only the dedication of the Martin Luther King Jr. memorial on the National Mall offered a similar opportunity, and Obama's address there does articulate a vision of productive citizenship and does model a mode of dual address; but even then, the sanctioned narrative of the civil rights movement and the singular focus on King that it promotes restrict the proliferation of duality into multiplicity and thus limit the democratic scope of the double-consciousness it presents.

The three addresses analyzed in this chapter are some of Obama's most significant statements on some of the most significant issues that he confronted during his first term. Certainly these are not the only subjects that a discourse of democratic double-consciousness might address, and neither are they the only examples of Obama's discourse that might be understood as providing these inventional resources, but they are representative of his speeches addressed to audiences imagined as representative of the entire polity, and they do invite us to address one another in a way that is a fitting adaptation to the diversity that characterizes contemporary public culture in the United States.

The previous chapter enhanced our understanding of democratic double-consciousness by emphasizing the limitations placed upon it when it is articulated in race talk. In addition to describing some of the potentialities and limitations of double-consciousness as articulated in discourse not explicitly about race, this chapter also emphasizes the importance of democratic double-consciousness being associated with an exemplary figure. In "A More Perfect Union," Obama presents Ashley and the old man as embodying this mode of address. In his address to Congress on health care reform, Obama presents Ted

Kennedy as an embodiment of a dual perspective that enlivens the sometimes detached quality of paratactic speech. In Obama's telling, Kennedy presents a mode of judgment and political engagement that is informed by duality but also animated by passion and empathy. In his Nobel Peace Prize Lecture, Obama presents a compelling discourse of ethical realism through which the relationship between war and peace might be reconceived and sets out a bold modification of the just-war doctrine that has long governed talk of war. But after presenting war and peace as interdependent and, in fact, in some ways similar, the speech does not seem to provide a robust mechanism for judgment among these comparable alternatives and thus illustrates a limitation of a discourse of duality. The speech on the economy at Osawatomie, Kansas, presents Theodore Roosevelt as an embodiment of robust civic duality. Roosevelt lends to Obama's doubled discourse the patina of tradition, so that democratic double-consciousness might be understood not as radical but instead as the revivification of essential but neglected modes of speech. While both the speech on health care reform and the speech on the economy present vivid exemplars associated with the invention of doubled address, the Nobel Prize Lecture does not, and this may account for some of its limitations, to the extent that judgment, at least as it is associated with double-consciousness, is more embodied act than abstract ratiocination.

Health Care Reform

In Obama's first book, *Dreams from My Father,* published in 1995 while he was still a young civil rights attorney in Chicago, he is portrayed sitting in a church basement with a woman named Mrs. Stevens. "By way of small talk," he asks her why she was "so concerned with improving health care in the area," and he is moved by her story of almost losing her sight in her twenties from cataracts because she couldn't afford the operation she needed.[3] In his second book, *The Audacity of Hope,* published in 2006, just after he was sworn in as a U.S. senator and just before he began to consider a run for the presidency, health care reform receives considerably more attention. Obama refers to the current system as "broken: wildly expensive, terribly inefficient, and poorly adapted to an economy no longer built on lifetime employment, a system that exposes hardworking Americans to chronic insecurity and possible destitution."[4] Obama calls health care reform "our most pressing task," even more important than "rais[ing] the wages of American workers and improv[ing] their retirement security."[5] And he proceeds to give details of "just one example of what a serious health-care reform plan might look like," a plan that bears many points of resemblance to the legislation that eventually was signed into law on March 23, 2010.[6]

Given that Obama has consistently showed himself as possessing an abiding interest in health care reform, it is not surprising that when he announced his candidacy on February 10, 2007, on the steps of the old statehouse in Springfield, Illinois, the issue was present as a key plank in his platform. He called on his supporters to "be the generation that finally, after all these years, tackles our health care crisis. . . . Let's be the generation that says right here, right now: We will have universal health care in America by the end of the next President's first term. We can do that."[7] After his victory in the Iowa caucuses, he promised that he will "be a President who finally makes health care affordable and available to every single American, the same way I expanded health care in Illinois, . . . by bringing Democrats and Republicans together to get the job done."[8] When he clinched the Democratic nomination, as a part of his praise for Hillary Rodham Clinton he promised that "you can rest assured that when we finally win the battle for universal health care in this country—and we will win that fight—she will be central to that victory."[9]

In the months immediately following his election, Obama began a politically costly effort to enact health care reform legislation. Most of the arguments he presented in public addresses on the subject were couched in a relatively dispassionate economic idiom. A few months after his inauguration, for example, in an address at Georgetown University, Obama declared that "nothing will be more important to this goal [entitlement reform] than passing health care reform that brings down costs across the system, including in Medicare and Medicaid."[10] Early the next month, on March 5, 2009, Obama announced the opening of the White House Forum on Health Care, referring to the "exploding costs of health care in America today" as "one of the greatest threats not just to the well-being of our families and the prosperity of our businesses, but to the very foundation of our economy."[11] On June 15, Obama addressed the American Medical Association at its annual convention in Chicago. He told the assembled medical professionals that digitizing medical records "will not only mean less paper-pushing and lower administrative costs, saving taxpayers billions of dollars; it will also mean all of you physicians will have an easier time doing your jobs." He promised that he wanted to invest "more in preventive care so we can avoid illness and disease in the first place." Health care reform must enable "every American [to] get coverage they can afford," he continued, "in part because it's in all of our economic interests."[12]

Though these addresses were seasoned with frequent references to individual men and women who would benefit from reform, these people were addressed primarily as economic case studies. In "A More Perfect Union," the relatively detached voice in the middle portion of the speech eventually was supplanted by an engaged and interested mode of citizenly address; a discourse that would foster democratic double-consciousness cannot merely diagnose but must also invite citizenly engagement by modeling and advocating for a mode of citizenly address. An economic discourse need not be dispassionate, of course, but these speeches generally inhabit an analytical and wonkish register that seems to leave little room for a more embodied discourse. Democratic double-consciousness requires the portrayal of a doubled mode through which citizens might address one another as citizens, but there is little in these addresses that is analogous to the intimate portrayals of the Ashley story or even the relatively human-scale portrayal of Martin Luther King Jr.

The dispassionate analysis that characterized Obama's speeches during this time cannot be said to have dominated the public sphere. During the August, 2009, congressional recess, a number of senators and representatives returned to their home districts and hosted town hall meetings on health care reform, apparently in an extension of Obama's efforts to correct some of the misinformation that was being circulated. In many cases, however, the images that filled TV screens and news blogs did not depict the calm dissemination of facts but instead revealed the raucous protests that often made it difficult for the administration representatives to speak.[13]

In Mehlville, Missouri, a suburb of St. Louis, the "back and forth between factions within the crowd created a carnival-like atmosphere inside and out between members of the movement opposing President Barack Obama's policies and groups who came to show support for the president's proposals."[14] Meetings were similarly disrupted in the Detroit suburb of Romulus, Michigan, and when House Speaker Nancy Pelosi visited a homeless clinic in Denver. In Boiling Springs, South Carolina, Representative Bob Inglis, a Republican, "was repeatedly interrupted when he said government could in some cases play a positive role in people's lives."[15] In the Tampa, Florida, suburb of Ybor City, some 1,500 people attended or attempted to attend a town hall meeting where a "freelance videographer was roughed up in an altercation, which damaged his camera equipment and glasses, and at least one man was treated for minor injuries after a scuffle left his shirt partially torn from his body." At this same rally, "Democratic lawmakers had a difficult time delivering their opening remarks as they were met with shouts of 'You work for us!' 'Tyranny! tyranny! tyranny!' and 'Read the bill!'"[16]

There was a strong visual component to these disruptive spectacles as many protestors dressed up to portray Uncle Sam, Benjamin Franklin, Native Americans, Revolutionary soldiers, and Captain America. A common poster at these protests showed a photo of Obama modified to resemble the Joker from the 2008 Batman film *The Dark Knight* and captioned with the single word "Socialism."[17] Other common visuals that emerged at various protests across the country included "the 'ObamaCare' poster featuring a dark 'witch doctor' with Obama's face digitally sutured to the image" and "the 'Barack the Barbarian' cartoon featuring Obama as a hard-bodied barbarian wielding a Bronze Age axe directed at a scantily clad white woman with long blonde hair."[18] At times, the threat of violence implied in these posters and slogans was much more explicit. A man at a town hall meeting in Maryland, for example, was arrested while holding a sign that read "Death to Obama" and "Death to Michelle and her two stupid kids." In New Hampshire, a man stood across the street from a town hall meeting holding his gun in plain sight.[19]

As the disruption and threats continued to escalate, Obama retained his characteristically calm demeanor. Obama's weekly radio address on August 15, 2009, is representative. He reminds his listeners that "TV loves a ruckus" but that actually there were "many constructive meetings going on all over the country where Americans are airing their hopes and concerns about this very important issue." He offers a pointed critique of some of the stories that were being told, such as "one of the scarier-sounding and more ridiculous rumors out there—that so-called 'death panels' would decide whether senior citizens get to live or die." He chastises "folks with a stake in the status quo" who "keep inventing these boogeymen in an effort to scare people," noting that "it's disappointing, but it's not surprising." These characterizations of the protestors do not suggest much opportunity for perspective-taking, setting them as irrational rather than as worthy of engagement, but Obama does finish that brief address with a call for reasoned dialogue, noting that there "are legitimate differences worthy of the real discussion that America deserves—one where we lower our voices, listen to one another, and talk about differences that really exist."[20] Where ridiculous people might cause a ruckus by telling scary stories and conjuring imaginary tribunals, Obama counsels instead that the situation calls for the hushed tones of rational debate.

He presents himself as "a participant observer" of these proceedings, "in, but not of" them, observing them from afar as though he were not a principal player, diagnosing their ills without modeling a mode of address designed to more productively engage them.[21] The call to dialogue is a nod toward the duality that characterizes "A More Perfect Union," but, as with so much of his public discourse on healthcare during the first months of his presidency, this call is all but muted because it is not followed up with a representative anecdote of doubled address. The "moral hesitancy" that can be an effect of detached observation can make an important contribution to democratic double-consciousness, as was illustrated in "A More Perfect Union," but it has to be supplemented by a mode of engagement.

Obama had announced that his goal was to enact comprehensive health care reform by the end of the calendar year, but by August the Congress, which was controlled by Democrats, had not been able to produce legislation, and ubiquitous video clips from unruly and unproductive town hall meetings had helped to create a strong oppositional narrative in the press; CBS news reported that "as angry protests erupted over health care at town hall meetings over the month of August, Americans in general became angrier on the issue."[22] Polls showed decreasing public support for health care reform, and yet Obama was, as Karen Tumulty, a reporter for *Time* magazine, put it, "on the verge of a lot more progress than we have seen in an issue that has defeated a lot of presidents."[23] As the summer dragged on, some observers became frustrated by Obama's repeated efforts to list calmly the provisions of his proposal and to appeal to rationality. David Corn, Washington D.C. bureau chief for *Mother Jones* magazine, observed that "with his health care reform effort hitting trouble on Capitol Hill, it may be that Obama does have an anger problem—as in, not enough of it."[24]

The speech that Obama delivered to Congress that fall was not angry in tone and in fact may be best remembered for an intemperate outburst that contrasted with Obama's demeanor. But it did supply the necessary modeling of a mode of address and did so in a way that both embodied that mode of address and infused it with human compassion. Presidential addresses to joint sessions, beyond the annual State of the Union address, are relatively rare events, and Obama's choice to convene such a session in order to address Congress on health care reform raised the stakes considerably, but it also provided the opportunity to address an audience imagined to represent the citizenry at large. When he addressed Congress on September 9, 2009, Obama not only delivered a powerfully emotional rejoinder to his opponents but, by associating that emotion with the recently deceased Ted Kennedy, also associated it with a peculiarly potent form of democratic duality.

Continuity and Calm

The speech begins by reminding the audience of the previous time that Obama had spoken to a joint session of Congress, on February 24, 2009, to address the economic crisis, but then asserts that "we did not come here just to clean up crises. We came here to build a future." This disarticulation of economic crisis and health care reform—one as a crisis, the other as a future—contrasts with his repeated attempts to link them throughout the spring and summer of 2009. The speech also announces a more impassioned tone than that which characterized most of those previous speeches on the topic: "I am not the first President to take up this cause," he says to thunderous applause, almost exclusively from the Democratic side of the aisle, "but I am determined to be the last."

A key theme is introduced with Obama's acknowledgment that a health care reform bill "was first introduced by John Dingell Sr. in 1943. Sixty-five years later, his son continues to introduce that same bill at the beginning of each session." John Dingell the son stands, himself in his early eighties, and receives a long standing ovation from both sides of the aisle. He stands as a living embodiment of the past, one that renders the past as actually within the present. Dingell Jr. is not a relic trotted out as an object of reverence, and he is not an exemplar of past action held up for emulation; he represents both himself and his father, an image of the past that continues to act in the present. When the members of Congress rise from their seats and applaud him, their emotional response is provoked in part by the fact that they are beholding a duality.

After this moment of bipartisan sentiment, Obama returns to describing the need for health care reform in terms that he and his proxies had been using for months. He reminds his listeners that the current system most negatively impacts "middle-class Americans," that it makes the United States "the only democracy—the only advanced democracy on Earth—the only wealthy nation" that does not provide some form of universal health care for its citizens, that its inefficiencies mean that we spend "one and a half times more per person on health care than any other country, but we aren't any healthier for it." The rearticulation of health care reform and the economy is solidified when Obama declares that the rising cost of health care is "our deficit problem. Nothing else even comes close." "Now, these are the facts," Obama concludes, in a clipped cadence meant to suggest, perhaps, that he is not engaging in fancy talk but merely telling it like it is. "Nobody disputes them. We know we must reform this system. The question is how."

As in "A More Perfect Union," a passionate and personal opening has given way to a more prosaic and detached series of observations that will, in the end, be supplanted by an invitation to citizenly engagement. But whereas in that earlier speech Obama is portrayed as capable of absorbing a full range of perspectives, here he is situated upon a middle ground characterized by the careful avoidance of extremes. This is not a duality that invites double-consciousness, because it does not invite the members of the audience to occupy simultaneously the two positions being described but instead recommends avoiding them. "There are those on the left who believe that the only way to fix the system is through a single-payer system like Canada's," Obama notes, while on the right, "there are those who argue that we should end employer-based systems and leave individuals to buy health insurance on their own." Continuing in a way that makes more explicit the ill effects of these extreme positions, Obama notes that during the previous months "we've seen Washington at its best and at its worst." On the one hand, we have seen "many in this chamber work tirelessly for the better part of this year to offer thoughtful ideas about how to achieve reform"; on the other, "what we've also seen in these last months is the same partisan spectacle that only hardens the disdain many Americans have towards their own government." Probably referring to the summer town hall protests, he acknowledges that "out of this blizzard of charges and counter-charges, confusion has reigned" but states firmly that "the time for bickering is over. The time for games has passed. . . . Now is the time to deliver on health care." This is not a dialectical synthesis, but neither is it an expression of democratic double-consciousness; it is, instead, a quiet middle ground that avoids the toxicity of extremes.

It is in this middling space, informed by rationality and goodwill, that Obama characterizes a mode of address through which he wants discussions to proceed. So in this speech we have a two-part process that is perhaps well suited to an effort to inject double-consciousness into a political controversy in which extreme positions threaten to congeal. First, space must be cleared in which the unproductive extremes are proscribed, because they lead only to a monovocal rigidity that is antithetical to double-consciousness. Then, a doubled address can be introduced that avoids the extremes without collapsing different perspectives into a homogeneous unity. Obama urges his "progressive friends" to "remain open to other ideas," and he urges his "Republican friends" to refrain from "making wild claims about a government takeover of health care." Note that Obama is describing not a utopia free from partisanship but a no-wake zone in which partisanship is throttled back to allow the flexibility and perspective-taking that civic discourse requires. This is a doubled discourse that takes into account the contributions "from many of the people in this room tonight—Democrats and Republicans"—but it also is a mode of address that retains a clear sense of purpose and clear limitations: "If you misrepresent what's in this plan, we will call you out."

As a resource for citizenship, thus far the speech models a firm dedication to the value of reasoned debate and to the potential destructiveness of extreme positions, misrepresentations of fact, and the lack of an overriding concern for the common good. It presents Obama, as it was put in a perceptive article in the *Economist,* "as a moderate in style and substance" and "as a reasonable and moderate adult in a room full of petty and partisan ideologues."[25] This speech also has introduced into this rational public space a mode of address that that takes differing views into account without hardening into extremes. Certainly this is a valuable antidote to the vituperation that is far more common in U.S.

political discourse. But this mode of address still lacks a representative body. The performative notion of citizenship that informs this book involves inhabiting a role, one that acknowledges both the "first persona" of the implied speaker and the "second persona" of the implied auditor.[26] Personae are not free-floating specters but embodied perspectives, and as a result the discourse attributed to them or modeled for them must be associated with a representative figure. In "A More Perfect Union" that role was assumed by the characters in the Ashley story; in Obama's dedication of the King memorial, that role was assumed by King; in this address, that role belongs to Ted Kennedy.

Kennedy's Ghost

Near the end of his speech, Obama invokes Senator Kennedy, who had passed away just fifteen days earlier, from brain cancer, on August 25. The passage recalls the earlier reference to John Dingell, in which the past and the present were portrayed as co-present and recovers some of the passion and appreciation for service and sacrifice with which the speech began. Obama mentions that he receives letters from "many Americans counting on us to succeed" and that he "received one of those letters a few days ago . . . from our beloved friend and colleague, Ted Kennedy." Kennedy had written the letter back in May, Obama explains, and had "asked that it be delivered upon his death." The letter was written *in* the past, but it was written *for* the present and thus sets Kennedy before the eyes of the audience while at the same time marking his absence. Kennedy also is associated with ordinary Americans, speaking, through his letter, from their position, sharing a channel commonly reserved for them.

Obama portrays Kennedy as able to bridge the personal and the political, particularly through the evocation of emotion. Kennedy's passionate public commitment to health care reform, Obama explains, did not flow from "some rigid ideology" but rather was a response to his "experience of having two children stricken with cancer" and the "sheer terror and helplessness that any parent feels when a child is badly sick." Unlike the protestors disrupting the town hall meetings, Kennedy is animated by an emotional commitment that is not an obstacle to civic duty but an aid to it. For Kennedy, his own personal passion was translated into a "large-heartedness" and a "concern and regard for the plight of others." Obama acknowledges that "people of both parties" who actually knew Kennedy and worked with him understood his capacity for crossing the aisle; Obama names Republicans Orrin Hatch, John McCain, and Chuck Grassley, each of whom worked together with Kennedy on various pieces of health care legislation and reform. This capacity for impassioned duality, at once both specific to Kennedy's own response to the health crises of his own children and also familiar to any parent, "is not a partisan feeling."

This is a feeling associated with civic friendship, with an ethic of fellow-feeling and reciprocity, and thus explicitly with democratic citizenship. As noted earlier, Danielle Allen suggests that civic friendship may lack the "emotional charge" of more personal relationships, but Kennedy, as Obama portrays him, is able to draw upon the emotional charge of his personal relationships to engage in political work. Certainly the feeling isn't precisely the same—no one would say that the feelings of fellowship that Kennedy felt with regard to Hatch or McCain or Grassley, however genuine, were the same as the emotions he felt for his family—but, as portrayed in Obama's speech, those private relationships are analogous to the public relationships and are inspired by analogous feelings. On a broader scale, this impassioned duality allowed Kennedy, for example, though wealthy and well insured, to "imagine what it must be like for those without insurance." To the extent that Kennedy was able to see others as "second selves," in Aristotle's terms, he was able to engage with them and care for them in a way that was like the way that he cared for his family and friends.[27]

Obama makes the connection to practices of citizenship explicit, arguing that no less so than rugged individualism, this form of civic fellowship "is part of the American character—our ability to stand in other people's shoes." Within this orientation, reciprocity is not merely a one-to-one exchange but proliferates into a broader cultural ethic in which multiple relationships are sustained. It fosters "a recognition that we are all in this together, and when fortune turns against one of us, others are there to lend a helping hand; a belief that in this country, hard work and responsibility should be rewarded by some measure of security and fair play; and an acknowledgment that sometimes government has to step in to help deliver on that promise." Kennedy emerges as an avatar of this form of duality, a doubled character able to hold within himself the sparring ideologies of American political philosophy as well as those that characterize contemporary American congressional politics and, through a sort of alchemy, draw out of these frictions an exemplary form of civic engagement.

Obama concludes by inserting this doubled version of the American character into history. Our "predecessors understood that government could not, and should not, solve every problem," but "they also understood that the danger of too much government is matched by the perils of too little." They realized that when "we can no longer even engage in a civil conversation with each other over the things that truly matter"—when we can no longer cross the empathetic divide, stand in one another's shoes, imagine ourselves in another's place, and recognize we're all in this together—we "lose something essential about ourselves." To the extent that it is true that "democratic citizenship consists primarily of reciprocity,"[28] these are tragic losses indeed. We cannot realize the character of our country without the enlarged perspectives and two-sided outlooks that Kennedy embodied. "I believe that we can replace acrimony with civility, and gridlock with progress," Obama concludes. "Because that's who we are. That is our calling. That is our character."[29]

Passionate Duality

Suzanne Mettler ascribes at least some of the resistance to Obama's health care reform proposal to the fact that health care is a part of what she calls the "submerged state," public policies "largely invisible to most Americans." Simply, many Americans erroneously believe that the privileges and benefits they enjoy flow to them without government intervention, and they therefore distrust policies that make that intervention visible. Commonly, Mettler summarizes, public policies are presented in ways that "obscure the role of the government and exaggerate that of the market, leaving citizens unaware of how power operates, unable to form meaningful opinions, and incapable, therefore, of voicing their views accordingly."[30] The problem of the submerged state is, in other words, a rhetorical problem—citizens are denied the inventional resources they need to craft effective public discourse. The economic frame that Obama clung to throughout most of his speeches and statements on health care reform may have contributed to this rhetorical problem, inadvertently reinforcing a market-based understanding of the issue while withholding models for addressing the issue as citizens.

This address on health care may offer an antidote to this invisibility, at least to the extent that it offers its auditors a model for speaking about health care in a way that includes the presence of a human-scale and empathetic government. By invoking Kennedy as a somewhat paradoxical avatar of impassioned reason, this discourse offers citizens a mode of addressing health care reform that does not encourage a submersion of the very apparatus through which it is delivered. This speech offers a discourse through which government involvement in health care might be made visible. The speech might be best remembered, though, for an interruption that can help draw our attention to the further limitations of a disembodied and dispassionate double-consciousness. Near the middle of the speech, as Obama was debunking some of the "bogus claims" spread by opponents of health care reform and just as he was turning his attention to the claim that his plan would benefit illegal immigrants, Representative Joe Wilson, a Republican from South Carolina, shouted "You lie!" Obama paused a moment and said in an even tone, continuing his train of thought and not explicitly addressing Wilson, "It's not true." He then continued with his speech. The reaction among the members of Congress contrasted clearly with Obama's; a loud bipartisan chorus of boos erupted, elicited by Wilson's breach of decorum. The moment could not have been better choreographed to illustrate Obama's foundational framing: he stands calmly in the center amid unproductive emotionality all around.

Within the masterful dramatic structure of this address, however, this interruption is merely a waypoint. The calm middle ground established in this middle portion of the speech is merely one step in a process of imbuing the paractic logic of double-consciousness with an impassioned embodiment. Except for the teaser at the beginning, in the form of the bipartisan show of appreciation for John Dingell Jr. and Sr., Obama mostly keeps affect and emotion offstage until the final act, when he suddenly brings out the memory of Ted Kennedy, whose sensitivity, empathy, and emotional investment are presented as the very foundation of his ability to appreciate both sides of an argument, to find moments of comparability between himself and his opponents, and to express and engage in a productive duality. Kennedy presents an impassioned form of double-consciousness animated by an ethical core that in turn explicitly is a mode of addressing others, particularly those who hold different political opinions, as an initial duality that fosters and acknowledges a complex web of reciprocity.[31]

Nobel Prize

On Friday, October 9, 2009, at about 5:03 A.M., Eastern Standard Time, the White House Situation Room forwarded an e-mail to White House staff with this subject line: "Item of Interest: President Obama Wins Nobel Peace Prize." About an hour later, White House press secretary Robert Gibbs awoke Obama with a phone call.[32] It would be an understatement to say that this news was not expected. "Obama had not been mentioned as among front-runners for the prize," CNN reported, "and the roomful of reporters gasped when Thorbjorn Jagland, chairman of the Nobel committee, announced that the president was the winner."[33] It was widely noted that nominations for the prize were due by February 1, 2009, only twelve days after Obama took office.

There were the many pro forma statements of recognition. John McCain, for example, released this brief notice: "I congratulate him on receiving this prestigious award. I join my fellow Americans in expressing pride in our president on this occasion." The Republican governor of Minnesota, Tim Pawlenty, noted that "there will be some people who are saying, 'Was it based on good intentions and thoughts, or is it going to be based on good results?' But I think the appropriate response is, when anybody wins a Nobel Prize, that is a very noteworthy development and designation, and I think the appropriate response is to say, 'Congratulations.'" Certainly, whenever "anybody" receives a Nobel Prize, it is "noteworthy." There also was the predictable vituperation. Rush Limbaugh advised that "The Nobel gang just suicide-bombed themselves" by awarding the prize to Obama, rendering the honor "now worth as much as whatever prizes they are putting in Cracker Jacks these days."[34] One opinion piece in the *Washington Post* suggested that it was unconstitutional for Obama to receive the Nobel Prize because it violated Article I, Section 9, of the U.S. Constitution, which prohibits officeholders from accepting an "emolument" from a foreign king.[35] Michael Steele, then chairperson of the Republican National Committee, sent out an e-mail observing that "President Obama won't be receiving any awards from Americans for job creation, fiscal responsibility, or backing up rhetoric with concrete action"—the e-mail subject line was "Nobel Prize for Awesomeness."[36]

But perhaps the most confounded reaction was from the White House itself. While the administration might have hoped that the prize would help to further Obama's agenda at a time when he was facing multiple challenges—health care reform, economic recovery, job formation, wartime strategy—they understood that it could have the opposite effect. David Axelrod, for example, noted: "I'd like to believe that winning the Nobel Peace Prize is not a political liability. . . . But this isn't something I gave a moment of thought to until today. Hopefully people will receive it with some sense of pride. But I don't know; it's uncharted waters."[37] The Obama administration found itself in the awkward position of trying to downplay one of the planet's most high-profile awards. Throughout the campaign, Obama's opponents had mocked him as an "international superstar with no accomplishments,"[38] and the awarding of the prize on the basis of admittedly slim accomplishments seemed to confirm the critique. An editorial in the Canadian *Globe and Mail* put it succinctly: "The prize could help Mr. Obama's cause or it could dash his hopes on the shoals of xenophobic domestic politics."[39] As Lynn Sweet noted dryly, "There was no celebration at the White House for the Nobel Peace Prize."[40]

As if to emphasize the irony of the moment, on Obama's calendar on the morning that he was notified that he had won the Peace Prize, time was blocked out to prepare for an afternoon meeting to make plans for war—specifically a "troop surge" in Afghanistan. Indeed, a common observation about Obama's Nobel acceptance speech, delivered on December 10 in Oslo, Norway, and officially referred to as the Nobel Peace Prize Lecture, was that for a speech given on the occasion of accepting a prize for peace, it actually has quite a lot to say about war. The speech is almost evenly divided, so that half of it talks about peace and the other half talks about war.[41] And it is this even division of attention that presents the key point of the speech—it invites us to attend equally to war and to peace, to imagine them as essentially parallel if not potentially similar, and ultimately to put our faith in a rather vaguely articulated "moral compass" as a means to navigate between the two. The world that Obama presents seems afflicted by "two warring ideals," as Du Bois put it, held together only through "dogged strength alone," to the extent that it is a world that is held in delicate balance, with power and reason, realism and idealism, might and right in an unstable symbiosis. It may be that this is an altogether fitting vision of peace for the twenty-first century, for a world destabilized among so many conflicting axes, a world that seems wildly unsuited to intractable rules. But this address also reveals a serious limitation of democratic double-consciousness when it lacks a robust mechanism for judgment.

Changing of the Guard

The speech opens by acknowledging "the considerable controversy that your generous decision has generated."[42] In part, Obama notes, this controversy "is because I am at the beginning, and not the end, of my labors on the world stage" and because thus far his "accomplishments are slight" compared to those of others who have won the award. "But perhaps the most profound issue surrounding my receipt of this prize," Obama notes, "is the fact that I am the Commander-in-Chief of the military of a nation in the midst of two wars." He has "an acute sense of the costs of armed conflict," and these have filled him with "difficult questions about the relationship between war and peace, and our effort to replace one with the other." These lines lay out the basic rhetorical form of the speech: Obama understands the horror of war and the fragility of peace to be indissoluble, so that even at an occasion when he is expected to celebrate peace he is not able to avoid a thorough discussion of the rationales for war; while he does not say here that he wishes to render them interchangeable, to say that we might "replace" war with peace does suggest at least some potential equivalencies.

Obama explicitly marks his debt to the "just-war" tradition: "War," he points out, "in one form or another, appeared with the first man," but "over time . . . [as] philosophers and clerics and statesmen" sought to "regulate the destructive power of war," the "concept of a 'just war' emerged, suggesting that war is justified only when certain conditions were met: if it is waged as a last resort or in self-defense; if the force used is proportional; and if, whenever possible, civilians are spared from violence." This is a compressed but accurate representation of key tenets of the just-war tradition—Obama, ever the academic, can be counted upon to cite his sources.[43]

In this speech just-war thought is credited with a long list of accomplishments.[44] It has not succeeded in bringing perfect peace, of course, for "terrible wars have been fought, and atrocities committed. But there has been no Third World War." It has contributed to the end of the Cold War, to the stitching together of the world by commerce, to the lifting of billions of people from poverty, and to the fact that the "ideals of liberty and self determination, equality and the rule of law have haltingly advanced." Despite this impressive record, however, Obama declares that "this old architecture is buckling under the weight of new threats"—"wars between nations have increasingly given way to wars within nations," there has been a "resurgence of ethnic or sectarian conflicts" and a "growth of secessionist movements, insurgencies, and failed states," and in "today's wars, many more civilians are killed than soldiers, the seeds of future conflict are sown, economies are wrecked, civil societies torn asunder, refugees amassed, children scarred." The predominance of just-war thought in world politics has made possible some tremendous successes, but the quality and quantity of violence today have made it untenable. We need, he tells us, "to think in new ways about the notions of just war and the imperatives of a just peace."

The new way of thinking that Obama models as a response to this dual assessment of the predominance and obsolescence of just-war thought is, predictably, doubled. On the one hand, we "must begin by acknowledging the hard truth: We will not eradicate violent conflict in our lifetimes. There will be times when nations—acting individually or in concert—will find the use of force not only necessary but morally justified." On the other hand, he doesn't wish completely to abandon the moral principles of the more pacifist public figures who have come before him. "As someone who stands here as a direct consequence of Dr. King's life work," he notes, "I am living testimony to the moral force of non-violence. I know there's nothing weak—nothing passive, nothing naïve—in the creed and lives of Gandhi and King." And yet, "as a head of state sworn to protect and defend my nation, I cannot be guided by their examples alone" because he must "face the world as it is" and recognize that, for example, a "non-violent movement could not have halted Hitler's armies."

Obama again has established himself in a middle ground, this time between a realist confrontation with an endemic threat and a more idealist notion that a world without war would be preferable to one with it, between a condemnation of war on moral grounds and a recognition that, sometimes, war is morally justified. However, this is not the quiet and detached middle ground set out in his speech on health care reform, free of ideological extremes that become hardened and resistant to dialogue, but a distinctively doubled space wherein the extremes of war and of peace are brought together for contemplation. Notably, however, unlike either "A More Perfect Union" or the health care reform speech, Obama does not present himself or any other figure as embodying this dual perspective.

Obama's phrasing recalls a realist ethics that bears the imprint of Reinhold Niebuhr, whom Obama identified in a 2007 interview as one of his "favorite philosophers," subscribing particularly to the Niebuhrian notions that "there's serious evil in the world, and hardship and pain," and that although "we should be humble and modest in our belief we can eliminate those things . . . we shouldn't use that as an excuse for cynicism and inaction." In his Nobel Prize Lecture, Obama says that "evil does exist in the world" and that "to say that force may sometimes be necessary is not a call to cynicism—it is a recognition of history; the imperfections of man and the limits of reason." John D. Carlson describes this line of thought as "a middle path between moralism and realism" and suggests that "Niebuhr appreciated the delicate tension that holds ethics and politics together"; in words that closely echo Obama's, Carlson notes that Niebuhrian ethics provides a "framework that sees politics as it is, not as one hopes it would be."[45] While this form of political realism does not completely reject the more pacifist idealism of a King or a Gandhi, as Colm McKeogh notes, a Niebuhrian ethics would acknowledge that "without coercion there could be no order, and without order there could be no justice" so that "all social cooperation on a larger scale than the most intimate social group requires a measure of coercion."[46] "So yes," Obama clarifies in Oslo, "the instruments of war do have a role to play in preserving the peace."

War and Peace

This form of ethical realism informs much of the core of the address, setting out a reciprocal relationship between war and peace. In keeping perhaps with the nature of the address as a lecture, it presents a well-ordered, three-part comparison between war and peace, balancing each point made about one with a point made about the other. Obama's argument follows the basic *topoi* of just-war thought but inserts his own Niebuhrian inflection. This is a paratactic logic insofar as it brings war and peace into view simultaneously and leaves uncertain the relationship between them; it does not determine any unidirectional relationship such as that one causes the other or necessarily follows upon the other. Instead, it presents them as parallel and interdependent, so that their distinctions threaten to blur.

The opening argument of this section of the speech falls under the heading of *jus ad bellum,* the criteria that govern the justification of war. "I believe," Obama declares, "that all nations—strong and weak alike—must adhere to standards that govern the use of force." While he, "like any head of state," reserves a right to unilateral action if necessary for national defense, he also is "convinced that adhering to standards, international standards, strengthens those who do, and isolates and weakens those who don't." With regard to peace, a similar importance of establishing and enforcing codes of conduct is marked:

"First, in dealing with those nations that break rules and laws, I believe that we must develop alternatives to violence that are tough enough to actually change behavior—for if we want a lasting peace, then the words of the international community must mean something." "Intransigence must be met with increased pressure," he continues, "and such pressure exists only when the world stands together as one."[47] This is not to be a particularly peaceful peace, then, but one that requires a well-organized phalanx of powerful nations that have placed themselves on constant alert, that have declared themselves willing to engage in efficient and decisive action, and that have pledged both blood and treasure.

Obama's second point also falls under the heading of *jus ad bellum,* the justification of war, and further muddies the distinction between war and peace. He asserts plainly that "force can be justified on humanitarian grounds, as it was in the Balkans," and that "militaries with a clear mandate" might play a role in keeping the peace. "I understand why war is not popular," Obama understates, "but I also know this: The belief that peace is desirable is rarely enough to achieve it." He even refers to NATO and UN "peacekeeping forces" as "wagers of peace." He does not elaborate, but waging peace would seem different from merely maintaining it or allowing it to flourish; it seems to suggest rather a preemptive action to create peace or a potentially peaceful regime where none now exists. The notion of waging peace ties peace indissolubly to war.

In making "one final point about the use of force," Obama turns to *jus in bello,* the criteria that address the conduct of war itself. "Even as we make difficult decisions about going to war," he notes, "we must also think clearly about how we fight it." When it confronts "a vicious adversary that abides by no rules . . . the United States of America must remain a standard bearer in the conduct of war. That is what makes us different from those whom we fight." One of the few moments of sustained applause is provoked by the line: "We lose ourselves when we compromise the very ideals that we fight to defend." Yet in one of the inverted parallelisms that characterize the doubled style, even the morality of peace sustains some bellicose advantage. While "true peace is not just freedom from fear, but freedom from want," it also is not merely an idealized goal but possesses strategic value. This is why, for example, "helping farmers feed their own people—or nations educate their children and care for the sick—is not mere charity." Obama argues that the United States is guided in these matters by "enlightened self-interest," because it recognizes "that development rarely takes root without security," "that security does not exist where human beings do not have access to enough food, or clean water, or the medicine and shelter they need to survive."

Moral Imagination

The core of Obama's speech, then, presents a balanced perspective on war and peace, setting the two in parallel. This dual point of view is reinforced by the structure of the speech, as discussions of war and of peace are juxtaposed at specific topical points, and by the language of the speech, as the audience is invited to consider a humanitarian war that wages peace and to reexamine the tensions between realism and idealism, condemnation and discussion, and self-interest and altruism. The audience is invited to contemplate both war and peace as ever-present modes of human conduct rather than as two starkly delineated options between which a choice must be made. War and peace are in this way figured in a play of signification, so that their meanings remain distinct while the precise moment when one shades into the other becomes unclear.

The device that Obama finally offers for navigating this murky path is "the continued expansion of our moral imagination; an insistence that there's something irreducible that we all share." This device is captioned, as in "A More Perfect Union," with the Golden Rule, "the one rule that lies at the heart of every major religion . . . that we do unto others as we would have them do unto us." Here, Obama insists that the Golden Rule asks us to recognize "how similar we are," despite the fact that "the dizzying pace of globalization [and] the cultural leveling of modernity" lead people instead to "fear the loss of what they cherish in their particular identities—their race, their tribe, and perhaps most powerfully their religion." The Golden Rule, as it is invoked in this speech, seems to require a rejection of single-mindedness in favor of the mixed motives of double-consciousness. It reminds us that "no Holy War can ever be a just war," for if you believe "that you are carrying out divine will . . . there is no need for restraint—no need to spare the pregnant mother, or the medic, or the Red Cross worker, or even a person of one's own faith." The Golden Rule would mitigate the tendency to "fall victim to the temptations of pride, and power, and sometimes evil," because following it would insist that we constantly view one another "through the revelation of the other world," to recall Du Bois's phrasing. It asks that we always stand just to one side of ourselves and resist becoming wedded to the single-minded "true self-consciousness" bestowed upon the privileged, unencumbered few who escape the burden of double-consciousness.

The idealism of King and Gandhi reenters the speech at this point, as a counterweight to bitter realism; Obama reminds us that their nonviolence "may not have been practical or possible in every circumstance, but the love that they preached—their fundamental faith in human progress—that must always be the North Star that guides us on our journey." In King's words from his own Nobel Prize Lecture, which Obama quotes here, we are invited to "refuse to accept the idea that the 'isness' of man's present condition makes him morally incapable of reaching up for the eternal 'oughtness' that forever confronts him."[48] In Obama's vision, the idealism of King and Gandhi must always be tempered by the realism of the present day; the dream of peace must always be tempered by the reality of war. Idealism may serve as "our moral compass," as he puts it, but of course to use a compass one keeps one eye on the immediate terrain and the other on a fixed point of reference. Plotting a course requires that we keep continuously in view both where we are and where we aim to be, that we tack back and forth between the two without allowing either to absorb our attention fully.

Obama's penchant for balanced phrases is in full flower, providing through this efflorescence of doubled figures a rich vocabulary upon which citizens might draw when addressing these issues and one another. He acknowledges that there is a "reflexive suspicion of America, the world's sole military superpower" but also urges that "the world must remember" that the "United States of America has helped underwrite global security for more than six decades with the blood of our citizens and the strength of our arms." A "soldier's courage and sacrifice is full of glory. . . . But war itself is never glorious." He urges that "part of our challenge is reconciling these two seemingly inreconcilable [sic] truths—that war is sometimes necessary, and war at some level is an expression of human folly." The cumulative effect is somewhat vertiginous, as we are presented with multiple juxtapositions between options that appear equally attractive, advantageous, or inevitable. Obama tells us that, while there is "no simple formula," still "we must try as best we can to balance isolation and engagement, pressure and incentives, so that human rights and dignity are advanced over time."

These doubled figures are valuable inventional resources for the crafting of a productive mode of citizenly address. But as has been illustrated in "A More Perfect Union," Obama's remarks at the Martin Luther King Jr. memorial, and his speech on health care reform, democratic double-consciousness seems to require embodiment within particular exemplary individuals. In this speech, the exemplary figures that are presented do not model modes of speech: "Somewhere today, in the here and now, in the world as it is, a soldier sees he's outgunned, but stands firm to keep the peace. Somewhere today, in this world, a young protestor awaits the brutality of her government, but has the courage to march on. Somewhere today, a mother facing punishing poverty still takes the time to teach her child, scrapes together what few coins she has to send that child to school—because she believes that a cruel world still has a place for that child's dreams." These individuals could be said to embody a Niebuhrian ethical realism, to illustrate a commitment to a middle path between moralism and realism that still keeps both in play, to model not only an appreciation for the delicate tension that holds ethics and politics together but also a manner of acting in the world that sustains that tension as a resource for the enactment of citizenship. Obama makes explicit their role as model personae: "Let us," he concludes, "live by their example." But with the possible exception of the mother teaching her child, these are silent figures; standing firm, marching on, facing poverty, and sustaining a dream are undeniably powerful actions and are as essential to the personal freedom of citizens as they are to the collective health of a democratic culture. But like the "beer summit" that followed the arrest of Henry Louis Gates Jr., these figures do not specifically present a mode of address, a way of speaking to one another as citizens; even the teaching of a child is here a private act, not a public one. These figures may inspire us as we confront a world held in the balance between war and peace, but they do not offer us a discursive mode of public judgment through which war might be avoided and peace cultivated.

An Uneasy Peace

After the address, the veteran journalist Tom Brokaw suggested that "this is as close as we've had to an Obama Doctrine probably, about how he sees the world," while both Rory Cooper of the Heritage Foundation and Howard Fineman of *Newsweek* suggested that this was a speech that, for the most part, might have been delivered by George W. Bush. Katrina Vanden Heuvel of the *Nation* thought that this speech framed Obama as an "ethical realist," recalling the paradoxical terms many others have used to refer to him. Fineman concurs, saying that Obama has "always been a realist," even in an address denouncing the invasion of Iraq back in 2002, and those who thought otherwise "weren't listening to everything he said."[49] Indeed, in that 2002 speech, delivered when Obama was an Illinois state senator, he said many things that would not have been out of place in his Nobel Prize Lecture; his first words on that day, in fact, were: "Let me begin by saying that although this has been billed as an anti-war rally, I stand before you as someone who is not opposed to war in all circumstances."[50]

But understanding this speech merely as an articulation of political realism distracts us from its value as a citizenly resource. While it may or may not present an accurate picture of Barack Obama's worldview, it does offer both a complex exemplar of democratic double-consciousness and an illustration of some of its limitations. This text explicitly presents itself as a discourse on citizenship, inviting its hearers to sustain a fluid ethical realism that may be especially well suited to a contemporary moment that seems characterized by a multiplication of instabilities and competing interests linked with a sometimes startling lack of perspectival flexibility and intercultural understanding. This doubled perspective is articulated in and through many figures of balance and equilibrium. And in this address the scope of this perspective is enlarged, so that it would encourage citizens of the United States and people everywhere else in the developed world to engage with one another as international citizens while still retaining their national identities, to see themselves as others see them without relinquishing their own perspectives, to strive for the ideal without losing sight of the practical.

On the other hand, however, this speech suggests some of the limitations of democratic double-consciousness when disconnected from a representative figure. As a resource for citizenly rhetorical invention, the address provides a thoughtful and innovative vocabulary through which to discuss war and peace, inviting its audience to perceive them as both inevitable and interdependent modes of human behavior that should be recognized as existing side by side on the world stage. But, as a consequence, in Obama's analysis war and peace become rather difficult to differentiate, shading into each other as they intertwine and change places. Difficult choices have to be made on this middle ground, because, Obama further noted in that 2007 interview, one should avoid "swinging from naïve idealism to bitter realism."[51] But the Golden Rule, as a compressed anecdote of reciprocity, may not be adequate as a device through which to manage the complexities of war and peace; a moral compass, however compelling it may be as an image, may not provide guidance sufficient to help us avoid war as we stumble toward peace. Obama has provided a vivid perspective, in other words, but one that lacks a robust mechanism for judgment.[52]

Indeed, as Joshua Reeves and Matthew S. May suggest, the balancing of perspectives that Obama demonstrates in this address actually may obscure decisions that tip the balance in favor of war by casting them as "the natural *response* to a violent and complicated planet."[53] That is, the vague moral compass Obama describes here may not only be inadequate as a model of judgment but actually render such judgment impossible, with the ironic result that the moral vision laid out in this speech on peace actually has the effect of making war more likely. This address invites citizens to see and to understand the precarious balance between war and peace, but what is needed is a mode of address that can help us invent ways to avoid the former and promote the latter. The representative citizens that Obama presents do not model this mode of address. And as Reeves and May remind us, Obama has presided over an era of aggressive U.S. military engagement that may be understood as a manifestation of the feeble inventive resources that Obama provided in Oslo.

The Economy

The causes of the global financial crisis of 2007 and 2008—the various interconnections and growing interdependencies among different sectors of the financial market, the specific actions and reactions that constituted the spiral of incomprehension and incompetence evident among so many of the individuals and institutions involved, and the particular points of both accidental and aggressive collusion among government agencies, corporate entities, and private citizens—are far too complex to review in detail here. On February 25, 2011, the National Commission on the Causes of the Financial and Economic Crisis in the United States issued its final version of *The Financial Crisis Inquiry Report,* a 662-page document, produced by a ten-member commission appointed by Congress. It located the ultimate cause of the crisis in "the collapse of the housing bubble—fueled by low interest rates, easy and available credit, scant regulation, and toxic mortgages." A few months later, the bipartisan United States Senate Permanent Subcommittee on Investigations released a 639-page report that reached similar conclusions, finding that "the crisis was not a natural disaster, but the result of high risk, complex financial products; undisclosed conflicts of interest; and the failure of regulators, the credit rating agencies, and the market itself to rein in the excesses of Wall Street." The National Commission concluded that the "profound events of 2007 and 2008" were "neither bumps in the road nor an accentuated dip in the financial and business cycles we have come to expect in a free market economic system" but rather "a fundamental disruption—a financial upheaval, if you will—that wreaked havoc in communities and neighborhoods across this country."[54]

The financial crisis certainly played an outsized role throughout Obama's first term in office and promises to continue to be a factor far into the future; as I write this, unemployment remains high, the national debt continues to accumulate, and economic growth, though showing increasingly positive vital signs, still remains less robust than many would prefer and disproportionately benefits economic elites. The financial crisis may also have helped to sweep Barack Obama into office, in part because it fanned dissatisfaction with the incumbent regime and in part because it allowed him to display to great advantage his trademark demeanor of calm and expertise. For example, on September 24, 2008, John McCain announced that he was suspending his campaign, canceling the televised presidential debate scheduled for September 26, and traveling to Washington to assist in addressing the crisis. In response, Obama expressed his opinion that a good president should be able to "multitask," attending to two or more things at the same time, which was a not very subtle way of suggesting that McCain was capable of focusing on only a single issue, either his campaign or the crisis, but not both.

Most of Obama's public address about the economy, however, exhibited little of this sort of duality. As was the case with regard to the mounting crisis surrounding the passage of health care reform, Obama's public address on the economy consistently displayed a singular focus on reiterating the facts of the crisis, its causes, and the steps taken by his administration to address it. For the most part, these speeches consist of a review of the key components of the American Recovery and Reinvestment Act, referred to colloquially as "the stimulus" and the signature piece of economic legislation in Obama's first term, together with explanations of other key actions and proposals yet to come. There is "a lot of misinformation," Obama explained in the White House rose garden in August, and he clearly saw his role as a purveyor of truth.[55] These speeches were, as he put it in an address at Georgetown University, "prose, and not poetry."

The poetry did not begin to emerge until after the 2010 midterm elections, in which a Republican rout perhaps suggested the limitations of the more prosaic approach.[56] Over the next year, Obama's addresses on the economy gradually began to offer not merely information but also an attitude about that information, culminating eventually in a perspective conducive to the invention of democratic double-consciousness. A preliminary shift in tone and tactic was apparent in December, when, during an address at Forsyth Technical Community College in Winston-Salem, North Carolina, Obama referred to the economic crisis as "our generation's Sputnik moment," a phrase that he repeated in his State of the Union address in January 2011. He meant that the economic meltdown offered an opportunity to "reinvent" the American economy by investing in "biomedical research, information technology, and especially clean energy technology."[57] As a metaphor, the Sputnik reference had the potential to invite the audience to understand Obama's proposal to reenergize the American economy by increasing funding for scientific and technology research as being as significant as the similar increase in funding that followed the launch of the first Soviet satellite in 1957. The metaphor invites a way of understanding the present in terms of the past and as such may have fostered an incipient form of duality. But, despite becoming perhaps the most often-referenced sound bite of the State of the Union address, the phrase failed to catch on as the guiding theme of Obama's economic rhetoric in the post-midterm era. As the political blogger Chris Weigant pointed out, "the concept of a 'Sputnik moment' is a risky political metaphor" for two reasons: because it suggests that the United States has some catching up to do in comparison to its global peers, which challenges "the general public's almost religious belief" that America always leads the world in all areas, and because the present moment is not informed by the same level of Cold War fear and loathing that met the news that the Soviet Union had achieved new technological capabilities.[58] There also was the fact that many Americans apparently did not know what Sputnik was.

At George Washington University in April 2011, Obama provided another framing device through which he invited his audience to view his economic policies and proposals, this one explicitly doubled. Here, he identifies two "threads." "From our first days as a nation," he offers, "we have put our faith in free markets and free enterprise as the engine of America's wealth and prosperity. More than citizens of any other country, we are rugged individualists, a self-reliant people with a healthy skepticism of too much government. But there's always been another thread running through our history," he continues, "a belief that we're all connected, and that there are some things we can only do together, as a nation."[59] These are the same two threads that also made an appearance in the speech to Congress on health care reform, and as in that speech they are woven together through an ethic of reciprocity manifest in a propensity for citizens to see themselves in the fortunes of their fellow citizens. "We recognize," Obama reminds us, "that no matter how responsibly we live our lives, hard times or bad luck, a crippling illness or a layoff may strike any one of us. 'There but for the grace of God go I,' we say to ourselves." These ideas might have been developed into a statement of democratic double-consciousness—as a result of seeing in fellow citizens a reflection of themselves, Obama's audience might have been directed to address one another in a way that acknowledges the ever-present potential to change places with the other, to stand where she or he stands, to feel the burden of our status as fellow citizens. But here this incipient duality is never associated with a representative figure and never developed into a mode of address.

Obama's fullest statement on the economy during his first term in office was delivered at Osawatomie, Kansas, on December 6, 2011. The speech was well advertised beforehand in the national media, and the location was highly symbolic. In 1910, Theodore Roosevelt had delivered his well-known "New Nationalism" speech in Osawatomie, a milestone progressive statement in which he called for "every man [to] have a fair chance to make of himself all that in him lies" and also for the "commonwealth [to] get from every citizen the highest service of which he is capable."[60] Writing on the eve of Obama's speech, David Jackson, in USA Today, noted that when "Obama speaks in Osawatomie, Kan., . . . we can be sure he will echo TR's calls for more income equality, restraints on powerful economic interests, and an end to the undue influence of special interests." Jay Carney, Obama's press secretary, promised that the "ideas that President Roosevelt put forward about the need for Americans of all kinds to get a fair shot and a fair shake are very much at issue today."[61]

The historian H. W. Brands, author of a widely acclaimed book on Theodore Roosevelt, noted after Obama's speech that "one of the ways of deflecting criticism is to put your own positions in the mouths of great figures from the past."[62] Brands implied that Obama had merely placed his own words in Roosevelt's mouth, making from Roosevelt's prestige and ethos a cloak for his own ideas. But actually what occurs in this speech is more complex than the form of rhetorical ventriloquism or *prosopopoeia* in which Obama engages in the dedication of the King memorial. There, Obama clearly is using King's mouth as a vehicle for his own ideas. Here he is engaged in something more akin to what he accomplishes in the speech on health care reform, in which he is not speaking through Kennedy so much as he is resurrecting or reanimating him, bringing him before the eyes of his audience as an exemplar. In this speech in Osawatomie, Roosevelt is presented as a doubled figure who possesses and embodies the appropriate antidote to the root cause of the financial crisis, which, in Obama's figuration, mainly consists of a single-minded devotion to free-market fundamentalism. Obama's central assertion, again similar to the health care reform address, is that the economic crisis was caused by a rhetorical deficiency, a way of speaking that overemphasized a narrow perspective and ignored a more complex dual-minded dedication to supporting free-market capitalism while at the same time acknowledging the need for its regulation.

Enter a Hero

Obama begins the speech by staking his claim on the territory in a way that recalls both "A More Perfect Union" and his speech at Brown Chapel in Selma, Alabama, but this time he stresses the white side of his biracial identity. "I like to say that I got my name from my father," he begins, "but I got my accent—and my values—from my mother. She was born in Wichita. Her mother grew up in Augusta [Kansas]. Her father was from El Dorado. So my Kansas roots run deep." His grandparents contribute a narrative that further establishes Obama's Kansas bona fides while also recalling a sense of collective sacrifice in a time of crisis: he notes that his "grandparents served during World War II," his grandfather as "a soldier in Patton's Army" and his grandmother as "a worker on a bomber assembly line" in Wichita.[63] Their sacrifice and hard work were rewarded, as his grandfather was able to attend college "on the G.I. Bill"; his grandmother, who "worked as a banker for most of her life," showed Obama that "the vast majority of bankers and financial service professionals, they want to do right by their customers."

This is a promising story about interdependence, reciprocity, and the eventual rewards of democratic sacrifice, and of course Obama's grandparents provide compelling embodiments of that ethic, but he quickly ushers them off the stage. They are relics of another time, not representatives of the present, and they are neither broad enough in their appeal nor robust enough in their fortitude to bring into the present the resources that are required. While "we're still home to the world's most productive workers," Obama asserts, "the basic bargain that made this country great has eroded." And the recession of 2008 exacerbated that erosion, allowing "the breathtaking greed of a few" and "irresponsibility all across the system" to plunge "our economy and the world into a crisis from which we're still fighting to recover." While contemporary U.S. citizens may be no less hardworking and selfless than were Obama's grandparents, the infrastructure that allowed their sacrifice to be rewarded no longer exists.

The story of Obama's grandparents paves the way for the emergence of a hero, a figure who might present this particular sort of democratic ethic but in a more robust form that might survive a translation from the past to the present. This hero begins to take shape through an implied comparison between Obama and Theodore Roosevelt. The comparison also continues, in a subtle way, the theme of sacrifice and redemption, as Obama reminds his listeners that when Roosevelt "came here to Osawatomie and he laid out his vision for what he called a New Nationalism" he was called a "radical," a "socialist," and "even a communist." "But today," he continues, "we are a richer nation and a stronger democracy because of what he fought for in his last campaign: an eight-hour work day and a minimum wage for women, insurance for the unemployed and for the elderly, and those with disabilities; political reform and a progressive income tax." As at Brown Chapel and Howard University, where Obama was building the comparisons between himself and Joshua and Martin Luther King Jr., here there is palpable audience response as his hearers laugh and applaud while they fill in the enthymeme—just as Roosevelt was called a socialist in his day but future generations enjoy the results of his sacrifice, so too is Obama called a socialist now so that future generations will benefit.

In particular, Obama cultivates a doubled perspective that he attributes to Roosevelt and that is articulated through a series of balanced phrases that recall in some ways his description of himself in "A More Perfect Union" and elsewhere. Roosevelt was the "Republican son of a wealthy family," who "praised what the titans of industry had done to create jobs and grow the economy" and believed "that the free market is the greatest force for economic progress in human history," but he also "knew that the free market has never been a free license to take whatever you can from whomever you can." To applause, Obama continues: "He understood the free market only works when there are rules of the road that ensure competition is fair and open and honest," so he "busted up monopolies" and "fought to make sure businesses couldn't profit by exploiting children or selling food or medicine that wasn't safe." In answer to those who felt that "massive inequality and exploitation of people was [sic] just the price you pay for progress," Roosevelt's response was neither a blind faith in the workings of the free market nor a outright rejection of the capitalist ideal but instead an embrace of a well-regulated market that entailed both an assertive enthusiasm for capitalism's wealth-generating potential and a healthy skepticism of its ability to sustain itself and to provide equal access and opportunity. He provides, in Obama's reading, a balanced perspective that seeks to stimulate economic prosperity while at the same time minimizing its collateral damage.

Building the analogy, Obama reminds us that Roosevelt, too, faced a moment of transition, both signified and precipitated by technological advances, including "railroads and factories." "Today, over 100 years later," Obama continues, "our economy has gone through another transformation." This time, instead of railroads, "huge advances in technology" are contributing to the "world . . . shifting to an innovation economy." These changes have allowed businesses to hire fewer workers and to move jobs overseas, including "even higher-skilled jobs, like accountants and middle management," and in general cause "painful disruptions . . . for a lot of Americans." Not only does the comparison build up the associations between Roosevelt and Obama, but it also begins to make the case for Roosevelt's relevance in the present.

The comparison extends to the realms of immediate reaction and delayed gratification as well. Today, "just as there was in Teddy Roosevelt's time, there is a certain crowd in Washington who, for the last few decades, have said, let's respond to this economic challenge with the same old tune." Obama admits that their solution is "a simple theory" that "fits well on a bumper sticker" and that "speaks to our rugged individualism and our healthy skepticism of too much government." But that simple ideology—"'The market will take care of everything,'" as Obama phrases it—speaks only to that one side of the American spirit, and because of this lopsided emphasis it simply "doesn't work," not "in the decade before the Great Depression" nor "when we tried it during the last decade" before the present recession. In ways that recall his rejection of Reverend Wright's one-sided views, this brand of free-market fundamentalism distorts our view. And, similar perhaps to the middle portion of a jeremiad, where the failures of the present are brought vividly before the eyes of the faithful, Obama's speech continues with a litany of the negative effects of this present-day single-minded perspective. It has caused slow job growth, massive deficits, cuts to education and infrastructure, weak regulation, financial irresponsibility, "a prosperity that's enjoyed by fewer and fewer of our citizens," CEOs who earn 110 times the salary of their workers and falling incomes and caused "the rungs on the ladder of opportunity" to grow "farther and farther apart." Middle-class families "can no longer afford to buy the goods and services that businesses are selling," which "drags down the entire economy from top to bottom."

Against the undifferentiated "crowd" that promulgates the simplistic, one-sided, bumper-sticker philosophy that enabled these outrages, Obama presents the dashing and heroic Rough Rider. Though he says, in his own voice, that "I am here to say that they are wrong," mostly he lets Roosevelt do the talking. Echoing what is perhaps the most-often quoted line from Roosevelt's speech at Osawatomie—the praise of "an economic system under which each man shall be guaranteed the opportunity to show the best that there is in him"—Obama declares that the most "fundamental issue" is the "promise" that "that this is a place where you can make it if you try."

Traditional Duality

Roosevelt is the embodiment of "a vision that's been embraced in the past by people of both parties for more than 200 years," a doubled vision that is deeply rooted in the American tradition, just as Obama—and Roosevelt—are deeply rooted in Kansas. This is neither "a view that we should somehow turn back technology or put up walls around America" nor "a view that says we should punish profit or success or pretend that government knows how to fix all of society's problems." It is, instead, "a view that says that in America we are greater together—when everyone engages in fair play and everybody gets a fair shot and everybody does their fair share." "Yes," Obama acknowledges, "business, and not government, will always be the primary generator of good jobs with incomes that lift people into the middle class and keep them there. But as a nation," he continues, "we've always come together, through our government, to help create the conditions where both workers and businesses can succeed." In this doubled vision, people and profit are to be viewed not one at a time but simultaneously and as interdependent in a dynamic give-and-take that is catalyzed through the intercession of the government.

Obama lays out a plan to "grow our middle class again," and, predictably, it relies on explicitly doubled actions. Rebuilding the economy "will require all of us to see that we have a stake in each other's success. And it will require all of us to take some responsibility." In part, this responsibility is personal, individual: "It will require parents to get more involved in their children's education." "It will require students to study harder." It also "will require greater responsibility from homeowners not to take out mortgages they can't afford." But also, in contrast to some of the speeches he made about race during his campaign, this collective responsibility "will require those of us in public service to make government more efficient and more effective, more consumer-friendly, more responsive to people's needs." And of course, in the area of enterprise and commerce, "it will require American business leaders to understand that their obligations don't just end with their shareholders."

The phrases are linked by their repeated first words "it will require," an example of the recurring paratactic logic of *anaphora*. It places ideas under a single heading so that they are presented not as items in a series or as points upon a hierarchy or as causally related, but as each co-equal with the other ideas with which they are grouped. The actions Obama lists present a range of possible reactions to the economy, differing economic perspectives and attitudes and traditions, and we are asked not to choose among them but rather to contemplate them simultaneously, to see individual responsibility and collective obligation, for example, as equally essential components of a whole.

This address at Osawatomie has presented a compelling notion of citizenship informed by a doubled understanding of economic policy. The speech has been light on the wonkish details that have informed most of Obama's prior addresses on the economy and much heavier on a rhetorical effort to invite his audiences toward sharing a double perspective about the economy. It primarily is an address about citizenship, about how to imagine oneself in relation to others, rather than a lesson about the complexities of a contemporary global economy. But as an exemplar of democratic double-consciousness, it also invites a proliferation of voices and perspectives that follow upon and that are made possible by that initial duality. Throughout the address, the emphasis is on the importance of displacing an oligarchic dichotomy that situates the few against the many with a more democratic and inclusive mode of citizen relationality. One of the bigger applause lines in the speech, for example, comes when Obama declares that he is "here in Kansas to reaffirm my deep conviction that we're greater together than we are on our own," that everyone should play "by the same rules," and that these "aren't 1 percent values or 99 percent values. They're American values. And we have to reclaim them."

This doubled perspective is not foreign to U.S. civic culture but endemic to it, just forgotten, and in need of recovery. It also is not a matter of "class warfare," as many of his critics have put it, because to understand it that way would be to understand it only with the simpleminded confines of division. It is, instead, a correction to the one-sided perspective that "distorts our democracy," as he puts it, again to applause, by giving "an outsized voice to the few who can afford high-priced lobbyists and unlimited campaign contributions, and it runs the risk of selling out our democracy to the highest bidder." Fragmenting the unitary faith in market principles, first through a doubled vision and then through the proliferation of perspectives made possible through that initial duality, opens up possibilities for the voices of the many to be heard.

Economic Duality

In the peroration, this citizen relationality is expressed as a mode of address, given voice by representative citizens. Andy Grove, "the legendary former CEO of Intel," is quoted as acknowledging that "everything I've achieved in my career, and a lot of what Intel has achieved . . . were made possible by a climate of democracy, an economic climate and investment climate provided by the United States." His personal success and the success of his business are due both to economic principles and to a manner of relating to one another as citizen equals. Marvin Windows and Doors, in Warroad, Minnesota, "did not lay off a single one of their 4,000 or so employees—not one," during the economic downturn, instead instituting cuts in pay among both the workers and the management. The CEO of Marvin is quoted as explaining that "these are people we went to school with. We go to church with them. We see them in the same restaurants. Indeed, a lot of us have married local girls and boys. We could be anywhere, but we are in Warroad." This means, according to Obama, that the CEO understands the value of "community," that his success depends upon the success of his employees.

And, of course, this dual-minded motive recognizes that the United States "has never just been about survival of the fittest" but is also "about building a nation where we're all better off," an idea most strongly embodied by Theodore Roosevelt. In a remarkable passage that completes the bridging of the past with the present, overcoming the march of time that left Obama's grandparents irrevocably behind, Obama suggests that it was these ideas, drawn from deep within the American tradition and embodied in Theodore Roosevelt, that "rallied thousands of Americans to Osawatomie—maybe even some of your ancestors—on a rain-soaked day more than a century ago." It was Roosevelt's speech that drew that audience to Osawatomie so long ago, and it is Roosevelt's speech, as revoiced by Obama, that speaks to the economic anxieties of the present. "We are all Americans," Obama quotes him as saying. "Our common interests are as broad as the continent." This capacious view of what might constitute what is held in common pushes against the boundaries of the homogeneous unity that Danielle Allen critiques. "The fundamental rule of our national life," Obama continues, again quoting Roosevelt, "the rule which underlies all others—is that, on the whole, and in the long run, we shall go up or down together." The rule isn't that we must imagine ourselves as being the same but that we must imagine ourselves as interdependent on one another and as sharing in a common destiny. Though Obama reminds us that today the "world is faster and the playing field is larger and the challenges are more complex," the importance of these values, "the values that got us this far," will never change. Roosevelt's doubled motives arrive in the present as relevant and vital as they ever were.

Roosevelt represents a revitalization of a forgotten attitude, drawn from the past into the present. This is a potent antidote to the single-minded devotion to free-market fundamentalism and an embrace instead of a more complex and flexible capacity for appreciating and sustaining dual perspectives without the imperative to reduce or resolve their seeming contradictions. The free market is good, but if left to its own devices it tends to career toward disaster; individual economic achievement is to be praised, but it must also be tempered by the obligations and sacrifices of citizenship. All these statements are true, so that the danger is not in a failure to choose among the alternatives but rather in being forced to choose.

Following this address, John Cassidy, in *The New Yorker*, wrote that "President Obama followed in the footsteps of Theodore Roosevelt and went to Osawatomie, Kansas, to deliver a populist speech about inequality and the middle class," and, in so doing, "at last, he found his voice."[64] That voice, so firmly grounded in both middle America and American tradition, smelled a bit dank for some, apparently, as the conservative *Weekly Standard* characterized the speech as "a trip to an intellectual mausoleum" that illustrates that the "American left has not had a significant new idea since the progressive period."[65] Such assessments may tell us as much about the divided political culture that Obama was addressing as they do about Obama's address itself. Yet, taken together, the idea that Obama found his voice in a graveyard does begin to suggest something of the rhetorical power of the speech. Obama not only reaches deeply into American political traditions to articulate his thoughts about the economy but explicitly portrays himself as doing so in an attempt to correct the "collective amnesia" of those who want "to return to the same practices that got us into this mess."

As James Kloppenberg notes, in Obama's second book, *The Audacity of Hope*, he "explicitly invokes the progressives' ideas of graduated taxation and government regulation of the economy," ideas that have been "embraced by Democrats from the election of Woodrow Wilson in 1912 through the presidency of Lyndon Johnson." These ideas stand in contrast to and have largely been displaced in the public sphere by a "bipartisan consensus" in favor of deregulating industry and lowering taxes—a consensus that retains its rhetorical power even after being "disproved by the catastrophic recession that began in 2008."[66] In fact, many passages in *The Audacity of Hope* in which Obama discusses the economy could be inserted into his speech at Osawatomie without revision, consistent both in the substance of their thought and in the symmetry of their construction. In that book, for example, Obama observes that, on the one hand, "the benefits of our free-market system have mostly derived from the individual efforts of generations of men and women pursuing their own vision of happiness," while, on the other hand, "in each and every period of great economic upheaval and transition we've depended on government action to open up opportunities, encourage competition, and make the market work better."

On the next page, he describes the "idea of social mobility" as one of the "great early bargains of American capitalism; industrial and commercial capitalism might lead to greater instability, but it would be a dynamic system in which anyone with enough energy and talent could rise to the top."[67]

Rather than point to a consistency in Obama's discourse about the economy, however, the parallels with *The Audacity of Hope* actually highlight the speech at Osawatomie as an anomaly. Just as "A More Perfect Union" was exceptional rather than typical, because most of Obama's discourse about race operated within the narrow boundaries imposed upon race talk in the contemporary U.S. civic sphere, so too was most of Obama's talk about the economy constrained by impositions on such talk. Just as Obama's admiration for Malcolm X, as he portrayed it in his memoir, never makes it into his speeches, so too these mixed motives regarding the economy are not generally articulated in his public address. "A More Perfect Union" was crafted to address an extraordinary circumstance that evolved out of a moment of crisis; while Osawatomie perhaps did not offer the same sense of "imperfection marked by urgency," still it offered some fertile possibilities—the hundredth anniversary of Theodore Roosevelt's "New Nationalism" address, the start of Obama's reelection campaign, a persistently sluggish economic recovery.[68] Like the racial neoliberalism that governs the articulation of race in the contemporary public culture, a discourse of economic neoliberalism sets the boundaries of a sanctioned narrative that might be trespassed only in exceptional circumstances. James Aune has described this phenomenon as "economic correctness," the rhetorical manifestation of a single-minded devotion to free-market ideals and the policing of discourse that diverges from that sanctioned narrative.[69]

Conclusion

Each of the speeches reviewed in this chapter has associations with race. Many of the comments made and signs carried during the protests at the town hall meetings on health care reform were undeniably racially offensive; the Nobel Prize Lecture delivered by Martin Luther King Jr. in 1964 was Obama's most explicit model for his own address; and the event at which Theodore Roosevelt spoke in 1910 in Osawatomie was a dedication of a memorial to John Brown, the militant abolitionist who in 1859 led the famous attack on Harper's Ferry (in 1856, Brown led a small force that attempted to defend Osawatomie when it came under siege by a proslavery militia).[70] None of these speeches specifically addresses race, however, and thus they suggest some of the ways that the inventional resources of democratic double-consciousness might inhabit discourse beyond confines of race talk.

The address to Congress on health care reform was crafted in an emotionally charged atmosphere stoked by a seemingly ever-widening gyre of outlandish charges. Obama's speech withholds an emotional response until the end, when it was manifest not in the person of Barack Obama but instead in the memory of Ted Kennedy. This speech presents a quiet middle ground governed by dispassionate rational debate while still providing the audience with a powerful emotional catharsis. When Obama reads from Kennedy's letter, he brings the recently deceased senator into the present, where Kennedy is portrayed as motivated, in part, by emotion and empathy. He is a distinctly doubled character—drawing on his intensely private emotions to animate his dedication to the public good, able to like his fellow members of Congress as well as disagree with them, acting from his own sense of ethics while also feeling the press of citizenly obligation, and seeing himself from the point of view of others. In Kennedy, then, an emotional response and a doubled perspective are brought together as a fitting civic strategy. The address offers citizens a way to talk about health care in a way that includes a communal role as well as an individual one, emotion as well as economics. Ted Kennedy is portrayed as embodying an impassioned and capacious dual perspective that is an appropriate antidote to the dysfunctional single-mindedness and narrow inflexibility that characterized discourse in Congress—and, by extension, in civic culture. Within the metabolism of the address, Kennedy's passion stands not in contrast to Obama's call for reasoned debate but as complementary to it, not occupying an opposite pole but instead among its essential ingredients, for if empathy and commitment were entirely banished from public discourse we could never find our way toward moral judgment.

When Obama was awarded the Nobel Peace Prize it presented a uniquely difficult and complex situation. To reject the award would have been a monumental political disaster, and yet to accept it also carried peculiar liabilities. Though he had run on a platform critical of U.S. military adventurism, he was now commander in chief of a military involved in two wars. In response, in the speech he displayed a careful balance of pragmatism and idealism, informed by both just-war theory and American exceptionalism and expressing an interest in both national self-interest and global stability. War and peace themselves are brought into a balanced and reciprocal relationship, so that they are portrayed not only as depending on one another but also as resembling one another. Both are inevitable, both are enforced by military or quasi-military action, and both have strategic value. War and peace stand before us on the world stage, still distinguishable from one another but linked in a way that begins to blur their distinction. Obama presents a "moral compass," encapsulated by the Golden

Rule, as a means for negotiating the balance between war and peace, but it seems inadequate to the task. The pressing problem regarding war and peace seems less about how best to describe their relationship than about how best to avoid the first and promote the second. This helps us to see some of the limitations of double-consciousness that arise from its foundations as a perspective or way of seeing; in this speech Obama has supplied us with a rich vocabulary through which to understand the relationship between these two inevitable states of human relations, but not with a mode of address through which we might privilege one over the other.

Just as he was beginning his reelection campaign, Obama traveled to Osawatomie, Kansas, to deliver a speech on the spot where Theodore Roosevelt had articulated a "New Nationalism." As with the speech before Congress on health care reform—and as in the King memorial dedication—we are presented with an exemplar of democratic double-consciousness other than Obama. While various figures are introduced, including Henry Ford, FDR, Bill Clinton, and Obama's own grandparents, ultimately Theodore Roosevelt emerges as the embodiment of an appropriately doubled attitude that is the antidote for the single-minded discourse of "economic correctness" that is responsible for the economic disaster. In this address on the economy, as in the address on health care reform, the means and the goal seem well aligned. Obama's argument is that the existing discourses through which we talk about the economy are insufficient and that the doubled style provides an alternative way of speaking; because the problem is a mode of address, the solution is an alternative mode of address. While Roosevelt does not display the emotional accouterments that Kennedy does in the heath care reform speech, he does present a markedly robust form of democratic double-consciousness, a vivid and heroic contrast to the undifferentiated "crowd" that expresses a single-minded devotion to the free market. These attitudes are illustrated as being deeply rooted in American traditions, as almost sprouting from the Kansas soil, and as such they present a valuable and fertile resource for rhetorical invention, encouraging citizens to revivify fundamentally American modes of address and action that have long been dormant in public culture.

In "A More Perfect Union," Obama presents himself as an exemplar of double-consciousness and then translates that experience into democratic double-consciousness when he asks his audiences to cultivate their own duality and to address one another accordingly. In two of the speeches analyzed in this chapter—the address to Congress on health care reform and the speech on the economy at Osawatomie—Obama instead produces a doppleganger, a surrogate who stands in for him as an doubled icon. Because democratic double-consciousness is a mode of address, it is most effectively presented when associated with a person; public address addresses speaking bodies and is addressed by bodies that speak. Kennedy is presented as a commoner, having written a letter to the president like so many other citizens before him; this is against type, of course, as Kennedy was a very wealthy man and a member of a prominent family, but as he is portrayed in the speech he possesses the ability to empathize with both everyday people and his colleagues in Congress. Roosevelt, on the other hand, is a hero, a dashing contrast to the undifferentiated crowd that stands opposed to Obama's ideals. This heroic persona seems to pack the ethical punch needed to transcend the barriers of time and thus to bridge the past and the present in a way that Obama's grandparents, who are portrayed as representing Roosevelt's values, are unable to do. It may be that the lack of an exemplary embodiment in the Nobel Prize Lecture contributes to the inadequacies of its portrayal of democratic double-consciousness, as it thus provides no sure locus of judgment. The speaking personae presented most strongly in the address, Gandhi and Martin Luther King Jr., are dismissed as inadequate, insufficiently realist for the task of addressing the world as it is, and in the end the address may be said to obscure judgment rather than invite it.

Together, these addresses expand upon Du Bois's formative rendering of double-consciousness, showing that although he understood it as an inevitable effect of being black in America, it also has potential as a valuable resource for the production of citizenly discourse. The topics and issues addressed here do not exhaust the possibilities, but they do, I think, indicate the flexibility and range of this mode of speech, freeing it from the narrow confines of discourse about race in the United States and suggesting its value as an inventional resource of citizenship more broadly.

— CHAPTER 6 —

Citizenship and Duality,
Rhetoric and Race

B arack Obama was sworn into office for his second term on January 20, 2013, as mandated by the Twentieth Amendment to the United States Constitution; because this date fell on a Sunday, the public inaugural ceremony took place on Monday, January 21. Approximately one million people gathered on the National Mall to hear Obama deliver his second inaugural address from the steps of the United States Capitol, and of course, as was the case with his first inaugural address, millions more watched it live and have watched it since through various media. Many who had watched Obama's first inaugural ceremony, in 2008, had hoped that the election of an African American president would help to heal some of the divisions that characterize civic culture in the United States. But as he stood behind the podium a second time, the electorate still was deeply divided, particularly with regard to race. Obama won 332 electoral votes to Republican candidate Mitt Romney's 206, but only 51 percent of the popular vote. He retained 93 percent of the African American vote, down from 95 percent in 2008, but earned only 39 percent of the white vote, down from 43 percent. A *Newsweek/Daily Beast* poll taken in April 2012 indicated that "majorities of both whites (72%) and blacks (89%) believe the country is divided by race" but that "twice as many blacks (40%) as whites (20%) say it is very divided" and that "just 19 percent of whites say that racism is a big problem in America, vs. 60 percent of blacks." As has surely always been the case and as Du Bois pointed out so many years ago, the color line is more visible to persons of color. The poll also found that "sixty-three percent of whites and 58 percent of African-Americans say race relations have either stayed the same or worsened" since Obama was first elected; "when asked whether or not Obama has been helpful or not in bridging the racial divide in the country, whites say not helpful (51%) while blacks say helpful (69%)."[1]

When addressing this divided people, as he had four years earlier, Obama delivered a speech that provides the inventional resources that invite what I have been referring to as democratic double-consciousness. This is one of the most important civic rituals in our political catechism, and this speech is even more directly and explicitly about citizenship than Obama's first inaugural. He takes as his text the preamble to the Declaration of Independence, what Stephen Lucas has described as "one of the best-known sentences in the English language": "We hold these truths to be self-evident, that all men are created equal; that they are endowed by their Creator with certain unalienable rights; that among these are life, liberty, and the pursuit of happiness." Obama asks his audience to "recall that what binds this nation together . . . is our allegiance" to these ideas. The choice of words may suggest, of course, another common U.S. civic ritual, the daily recitation of the Pledge of Allegiance that many remember from school. But, as Lucas points out, "part of the rhetorical brilliance of the Declaration is that it was written so people who differed on a wide range of political issues could accept the general ideas stated in the preamble."[2] Obama does not explore or clarify the definitions of the terms used in the passage that he quotes, leaving their ambiguity intact.

While the speech contains several instances of antithesis, such as this strong echo of John F. Kennedy's inaugural—"we will show the courage to try and resolve our differences with other nations peacefully, not because we are naïve about the dangers we face, but because engagement can more durably lift suspicion and fear"—the dominant rhetorical motif is a more paratactic form of parallelism. For example, Obama tells his audience that we have always understood that "fidelity to our founding principles requires new responses to new challenges" and that "preserving our individual freedoms ultimately requires collective action." The founding principles and the new challenges, the individual freedoms and the collective action, are established as co-present and interdependent, not subject to a transcendent synthesis or intended to supplant one another. Similarly, the audience is told to "reject the belief that America must choose between caring for the generation that built this country and investing in the generation that will build its future." It is the forced choice that is rejected—care for the old and for the young are to be considered and sustained together, not traded off one for the other. In a balancing of war and peace that recalls the Nobel Peace Prize Lecture, he says that he and his fellow "citizens, seared by the memory of those we have lost, know too well the price that is paid for liberty" at the same time that "we are also heirs to those who won the peace and not just the war; who turned sworn enemies into the surest of friends."

The first significant applause greets Obama's assertion that his hearers are "one nation and one people." But within the context of this address and of Obama's public discourse more generally, this assertion does not carry the assumption that becoming "one people" means that we must become homogeneous. "Being true to our founding documents," Obama continues, "does not require us to agree on every contour of life. It does not mean we all define liberty in exactly the same way or follow the same precise path to happiness." We can be dedicated to the same principles and still disagree, we can be one and many at the same time, with no contradiction. Obama gives voice to the multiple perspectives that such a conception would accommodate and cultivate, citing "our forebears through Seneca Falls, and Selma, and Stonewall" as well as paying homage to "all those men and women, sung and unsung, who left footprints along this great Mall, to hear a preacher say that we cannot walk alone; to hear a King proclaim that our individual freedom is inextricably bound to the freedom of every soul on Earth."[3] In surrounding King with these other voices, setting him among them in a series, this speech offers a more multivocal presentation of the civil rights movement than in the 2008 campaign speeches; notice that the sung and unsung men and women are the subject of that sentence, not King.

The speech begins with a subtle reference to the Pledge of Allegiance and concludes with its overt enactment, as it aligns Obama with his audience in a collective speech act. "My fellow Americans," Obama says, "the oath I have sworn before you today, like the one recited by others who serve in this Capitol, was an oath to God and country, not party or faction—and we must faithfully execute that pledge during the duration of our service." Understood in this way, the oath marks Obama, like other elected public officials, as different from his fellow citizens; the taking of the oath just witnessed by his audience divides him from them, settling on his shoulders a mantle of unequaled power and prestige.[4] This is citizenly discourse of a kind, to the extent that it marks a significant civic ritual, but one that might be understood to invite the rather monarchical preeminence of a single voice and single perspective. But then in a remarkable conflation, the speech draws Obama's oath into parallel with more everyday oaths of citizenship. Obama continues, saying that "the words I spoke today are not so different from the oath that is taken each time a soldier signs up for duty, or an immigrant realizes her dream. My oath is not so different from the pledge we all make to the flag that waves above and that fills our hearts with pride." The beginning and the end of the speech, then, frame it as being explicitly a discourse on democratic citizenship, and the ending in particular emphasizes this discourse as a mode of address. Obama's oath is not merely a single statement said by a single elite person on a single and rarified occasion but is parallel and analogous to the oaths spoken by many different people on many different and more common occasions. Yet these occasions still resonate with personal and collective significance; they represent not mere everyday talk but speech performances of solemnity and force. "They are," Obama concludes, "the words of citizens, and they represent our greatest hope. You and I, as citizens, have the power to set this country's course. You and I, as citizens, have the obligation to shape the debates of our time—not only with the votes we cast, but with the voices we lift in defense of our most ancient values and enduring ideals." Obama casts his voice as an imitation of the voices of his audience, then encourages his audience to imitate his own, and reminds them of their obligation to participate in further discussion, to use their own voices, shaped through their imitation of his own doubled style, to address themselves and one another as citizens. This is a vivid invitation to democratic double-consciousness, exhibiting the reciprocity and obligation, collective sacrifice and individual distinction, and commitment to a plurality of voices speaking together as an agonistic whole that characterize this mode of civic engagement.

In this concluding chapter, I summarize the arc of my argument before discussing some of the implications of democratic double-consciousness, first with regard to its manifestation in Obama's public discourse and then, more broadly, as an inventional resource that may be made available as a productive antidote to one-sided, single-minded, monovocal—and as a result dysfunctional and undemocratic—public discourse. I end by discussing the implications for understanding this mode of speech specifically as a *rhetoric,* indeed as an integral component of the rhetorical tradition, and thus as perhaps a promise for the revitalization of rhetorical competence within our civic culture.

Citizenship and Double-Consciousness

As a representative figure of public duality, Barack Obama is perhaps unparalleled in contemporary politics. His mixed ethnicity is complemented and amplified in his public address through his penchant for balanced phrases, doubled figures, and other manners of speech that encourage a doubled point of view. I have responded to Obama's public address not primarily to appreciate its artistry, to decode its appeal, or to gain insight into its maker; rather, my aim has been to explore it as an inventional resource upon which citizens might draw when crafting ways to speak with one another. I have been interested in what approaches to public issues and, in particular, what ways of speaking about those issues might be made available through the close analysis of his public discourse. I have been interested, in other words, in what practices of citizenship might be cultivated by Obama's public address.

The particular inventional resources upon which I have focused I have organized under the heading *democratic double-consciousness.* As a phenomenon and a practice, it is rooted in the work of W. E. B. Du Bois, and especially *The Souls of Black Folk.* He formulated the concept as a way to describe the alienation and self-consciousness that arise from being a black person in a predominantly white culture but also as a way to describe the particular insights into U.S. culture and democratic practice that may arise from this experience. From the exclusion from full participation in U.S. citizenship might arise points of view and modes of speech that can contribute not only to a critique of that exclusion but also to a manner of addressing one another as citizens that diminishes the potential for exclusion. For Du Bois, then, double-consciousness is not simply an affliction to be cured or a burden to be lifted, for it also offers some amelioration of the very circumstances that have contributed to its formation; it is a burden with benefits, imposed unilaterally upon the marginalized yet at the same time offering some of the practices and perspectives that might produce an appropriate response to that imposition. We can assume, of course, that Du Bois would have preferred never to have experienced double-consciousness in the first place, but it is also clear that he sees in it a source of some part of the unique gifts that he believed African Americans might offer to the world.

The interpretive frame that has governed my analyses is the result of a "casuistic stretching" of double-consciousness toward a practice of citizenship.[5] In the stretching I intended to remain faithful to Du Bois's original principles while at the same time opening the concept outward to broader applications. As defined here, public discourse that may serve as an inventional resource for democratic double-consciousness possesses three fundamental qualities. First, it is expressly concerned with citizenship, with the kinds of relationships individuals might have with one another and through which they recognize one another. Citizenship is conceived here as a performative role, a mode both of addressing and of being addressed, that emphasizes interdependence and collective sacrifice. This form of citizenship is enacted most strongly and particularly when *"speaking to one another in public,"*[6] which leads to the second fundamental quality of discourse that might foster democratic double-consciousness: that it is *addressed*. It refers not to a state of mind or latent disposition but to a way of speaking to one another as citizens. Of course, this discourse, like any discourse, is addressed within constraints both implicit and explicit; though citizens invent such discourse, they do not invent it in circumstances entirely of their own making. Even so, democratic double-consciousness emphasizes the potential of citizens to act as agents in civic culture, particularly discursively. Finally, public discourse that might serve as an inventional resource for democratic double-consciousness does not stop at being merely doubled. Because the parataxis that informs democratic double-consciousness is not limited by a binary logic, it fosters a proliferation of voices and points of view. Duality is the starting point, the initial countermode and critique of single-voiced discourse, but the end point is a continuing multiplicity of voices and perspectives as the primary duality compounds upon itself.

Contemporary political theorists have begun to explore the idea that the burdens of citizenship, such as those that might precipitate democratic double-consciousness, might themselves help to produce the very attitudes and practices that, in turn, help to lessen some of the more inequitable and undemocratic consequences of this burden. In many cases these theories recall Du Bois's ideas, often implicitly but, increasingly, explicitly. A frequent theme in this line of thought is that the racial problematics of U.S. citizenship should be drawn upon as a resource for discovering ways to address those very problematics; that is, in a way parallel to Du Bois, many who study the contemporary practice of democratic citizenship believe that the exclusionary history of U.S. race relations can be an inventional resource for ways of thinking and acting that can begin to address some of the divisions that characterize U.S. civic culture. As Lawrie Balfour puts it, both echoing Du Bois and making a case for attending to his thought, if we aim "to construct a democratic theory that is itself broadly democratic,"[7] then we cannot avoid drawing upon the "mixed inheritance" that is the legacy of U.S. citizenship.

I have joined in this larger project in one way that a rhetorical critic can, which is through searching out exemplars of rhetorical public discourse that are performing this sort of civic labor. Because I am concerned with describing and making available a discursive practice, I am required to engage with discursive practice; democratic double-consciousness cannot be adequately formulated through theoretical work alone. This book, in other words, is an explicitly rhetorical intervention, intended to locate manners of speech through which a more robust practice of citizenship might be articulated. The speeches of Barack Obama provide a remarkably rich site for exploring the various manifestations and potentialities of doubled discourse, as they are alive with the tropes and figures through which this civic labor might be accomplished. The speech titled "A More Perfect Union," delivered by Obama at a moment of crisis in his 2008 presidential campaign, is the most fully realized performance of democratic double-consciousness analyzed here. It begins by presenting Obama's own bifurcated body as an avatar of double-consciousness, suggesting that he and the perspectives that he possesses are capable of encompassing and synthesizing the tensions present within contemporary U.S. civic culture, particularly with regard to race. This heroic manifestation immediately is discarded, however, as the speech then invites the members of its audience to experience their own double-consciousness, to cultivate for themselves the perspectival mobility that is fostered through a doubled point of view. It is at this moment, near the middle of that speech and the center of this book, that the Du Boisian double-consciousness that Obama is expressing as a way of describing his own perspective is translated into a democratic double-consciousness that his hearers are asked to cultivate and to express as a way of addressing one another as citizens. Obama cultivates this duality in his audience by presenting pairs of points of view, within which one viewpoint is not intended to dominate or supplant the other and whose tensions or contradictions are to be neither transcended nor synthesized; rather, Obama's audience is asked to inhabit them both and to understand both as comparable in terms of reasonableness yet never collapsible into homogeneity. The speech introduces these points of view through characteristically balanced phrases—parallel, paradoxical, chiasmic, paratactic—that emphasize this form of double-consciousness as a mode of speech. In his peroration, Obama presents the Golden Rule as thumbnail condensation of the ethic of reciprocity that governs this form of double-consciousness and its associated ways of speaking.

Most of Obama's other discourses about race, however, throughout the campaign and into his first term, did not invite his audiences toward democratic double-consciousness. They mostly were concerned with positioning Obama and his campaign as an extension of a peculiarly narrow conception of the civil rights movement. This conception focused primarily on Martin Luther King Jr. and on particular events—most prominently the 1963 March on Washington for Jobs and Freedom—that have become relatively safe ways to talk about race, much of their original edge rubbed away through the process of their becoming accepted within the canon of mainstream U.S. civic culture. Obama delivered these speeches primarily to African Americans whom he was seeking to draw together as a voting bloc, and, as a result of this attribution of homogeneity, these texts are almost entirely devoid of the doubled style of speech through which double-consciousness might be fostered and sustained. These speeches present a more linear and monovocal mode of speech, a line of descent from King to Obama and a civic culture that privileges the speech of a single leader. These speeches illustrate the confines of race talk in the United States. Not even a person with the undeniable rhetorical gifts of Barack Obama, not even after his election to the highest office in the land—and arguably the most powerful office in the world—can stray far from the proscribed limits of race talk. This limits the scope and value of democratic double-consciousness as long as it is tied to public discourse that is explicitly about race. Obama's address at the dedication of the Martin Luther King Jr. memorial is a partial counterexample; Obama attempts to recover some of King's edge, to recast him as the controversial figure that he was in life, in a speech that is imagined to be addressed to the "second persona" of the public at large, and in the process attributes to King a vivid enactment of democratic double-consciousness.[8] Yet even here the transformational potential of this portrayal is blunted because it is confined within the sanctioned civil rights narrative, its association with King, and its limitation to discourses of race.

Further aspects of the variation and limitation of democratic double-consciousness become apparent when it is manifest in texts not explicitly linked to race. In his address to Congress on health care reform, Obama presents a powerful exemplar of double-consciousness in the person of the recently deceased Senator Ted Kennedy. As he reads from a letter written by Kennedy, he elicits the emotional and empathetic response essential to ethical judgment and associates it with the productive duality that Kennedy is portrayed as exhibiting. This text counters the detached mode of address in which Obama sometimes engages with an impassioned persona capable of translating personal trauma into a form of civic friendship. This speech also emphasizes the need for democratic double-consciousness, as a mode of address, to be associated with a person; it is not an abstract category but a way of speaking that attains recognizable form when it is associated with a public body. Obama's Nobel Peace Prize Lecture asks his audience to cultivate an ability to hold opposites in view simultaneously, so that war and peace, together with force and diplomacy, ethics and advantage, charity and self-interest, might be seen as mutually dependent and equally viable options in the contemporary world. However, while the Golden Rule seemed entirely appropriate in "A More Perfect Union" as an ethic of reciprocity that encouraged the perspective-taking essential to improved race relations, it seems inadequate as a mechanism through which we might be guided toward peace and away from war. Speaking on the economy at Osawatomie, Kansas, Obama renders democratic double-consciousness a traditional practice of citizenship in the United States, presenting Theodore Roosevelt as the exemplary figure. This lends double-consciousness a robust persona and an association with the progressive movement in the United States as well as a place among U.S. political traditions generally, thus making this speech at Osawatomie an unusually potent articulation of the way that duality as a civic resource can be connected both to a heroic figure and to endemic U.S. political traditions while still retaining a connection to the human-scale performances of everyday citizenship.

These are examples of public discourse that supply the inventional resources of democratic double-consciousness and as such might be deployed as an antidote to the tropes of "oneness," the ideal of homogeneity, and the valorization of single-minded, single-voiced "straight talk" that characterizes of much of contemporary public discourse.[9] The problem isn't that sincerity and plain speaking are pathological but rather that they have achieved a kind of hegemony as discursive norms. Much of the public discourse that circulates in contemporary civic culture adheres to these norms, and as a result the discourse upon which citizens might rely as models for their own rhetorical invention presents only a narrow and anemic pool of possibilities. As Elizabeth Markovits points out, the ideal speaker is imagined to be "sincere," "unitary," exhibiting "no split self, no self-consciousness that would allow the speaker to manipulate her own words for greatest effect."[10] We are in the throes of a "cult of plain speaking," as John Haiman puts it, policed by "a kind of adulation of the unaffected vigor of the one-syllable words in which 'real people' express themselves."[11] Woe unto any public figure or any private person who would address a public who speaks in a manner that suggests that she or he is of more than one mind on a controversial matter. A tendency to see things from more than one perspective and to talk in ways that recognize that an undifferentiated, homogeneous unity is both impossible and undesirable would defy our expectation that "the sincere speaker is one with an authentic, unitary self."[12]

A recurring argument in Obama's oratory is that a single-minded and monologic discourse simply is not up to the task of addressing contemporary political and cultural pluralism. It is not, in other words, a style of discourse capable of promoting or sustaining effective contemporary citizenship. As Peter Meyers puts it, citizens "had better be trained to see the world in two ways at once" if we are to forestall the tendencies toward what he refers to as "monocracy," the progressive narrowing of voice and perspective until only one individual is able to speak.[13] What is needed is a style of discourse within which differing perspectives can be articulated in mutually understandable terms, a rhetorical action encompassing the various figures that characterize a doubled style. Such a discourse would allow us to recognize that differing points of view need not always be brought into alignment, that oppositions need not always be dialectally transcended, that we need not all be essentially similar in order to be fundamentally connected. This is a discourse that recognizes that in order to become more unified we must learn how to divide ourselves by speaking in a manner that recognizes and encourages a form of double-consciousness. This is a discourse, in other words, and finally, that invites us to articulate one another as democratic citizens.

Rhetoric and Duality

I have been arguing that a critical engagement with Obama's public discourse might render it as performing a civic pedagogy. The underlying assumption is that civic discourse is a species of public discourse and that like all public discourse it is produced in response to other public discourse. That response may take the form of opposition, critique, revision, extension, quotation, or paraphrase, but, to the extent to which we understand citizenship as a discursive role, as a rhetorical enactment of civic agency, it depends upon a dialogic engagement with the discourse of others. Obama's public discourse, or at least certain examples of it, can be read as providing resources through which this public dialogue can be encouraged to develop in directions that are especially well suited to contemporary democratic citizenship. The central argument of this book, in other words, is that some of Obama's discourse can be understood as providing resources through which citizens might address one another and recognize one another as being addressed.

My analytical approach has been animated by the intention of making these resources available as equipment for civic life. This is a work of *inventional criticism,* characterized by an effort to describe and to think about the implications of the inventional resources that might be made available through an analysis of public discourse. As an approach to rhetorical criticism that is distinguished primarily by its *purpose,* this is intended to complement other approaches that are defined mostly by *object* or *method.* Whatever the nature of the public discourse brought under critique, the methods through which it is analyzed, or the theoretical vocabulary employed, this mode of rhetorical criticism is animated by the purpose of making public discourse available as inventional resources for the discursive practice of citizenship. If it is true, and I think that it is, that "it is not an exaggeration to characterize the history of rhetoric as a twenty-four-hundred-year reflection on citizen education,"[14] then it should be clear that this mode of criticism is intensely rhetorical. In this sense, my critical stance is analogous to that of the rhetorical pedagogue who presents analyses of exemplars to her students as an aid in their own rhetorical production. Public discourse is viewed as an archive of potential and possibility, and the critic's task is not only to appreciate its artfulness, its appropriateness to a particular situation, its possible effects, its relationship to the rhetor, and so on but also, and more particularly, to articulate the potentials of the discourse to serve as a resource for the invention of further discourse. Indeed, within this critical project, the interpretive engagement with public discourse that animates the analysis can be understood as itself modeling some aspects of a discursive performance of citizenship. The critical act parallels or is in reflective dialogue with the discourse under analysis, entering into the worldview of that discourse, however partially and temporarily, in a way that is analogous to the ways that citizenly discourses engage with one another.

It is true, as Joy Connolly reminds us, that "each of us is a member of a political community. At the same time, we are all individual subjects, isolated bundles of sensation, imagination, memory, and desire."[15] This interstitial space between individual and community, between personal identity and collective identification, between neoliberal autonomy and communitarian responsibility, is a locus of rhetoric. Rhetorical discourse, in this conception, is the medium through which the dualities of citizenship are addressed, for, as citizens draw upon the available cultural resources to craft public discourse with the capability of inducing action in themselves and others, they must necessarily modulate their own interests and goals through the interests and goals of their peers. If they do not do so, their auditors may not see themselves articulated in or interpolated by the discourse produced, and the discourse will fail. This is the fundamental motive of rhetorical invention and as such is the motive that ties rhetorical competence to democratic double-consciousness.

Rhetoric, as Iris Marion Young reminds us, even in her relatively narrow conception of it as encompassing only the "affective, embodied, and stylistic aspects of communication," necessitates "attention to the particular audience of one's communication, and orienting one's claims and arguments to the particular assumptions, history, and idioms of that audience." It is for this reason, this ability to divide one's attention between one's own aims and those of one's audience, that rhetoric "constitutes the flesh and blood of any political communication, whether in a neighbourhood meeting or on the floor of Parliament."[16] The connection between effective citizenship and rhetorical competence is further emphasized by Gerard Hauser, who insists that citizens "must be receptive to alternative modes of expression, engage in active interpretation to understand what is being said and how it relates to them, and be open to change."[17] "To be a good rhetorician," Danielle Allen concurs, "one must see oneself as strangers do. The effort to do so entails understanding how one is implicated in strangers' lives, and how calculi of goods and ills look different from other experiential positions."[18] Skilled speakers, she notes, must imagine "how a proposal will look from all the perspectivally differentiated positions within the citizenry" and thus take into account the perspectives of those citizens different from themselves.[19] An ethical citizen and an effective rhetorician are marked by some similar habits and attributes, and among these is the ability to observe issues from multiple perspectives and to see oneself from the point of view of the other. The citizen possessed of rhetorical competence would gain "a certain ethical fluidity" and with it an ability, indeed a propensity, "to think [herself or] himself into another's subject position."[20]

In this case, the inventional resources that have been made available through an analysis of Barack Obama's public address parallel those that are emphasized in rhetorical education generally. That is, a rhetorical education would cultivate certain forms of duality that are not dissimilar from those cultivated through a close study of Obama's public address. As I noted in the first chapter, rhetoric as a field of study arose in ancient Athens in part as a response to the need for democratic citizens to be able to invent appropriate and effective discourses through which to address one another. To the extent that both the art of rhetoric and democratic double-consciousness, as I have defined it, emerge from the problematics of citizenship, it may be expected that rhetorical training tends to cultivate a form of double-consciousness. In the first chapter I distinguished an instrumental sense of rhetorical competence from a sense of rhetoric as a *habitus* or sensibility; here, I refer to a rhetorical education that would cultivate a more expanded form of rhetorical competence as a sensibility manifest in and dependent upon a discourse of duality.

The associations between rhetoric and duality are myriad. Some of the most pervasive and persistent pedagogical practices associated with training in rhetoric are designed to produce something like a double-consciousness, or at least a consciousness of the doubled qualities of public discourse and of civic life. The *dissoi logoi,* for example, involves asking each student to argue two opposing sides of a single issue and might be taken as a foundational rhetorical enterprise. Jeffrey Walker notes the importance of *dissoi logoi* in Isocrates's teachings. Near the end of Isocrates's text titled *Panathenaicus,* Walker points out, Isocrates says that as he was finishing the treatise he invited a skilled former student to debate with him, "in order that, if any false statement had escaped me, he might detect it and point it out to me."[21] And Walzer argues persuasively that two extant speeches by Isocrates—*Archidamus* and *On the Peace*—functioned as exemplars illustrating two sides of a single issue (specifically, whether to accept a peace treaty). They were, in other words, "companion pieces—antilogies presenting opposite theses on the same themes."[22] As Walker reminds us, the "entire force of the art of rhetoric—the *impact* of its training regimen—lies in this fundamental activity," so it is notable but not surprising that arguing on both sides of an issue and the double-consciousness that such practice encourages would be prominent in an Isocratean pedagogy.[23]

Thomas O. Sloane concurs that "contrarianism is of the essence in rhetoric," and it also is "of the essence in traditional rhetorical education."[24] "At its core," in fact, "rhetorical invention is pro and con thinking."[25] The purpose of such pedagogy is to hone a rhetor's ability to invent arguments; by switching perspectives, making the strongest arguments possible from opposing points of view, students gain the rhetorical competencies of both flexibility and *copia;* that is, it helps to protect the rhetor from a tendency to become locked into any single mode of thought or speech, and it enables the rhetor to round out her or his discourses by expounding on ideas from several different perspectives. A significant effect of this exercise, of course, is a faculty for multiperspectivalism, for seeing an issue or situation from (at least) two perspectives at a time. This faculty, in turn, can be manifest in a capacity for standing temporarily in another's shoes. This perspectival flexibility may be considered a side effect of rhetorical training to the extent that it is a skill that cannot be taught directly, as by formula or precept, but instead must be habituated through repeated exercise over a number of years. But it is not a side effect with regard to the purpose and goal of a rhetorical education, for this sort of perspectival flexibility is an essential faculty for the would-be rhetorician just as it is for the would-be citizen.

Another age-old practice associated with rhetorical pedagogy is *imitatio*. In the first chapter, I noted that inventional criticism, as I have practiced it in this book, draws in part from the tradition of imitative pedagogy in rhetoric, as it seeks to locate within public discourse rhetorical strategies and attitudes that are worthy of emulation so that such discourse might "serve as equipment for future rhetorical production."[26] The object of *imitatio* is to produce a new text that stands alongside the original, shaped and informed by it, and thus engaged in an intimate response to it but not overlying or merely mimicking it. The texts that students produce through imitative practices, Quintilian reminds us, should "rival and vie with the original" and thus avoid merely repeating them.[27] While my analyses certainly will not vie with Obama's speeches in either reach or significance, they do, I hope, illustrate as a critical approach the pedagogical practice through which students tack back and forth between the analysis of existing discourse and the genesis of new discourse, pivoting between the two in an inventional process that does not allow them to become fully immersed in the world addressed by the model text because their attention repeatedly and insistently is drawn to the world they wish to address in their own critical texts.[28] A student rhetor, in other words, learns to oscillate between the roles of interpreter and performer in a way that is analogous to the give-and-take of citizenly practice. As a student of rhetoric learns how to slip between the voice of the other and the voice of her self, she also is learning how to slip between her own perspective and that of another.

Kenneth Burke famously positions "identification" at the center of rhetorical theory, in so doing simultaneously summarizing and reframing much of the rhetorical tradition. Identification, as Burke describes it, retains, as perhaps it must, the duality at the heart of the rhetorical tradition. "You persuade a man," he reminds us, in his most succinct description of the rhetorical force of identification, "only insofar as you can talk his language by speech, gesture, tonality, order, image, attitude, idea, *identifying* your ways with his."[29] This line, of course, would not at all be out of place in one of Barack Obama's speeches; it could serve, indeed, as a short summary of "A More Perfect Union." To become identified with others, Burke explains in terms that resonate with Danielle Allen's notion of "wholeness," is to become "consubstantial" with them—but not identical to them. As with *imitatio,* identification is not a melding of minds but depends upon a pivot or oscillation between one's own interests and those of the other, an ability to see in each particular case the available means through which points of commonality might be persuasively cultivated. *Identification,* in other words, does not entail a loss of *identity*.[30] It is possible and in fact desirable to ask citizens to recognize their mutual obligations and consubstantiations without requiring them to assume homogeneity.[31]

There are any number of further terms and concepts associated with the study of rhetoric that refer to or cultivate a doubled style of speech. But the point is that democratic double-consciousness, as I have described it and as Obama enacts it, is tightly integrated with rhetorical competence. Rhetorical competence is both an effect and a source of democratic double-consciousness, and as such it is both an effect and a source of citizenly competence.

Rhetoric and Race

The rhetorical resources made available in Obama's public discourse can be understood as closely parallel to those made available through a rhetorical education, which suggests that the form of double-consciousness promoted through a critical encounter with Obama's discourse is analogous to some of the habits of thought and speech that are cultivated through acquiring rhetorical competence. But as I noted in the second chapter and have argued throughout, it will not do to stretch the concept of double-consciousness so far that its rootedness in U.S. race relations is lost. Double-consciousness obtains much of its value as a critical heuristic through which to invent more inclusive practices of U.S. citizenship from its association with the exclusionary racial practices that characterize U.S. citizenship. That is why I want to end this chapter and this book with a reflection on double-consciousness as a racialized trope.

For some, Obama's election signaled the start of a postracial era in which race would now become either insignificant or irrelevant in U.S. political affairs. As Richard Thompson Ford puts it, part of Obama's appeal "was that he implicitly promised to bring the United States' long, ugly racial struggle to a heroic conclusion: the charismatic Black president would heal the nation's racial wounds, just as he promised to bridge its ideological chasm. But some had begun to suggest that if dust bowl aggies and high-plains cowboys were ready for a Black president, the nation had *already* gotten beyond race. Obama's surprising success suggested that the nation was already *postracist*."[32] Though Obama did not encourage this sort of thinking, his political fortunes may have depended, at least in part, on his not actively *dis*couraging it. As I have illustrated, the difficulties of explicitly addressing racial issues are immense, and the risks of doing so are substantial. And yet, there are distinct advantages to allowing these racial dynamics to play out in the public consciousness without explicit acknowledgment. "At least some of Obama's considerable support among White voters," Ford concludes, "was the result of an implicit promise: that if the United States could elect a Black president, this would prove that the nation had finally over-come the long-lived evil of racism. Voting for Obama was like reparations on the cheap."[33]

Many critics and observers have argued that Obama succumbed to the limi-tations of this bargain and as a result has not addressed race directly in any very satisfactorily transformative manner. Mark McPhail, for example, suggests that Obama's discourse presents not a productive acknowledgment of racial differ-ence but instead "an old vision of racelessness." Obama tends to ignore "the historical and social realities of American racism," McPhail continues, and thus his discourse "will do little to inspire white Americans toward a resigning of the racial contract."[34] Darrel Wanzer, similarly, notes that, while "Obama's detrac-tors certainly deserve critical attention for their invective, Obama also deserves critical attention for operating within a racially neoliberal discursive field that binds him to antiracial (as opposed to antiracist) responses to subtly (and not so subtly) racist discourses."[35] Stephanie Li attributes much of Obama's political success to his use of a "race-specific, race-free language": "He is race-specific be-cause his racial identity is widely known, but he is race-free in that he routinely ignores racial matters."[36] Ebony Utley and Amy L. Heyse argue that Obama's discourse displays a "lack of recognition for black speaking traditions" and that even though "A More Perfect Union" was a "masterfully given speech" it still "belied the contours of race and the effects of racism in the United States."[37] My analysis, to some extent, bears this out. Obama rarely speaks about race directly, generally does so only within the tight confines of a sanctioned civil rights movement narrative, and is soundly disciplined in the public sphere when he strays beyond this narrative.

But my analysis also offers a different assessment. While Obama may gen-erally avoid addressing race as an explicit subject in his speeches, I have argued that his rhetoric actually is steeped in African American rhetorical traditions. His most potent public discourse, regardless of the subject being addressed, draws from the deep discursive wells that have been excavated by the historical and continuing racial problematics of U.S. citizenship and as a result provide rhetorical resources well suited to addressing the divisions and dysfunctions of contemporary civic culture. The remarkable thing about Obama's discourse, in other words, is not how little it explicitly confronts issues of race but how thoroughly it addresses so many issues through an idiom that is rooted in race.

Not only does Obama rely upon doubled tropes that are strongly associ-ated with African American literary theory and social critique, but he actually invites his audience to employ these tropes and, thus, to some extent, experi-ence double-consciousness. Like Du Bois, Obama sets "his own life in relation to the race concept in order to engender double-vision in his readers."[38] Obama would have his audience feel their own two-ness, not only to become doubled in emulation of his own dark body but also to hone their powers of observation, to see parts of themselves reflected in the eyes of the other without collapsing that other point of view into their own. He would have us feel the gaze of the other and become self-conscious of the power of our own gaze, to experience the centrifugal forces of our collective obligations as they threaten to rend our souls while balanced by the centripetal exertions of our own sense of identity. We should bear our fair share of the burdens of citizenship to feel their weight upon us and know that it is only out of this collective sacrifice that we might invent new insights into the practice of citizenship. Obama's public discourse, in other words, would have us experience the world as W. E. B. Du Bois theorized that African Americans do.

The democratic double-consciousness that I have described through my analysis of Obama's public address, like Du Bois's famous articulation, is not only an adaptation to division but also a remedy for it, at least potentially; if we were to develop a capacity to see ourselves from the perspective of another and to view one another as comparable without the requirement of being absorbed into a homogeneous mass, to understand this initial duality as opening up the potential for the proliferation of multiple voices and perspectives, and, most important, to address one another in a manner that would acknowledge and sustain these perspectives, then we might begin to see ourselves as members of a coherent whole. The discursive forms deployed in Obama's public address, drawn from the racial divisions that characterize the evolving history of U.S. citizenship, provoke and sustain the ethic of reciprocity that is at the heart of democratic citizenship. These tropes encourage each of us to *turn* our attention, to twist our speech and our gaze, so that the burden of our commitments to our fellow citizens is revealed to be not only an effect of democratic life but also an inventional resource for the discursive practices of rhetorical citizenship. The most radical quality of Obama's rhetoric may be the fact that it brings this raced discourse into mainstream American public culture and asks its hearers to speak in its idiom.

Obama's public address asks each of us to feel the imposition of democratic citizenship and to speak accordingly. This is a mode of speech that asks citizens to understand themselves as always already, perpetually and inevitably, implicated in the public lives of others, responsible for one another, and obligated to respond to one another. It draws upon the complexities of citizenship and in particular the problematics of racial difference that have troubled U.S. citizenship since its very inception in order to craft a more inclusive style that addresses those complexities without eliminating them. It reminds us that we are burdened by the intricacies of citizenship and that not only is it often impossible to slough off those burdens through strategies designed to resolve ambiguity or to transcend division but also that it is undesirable to do so, for it is only through shouldering those burdens, however unpleasant they may be, that we may uncover the means through which they may be shared and, thus, lightened. This is the price and promise of citizenship.

Epilogue

On August 9, 2014, Michael Brown, an unarmed eighteen-year-old African American man, was shot and killed by a white police officer on a street in Ferguson, Missouri. I am grateful to have the opportunity to add a brief discussion of Barack Obama's response to this incident and its aftermath. As I write this, specifics continue to come into focus, but it seems generally agreed that around noon on that Saturday, Ferguson police officer Darren Wilson saw Brown walking in the street with another African American man. Wilson pulled his patrol car alongside and told them to move to the sidewalk. He may or may not have suspected that Brown had been involved in a robbery earlier that day. Some sort of scuffle ensued, perhaps as a result of Brown's reaching in through the window, and it seems that Wilson's gun was discharged inside the car, possibly injuring Brown. Brown then moved away, but within a few moments, perhaps in response to a command from Wilson, he turned to face Wilson and may have begun to move toward him. Many witnesses have said that Brown had his hands raised. Wilson then shot Brown several times, and Brown fell, already dead or dying in the street. His body lay there for hours while a crowd gathered, an ambulance arrived, and police officers investigated the scene.

The next several weeks brought clashes between protestors and police. The local police force was augmented by reinforcements from the greater St. Louis area, together with armored vehicles, SWAT teams, and the National Guard. A week after the shooting, Missouri's governor, Jay Nixon, declared a state of emergency and set a curfew for all residents between the hours of midnight and 5:00 A.M. Al Sharpton and Jesse Jackson traveled to Ferguson, and President Obama sent Attorney General Eric Holder. A grand jury was convened. Months after Michael Brown was killed, protests and arrests continue.

In contrast to Obama's comments about the arrest of Henry Louis Gates, Jr., and the death of Trayvon Martin, both of which appeared to be off-the-cuff remarks given during question-and-answer sessions following addresses on other topics, Obama presented two quite similar prepared statements on the shooting of Michael Brown and the subsequent unrest in Ferguson, the first on August 14, from Martha's Vineyard, where the president was vacationing with his family, and the second on August 18, from the White House.[1] These statements are best understood as a continuation, and perhaps a culmination, of the story told in chapter 4 of this book, which describes the limitations imposed on talk about race in the United States and the effect of those limitations on Obama's public address. The speeches reviewed in that chapter show that during the 2008 campaign and extending through his first year in office, Obama discussed race only within the context of a safe and narrow narrative of the civil rights movement, one focused almost exclusively on the leadership of Martin Luther King, Jr.; in his statements about Ferguson, Obama avoided the mention of race almost entirely.[2]

Both statements begin with Obama ticking off actions and observations in a clinical and bureaucratic style. Obama reveals that he has instructed the attorney general to "determine exactly what happened," tells us that he has expressed his "concern" to Governor Nixon, and recounts the measures taken thus far by the FBI and the Department of Justice. He informs us, as a newscaster might, that local authorities are developing strategies to "maintain public safety without restricting the right of peaceful protest and while avoiding unnecessary escalation." Even the shooting is described in language that might as easily describe a traffic accident: "We lost a young man, Michael Brown, in heartbreaking and tragic circumstances." Local authorities have been reminded that they "have a responsibility to be open and transparent about how they are investigating that death." This is a discourse of expertise, portraying qualified and capable people addressing a complicated and volatile situation. It deploys a phalanx of political surrogates and government agencies that insulate Obama from the events. Within this discursive context, Obama's admonishments that looting and violence undermine justice, that the police should not deny the right to peaceful protest, and that we all should "seek some understanding rather than simply holler at each other" sound distant and even paternalistic, the voice of a wise elder insisting from on high that his flock call itself to order. The disengaged tone is reinforced when both statements close by trailing off into abstract platitudes: "we all need to hold ourselves to a high standard" and recall that disagreement is "part of our democracy"; and because "we're all part of one American family . . . united in common values," we must "seek out our shared humanity" and learn to "understand each other." The only mention of race comes at the end of the August 18 address, but even this is expressed in generalities. Obama reminds us that "too many young men of color are left behind and seen only as objects of fear" and that "people of good will of all races are ready to chip in" to effect change.

It is perhaps unfair to expect too much from these statements. They seem intended to assure Obama's listeners that he is aware of the situation and that his administration is taking appropriate action. These innocuous but carefully crafted statements seem designed to offend as few as possible, to eschew taking sides, and perhaps to sidestep the vehement criticisms that have followed some of Obama's more extemporaneous remarks. It may be that they model calm detachment as an antidote to escalating tensions. But whatever the intention, the fact is that none of these phrases places the events in Ferguson within the context of the long histories of racial profiling, differential sentencing, and the increased likelihood of deadly force that characterize the experiences of many African Americans, and especially African American men, with law enforcement and the judicial system. Obama tells us that he understands "the passion and the anger that arise over the death of Michael Brown," but he does not tell us that he identifies with these emotions, and he does not say that he feels them. And nothing that Obama says here recognizes racial difference, or even racial identity, in any specific way, and certainly he does not acknowledge that race produces differential experiences of citizenship.

The descent has been precipitous. From the heights of "A More Perfect Union," which offered a nuanced way of speaking about race that retained a recognition of difference without rejecting an ideal of unity and that explicitly tied this dual recognition to practices of democratic citizenship, Obama has arrived a little more than six years later at an anemic discourse through which he can address a highly racialized incident while mentioning race hardly at all. It may be tempting to lay responsibility for this sheer rhetorical drop firmly at Obama's feet. No other president, no other elected official, and probably no other public figure has ever presented so clearly, and even explicitly, a promise to enrich the inventional resources through which we might talk about race and thus correct our collective racial aphasia. And as a result, of course, few have been given the opportunity to disappoint so many so profoundly. But we must acknowledge as well that the responsibility exceeds Obama and extends to ourselves and to the narrow confines we have reserved for race talk in the United States, boundaries that are so thoroughly policed that even so gifted and powerful a man as he does not seem emboldened to trespass against them.

A brief comparison is instructive. On October 21 Governor Nixon announced a Ferguson Commission, charged with offering "specific recommendations for making this region a stronger, fairer place for everyone to live."[3] In his remarks the governor places the protests in Ferguson within a historical context, acknowledging that they "echo others within our lifetime," and he characterizes them as "a cry from the heart, heard and felt around the nation and around the world. A cry for justice. A cry for change in the schoolhouse and the courthouse. A cry for change in the social and economic conditions that impede prosperity, equality, and safety for all of us." He describes the issues addressed by these protests as "shared problems," and he illustrates the notion in statements linked in close grammatical parallelism:

> I think of the mother of an African-American teenager, as she kisses him goodbye each morning, hands him his backpack and watches him head off to school, knowing that he might never come home again. She lives with that fear every day.
>
> I think about the wife of a cop, as she kisses her husband goodbye, hands him a cup of coffee and watches him drive off to work, knowing he might never come home again. She lives with that fear every day.

These phrases almost might have been cribbed from Obama's "A More Perfect Union" to the extent that they set these vignettes beside each other, in *parataxis*, inviting the audience to compare the two without explicitly equating them. They solicit an effort to identify with one another at the level of affect and emotion. They ask listeners to view one another, for a moment, through the eyes of the other, and thus to experience a doubled perspective. Certainly these phrases lack the elegance and subtlety of Obama's best oratory. But they do at least gesture toward a way to talk about race that might provide inventional resources for citizens who, as the governor puts it, "come together in good faith, endure the fierce crucible of public opinion, and lead the hard work of change."

Jay Nixon is a white man and the governor of a relatively small state, and as a result he does not face the same constraints and expectations that Obama does as the first African American U.S. president. We should be cautious in our comparison, as the governor may have opportunity, and even privilege, not available to the president. Yet still the governor's comments suggest the possibility that events such as those in Ferguson, Missouri, might be addressed in a way that contributes both to our ability to talk about race and to our ability to address one another as citizens.

Any robust discourse of citizenship in the United States must draw upon the problematics of race that have stained American citizenship since its inception. We cannot hope to invent a viable mode of addressing one another as citizens that somehow fails to not only acknowledge but actually to integrate the experiences of our fellow Americans who have been, and continue to be, excluded from full citizenship. Obama's statements on Ferguson make little room for the recognition of race, and even less for so complex a part of our collective racial heritage as double-consciousness. In this book I have argued that some of Obama's speeches, particularly those analyzed in chapter 5, may contribute to practices of citizenship without explicitly addressing race—but that is possible only because a speech such as "A More Perfect Union," which does address race, has provided rhetorical resources that may enable such discourse. Statements such as Obama's in response to Ferguson achieve none of this rhetorical work. The near-total evacuation of race from these remarks renders them incapable of contributing to the cultivation of a durable and productive discourse of citizenship. In the end public discourse such as this may instruct us about how to manage our relationship to authority, and they may assure us that appropriate decisions are being made on our behalf, but they can offer little that might help us to address one another.

Notes

Preface

1. There does not seem to be agreement in the extant literature about whether to spell "double-consciousness" with the hyphen or without. I will spell it with the hyphen, because this follows Du Bois's usage in the 1903 edition of *The Souls of Black Folk*.

Chapter 1—Inventional Criticism

1. Campbell and Jamieson, *Deeds Done in Words*, 15–16. See also Ryan, *The Inaugural Addresses of Twentieth-Century American Presidents;* Beasley, "The Rhetoric of Ideological Consensus in the United States."

2. Barack Obama, "President Barack Obama's Inaugural Address," *Whitehouse.gov,* January 21, 2009, http://www.whitehouse.gov/blog/inaugural-address (accessed March 3, 2009).

3. D'Souza, *The Roots of Obama's Rage*, 2.

4. D'Souza, *Roots of Obama's Rage*, 25, 59, 77. D'Souza argues, for example, that the truth about Obama's character lies in the influences of the anticolonialism of both his African father and his Indonesian stepfather. Jack Cashill, in *Deconstructing Obama,* provides an especially intense variation on this theme, studying Obama's memoir *Dreams from My Father* not to discover the "real" Obama behind the mask but rather to show that in fact the "real" Obama didn't even write it.

5. Corsi, *The Obama Nation,* ix, 124, 177, 282.

6. Abramsky, *Inside Obama's Brain,* 9.

7. Jack Kelly, "Obama Goes from Blank Slate to Empty Suit," *Real Clear Politics,* March 6, 2011, http://www.realclearpolitics.com/articles/2011/03/06/obama_from_blank _slate_to_empty_suit_109134.html (accessed July 30, 2012).

8. Frank, *Obama on the Couch,* 3.

9. Frank, "The Prophetic Voice and the Face of the Other in Barack Obama's 'A More Perfect Union' Address," 170.

10. Medhurst, "Barack Obama's 2009 Inaugural Address," 195, 214.

11. Kloppenberg, *Reading Obama,* xv.

12. Kloppenberg, *Reading Obama,* 40.

13. Leeman, *The Teleological Discourse of Barack Obama,* 13–14, 243–45, 249–50. A notable exception to these approaches to Obama's public address is John Murphy, who argues that Obama "teaches his audience how to interpret his campaign and American public life through the performance of Joshua and the renewal of covenant." Murphy, "Barack Obama," 388. Peter Simonson, in "The Streets of Laredo," provides an ethnographic account of some of the ways that citizens have made use of Obama's discourse and the phenomenon of his 2008 campaign.

14. Inventional criticism is intended to circumvent the "dialectic between object and method" that Dilip Gaonkar argues was set in motion within the field of rhetorical criticism by Herbert A. Wichelns's landmark essay, "The Literary Criticism of Oratory." While it would have been correct to note during the last decades of the twentieth century, as James Jasinski has it, that "method rules," I would argue that now the pendulum has swung back again to a situated "object" as the locus of interest among rhetorical critics. I mean to interrupt this dialectic by introducing a mode of critique that is characterized not by object or method but by *purpose*—in this case, the purpose of inventing resources capable of fostering democratic citizenly engagement. Gaonkar, "Object and Method"; Jasinski, "The Status of Theory and Method"; Wichelns, "The Literary Criticism of Oratory." For a thorough discussion of the problematic entailments of "method" in rhetorical criticism, see Nothstine, Blair, and Copeland, *Critical Questions*.

15. Walzer, "Teaching 'Political Wisdom,'" 113.

16. For a succinct review of this standard origin story, together with a revision of it, see Schiappa, *The Beginnings of Rhetorical Theory*. See also Kennedy, *A New History of Classical Rhetoric*.

17. Hauser, *Vernacular Voices*, 33.

18. For a recent argument in support of this position, see Keith and Mountford, "The Mt. Oread Manifesto."

19. Garsten, *Saving Persuasion*.

20. Young, *Inclusion and Democracy*, 7, 64, 70.

21. Markovits, *The Politics of Sincerity*, 9, 39.

22. Young, *Inclusion and Democracy*, 65.

23. Markovits, *The Politics of Sincerity*, 11.

24. McKeon, "The Methods of Rhetoric and Philosophy," 59.

25. For a succinct summary of these ancient canons, see Watson, "Invention," 360.

26. Lyon, "Rhetoric and Hermeneutics," 47.

27. Copeland, *Rhetoric, Hermeneutics, and Translation*, 151.

28. Hauser, *Vernacular Voices*, 33.

29. Jasinski, *Sourcebook on Rhetoric*, 327–31. As Sharon Crowley points out, this sense of the fundamental intertextuality of public discourse is at odds with "the modern belief that knowledge resulted from the actions of individual minds on the things of the world." Crowley, *The Methodical Memory*, 4.

30. Leff, "Hermeneutical Rhetoric," 201. See also Crowley, "Rhetoric, Literature, and the Dissociation of Invention," 25. The mode of rhetorical criticism that I am describing owes some debt to and as a result bears resemblance to the "hermeneutical rhetoric" as described by Leff. It exceeds that conception, however, because it takes as its motive not the intrinsic discovery and appreciation of rhetorical artistry but the invention, through the criticism of rhetorical art, of discursive resources with extrinsic value.

31. Campbell, "Agency: Promiscuous and Protean," 1–19.

32. In this paragraph I am aligning my critical practice with some elements associated with "critical rhetoric" and "productive criticism." McKerrow, "Critical Rhetoric"; Ono and Sloop, "Commitment to Telos"; Ivie, "Productive Criticism"; Ivie, "Productive Criticism Then and Now."

33. Wilson, "The Racial Contexts of Public Address," 213. Michael McGee's oft-quoted dictum, that "*text construction is now something done more by the consumers than by the producers of discourse*," suggests perhaps that this was a recent phenomenon at the time he wrote, when actually it is a reminder of one of the fundamental qualities

of public discourse. McGee, "Text, Context, and the Fragmentation of Contemporary Culture," 288.

34. Copeland, *Rhetoric, Hermeneutics, and Translation*, 179.

35. Walker, *The Genuine Teachers of This Art*, 80–81; Walzer, "Teaching 'Political Wisdom,'" 114. In the *Institutio Oratoria*, Quintilian suggests that teachers of rhetoric should in the lectures "point out the beauties of authors, and, if occasion ever present itself, their faults" and "should leave nothing unnoticed which is important to be remarked, either in the thought or the language" (II.v.4–9).

36. Walker, *The Genuine Teachers of This Art*, 73–74.

37. For a particularly instructive description of this process, see Leff, "The Idea of Rhetoric as Interpretive Practice," 97–99.

38. Walzer, "Teaching 'Political Wisdom,'" 121.

39. Inventional engagements with vernacular discourses, those that resonate within local communities and through which citizens make their concerns known among themselves, are especially productive. See Ono and Sloop, "The Critique of Vernacular Discourse"; Hauser, *Vernacular Voices*; McCormick, "Earning One's Inheritance."

40. Burke, "Literature as Equipment for Living," 293–304.

41. Gencarella, "Purifying Rhetoric."

42. Connolly, *The State of Speech*, 2.

43. Asen, "A Discourse Theory of Citizenship"; Kock and Villadsen, "Introduction: Citizenship as a Rhetorical Practice."

44. Cohen, *Semi-Citizenship in Democratic Politics*, 21.

45. Meyers, *Civic War and the Corruption of the Citizen*, 4, 241. Of course, other modes of communication, including the visual, aural, and tactile, may be considered forms of "speech," where speech is understood as the umbrella term for human symbolic interaction.

46. Asen, "A Discourse Theory of Citizenship," 196.

47. Asen, "A Discourse Theory of Citizenship," 203–4.

48. Meyers, *Civic War and the Corruption of the Citizen*, 1–2.

49. Black, "The Second Persona," 111–13. See also Charland, "Constitutive Rhetoric"; McGee, "In Search of 'the People.'"

50. After earning a reputation for soaring oratory during the campaign, Obama faced high expectations for the inaugural address, but he and his speechwriters deliberately crafted a speech that was notably muted in tone, intended to fulfill these expectations without exceeding them. Alter, *The Promise*, 106; Wolffe, *Renegade*, 308.

Chapter 2—Democratic Double-Consciousness

1. Obama, *Dreams from My Father*, 86.

2. Obama, *Dreams from My Father*, 87.

3. Obama, *Dreams from My Father*, 89.

4. Ben Wallace-Wells, "Destiny's Child," *Rolling Stone*, February 22, 2007, http://archive.rollingstone.com (accessed July 21, 2009).

5. Obama, *The Audacity of Hope*, 11. Obama's friend Cassandra Butts is reported to have characterized Obama as a "cultural Rorschach test." Abramsky, *Inside Obama's Brain*, 17.

6. Abramsky, *Inside Obama's Brain*, 53, 55.

7. Abramsky, *Inside Obama's Brain*, 163.

8. Romano, *America the Philosophical*, 601.

9. Remnick, *The Bridge,* 431.

10. Wolffe, *Renegade,* 25.

11. Quoted in Remnick, *The Bridge,* 195.

12. Alter, *The Promise,* 152.

13. Kitwana, "Between Expediency and Conviction," 94.

14. Remnick, *The Bridge,* 101.

15. Frank, *Obama on the Couch,* 23.

16. Wallace-Wells, "Destiny's Child."

17. Remnick, *The Bridge,* 237, 433.

18. Abramsky, *Inside Obama's Brain,* 53; Steele, *A Bound Man,* 98.

19. Remnick, *The Bridge,* 408.

20. Maureen Dowd, "Why Is He Bi? (Sigh)," *New York Times,* June 26, 2011, http://www.nytimes.com/2011/06/26/opinion/sunday/26dowd.html (accessed June 26, 2011).

21. Maraniss, *Barack Obama,* xx; Remnick, *The Bridge,* 456.

22. Frank, *Obama on the Couch,* 85.

23. Krugman, "The President is Missing," *New York Times,* April 10, 2011, http://www.nytimes.com/2011/04/11/opinion/11krugman.html (accessed August 18, 2012). Frank describes an item in the satirical publication the *Onion* suggesting that "the real President Obama had been kidnapped hours after the election and replaced by an imposter." Frank, *Obama on the Couch,* 4.

24. Vaughn and Mercieca, *The Rhetoric of Heroic Expectations.*

25. Conley, "Virtuoso," 309.

26. Medhurst, "Barack Obama's 2009 Inaugural Address," 199–202.

27. Frank, "Obama's Rhetorical Signature," 615. Susanna Dilliplane also notes that Obama engages in a "rejection of mutually exclusive binaries," which is "consistent with Obama's subsumption of different parts or perspectives." Dilliplane, "Race, Rhetoric, and Running for President," 142.

28. Remnick, *The Bridge,* 192.

29. Quoted in Renmick, *The Bridge,* 195. The article Tribe is discussing was about abortion.

30. Remnick, *The Bridge,* 265. Remnick also reports that a leading conservative legal scholar judged Obama's course syllabi when he taught at the University of Chicago to be "leading his students in an honest assessment of competing views" (264).

31. Alter, *The Promise,* 152. Tom Coburn, a Republican senator from Oklahoma, reportedly enjoys a friendship with Obama. Coburn, like Obama, was elected to the U.S. Senate in 2004. He retired at the end of 2014 because of a recurrence of cancer.

32. Kloppenberg, *Reading Obama,* 148.

33. William Finnegan, "The Candidate: How the Son of a Kenyan Economist Became an Illinois Everyman," *New Yorker,* May 31, 2004, http://www.newyorker.com/archive/2004/05/31/040531fa_fact1 (accessed October 24, 2012).

34. Stanley Fish, "Barack Obama's Prose Style," *New York Times,* January 22, 2009, http://opinionator.blogs.nytimes.com/2009/01/22/barack-obamas-prose-style (accessed March 8, 2010). Fish is quoting the *Oxford English Dictionary.* On parataxis, see also Lanham, *A Handlist of Rhetorical Terms,* 108; Jasinski, *Sourcebook on Rhetoric,* 539–40; Hariman, "Allegory and Democratic Public Culture in the Postmodern Era," 267–96.

35. Lanham, *Analyzing Prose,* 29; Jasinski, *Sourcebook on Rhetoric,* 539.

36. Compromise and synthesis would seem to require a hypotactic style and perhaps a polysyndic one.

37. Wolffe, *Renegade*, 151.

38. Kloppenberg, *Reading Obama*, 13, 19, 250–51. Jonathan Alter similarly notes: "In his books and speeches Obama had long been willing to explore what W. E. B. DuBois [*sic*] called the 'double-consciousness' of well-educated minorities who came to thrive in both black and white worlds." Alter, *The Promise*, 284.

39. I might note that Barack Obama is only a few weeks younger than I am.

40. Gates, "Introduction: Darkly, as through a Veil," xix.

41. Naturally, the form of double-consciousness that I describe in this book has some affinity with the "double-voicedness" described by Mikhail Bakhtin, particularly the form of heteroglossia that he refers to as a "hybrid construction," which he defines as "an utterance that belongs, by its grammatical (syntactic) and compositional markers, to a single speaker, but that actually contains mixed within it two utterances, two speech manners, two styles, two 'languages,' two semantic and axiological belief systems." Bakhtin, "Discourse in the Novel," 304. Du Bois's formulation of double-consciousness offers several qualities that are especially valuable to the present study, most particularly the intimate associations with racial alienation and U.S. citizenship.

42. For an analysis that takes the duality manifest in Du Bois's *The Souls of Black Folk* as fundamental feature of its political critique, see Terrill and Leff, "The Polemicist as Artist." See also Terrill and Watts, "W. E. B. Du Bois, Double-Consciousness, and Pan-Africanism."

43. Dickson D. Bruce Jr. offers perhaps the most succinct analysis of the sources upon which Du Bois likely drew: Bruce, "W. E. B. Du Bois and the Idea of Double Consciousness," 299–309.

44. Adolph Reed calls this passage "probably—excepting perhaps his statement designating the 'color line' as the twentieth century's distinctive problem—the most widely known and most frequently cited statement of any in Du Bois's entire corpus." Reed, *W. E. B. Du Bois and American Political Thought*, 91. This is really saying something, given that, by Henry Louis Gates's estimation, "Du Bois wrote on average one work of one sort or another *every twelve days* between the ages of thirty and ninety-five." Gates also remembers copying this passage out, in full, into his private commonplace book. Gates, "Introduction," xi, xxiii–xxiv.

45. Du Bois, *Souls*, 3.

46. Reed, "Du Bois's 'Double Consciousness,'" 135.

47. Du Bois, *Souls*, 148.

48. Obama, *Dreams from My Father*, xv.

49. Obama, *Dreams from My Father*, xv.

50. Lewis, *W. E. B. Du Bois*, 144–45.

51. Lewis, *W. E. B. Du Bois*, 196.

52. Allen, "Ever Feeling One's Twoness," 261–75. See also Allen, "Du Boisian Double-Consciousness." Paul Gilroy, similarly, argues that Du Bois—and Richard Wright, in drawing upon Du Bois—viewed double-consciousness as "neither simply a disability nor a consistent privilege." Gilroy, *The Black Atlantic*, 161.

53. "Du Bois does not *adopt* Hegel but *adapts* him to his own ends." Zamir, *Dark Voices*, 114. Zamir argues similarly that although Du Bois was influenced by the psychological ideas of William James and the transcendentalism of Ralph Waldo Emerson, those ideas are helpful "only inasmuch as they help map out a discursive field in which Du Bois's work can be critically differentiated," because Du Bois was not interested in resolving the divided self (116; 154–63). Bruce refers to two strands of influence on Du Bois's ideas of

double-consciousness, the "figurative," deriving from Emerson, and the "medical," deriving from James. Bruce, "W. E. B. Du Bois and the Idea of Double Consciousness," 299–309.

54. Holt, "The Political Uses of Alienation," 306.

55. Obama, *Dreams from My Father,* 82.

56. Obama, *Dreams from My Father,* 82.

57. Obama, *Audacity of Hope,* 10.

58. Obama, *Audacity of Hope,* 66.

59. Obama, *Audacity of Hope,* 67.

60. Obama, *Audacity of Hope,* 68.

61. It would be in keeping with the doubled effects of double-consciousness to note that because Obama "looks like" (appears similar to) those who are alienated from mainstream American culture, he gains an ability also to "look like" them (to see from their perspective).

62. Balfour, *Democracy's Reconstruction,* 17. Balfour is quoting from Norton, "Seeing in the Dark."

63. Du Bois did not formulate his ideas about double-consciousness as an orator running for public office, though he did run for U.S. senator from New York in 1950, at the age of eighty-two, on the American Labor Party ticket.

64. Burke, *Attitudes toward History,* 229; Jasinski, *Sourcebook on Rhetoric,* 89–90.

65. Reed, *W. E. B. Du Bois and American Political Thought,* 92.

66. Reed, *W. E. B. Du Bois and American Political Thought,* 97–98.

67. Lincoln, "The Du Boisian Dubiety," 196, 200.

68. Zamir, *Dark Voices,* 116. Zamir goes on to note that the "account of 'double-consciousness' in the first chapter of *Souls* represents the black middle-class elite facing the failure of its own progressive ideas in the late nineteenth century, in the aftermath of failed Reconstruction and under the gaze of a white America" (116). Zamir also provides a thorough and authoritative overview of the cultural and intellectual milieu within which Du Bois developed his concept. The most valuable survey of the various appropriations of double-consciousness is Reed, *W. E. B. Du Bois and American Political Thought,* 91–99. A variation on this theme comes from Wilson J. Moses, who dismisses the "two-souls paradigm" as "essentially reductive" because it is inadequate as a way to account for the fact that the "personality of every human being is complex and contradictory." Moses, "Ambivalent Maybe," 274–75.

69. Stewart, *Strange Jeremiahs,* 218.

70. Reed, *W. E. B. Du Bois and American Political Thought,* 109.

71. McPhail, "Double Consciousness in Black and White," 5.

72. Balfour, *Democracy's Reconstruction,* 6.

73. Allen, *Talking to Strangers,* xxi.

74. Lape, *Race and Citizen Identity in the Classical Athenian Democracy.*

75. Jun, *Race for Citizenship,* 17.

76. Roman, *Citizenship and Its Exclusions,* 6. Punctuation as in original.

77. Smith, *Civic Ideals,* 14.

78. Shklar, *American Citizenship,* 15–18, 48–55.

79. Karst, *Belonging to America,* 43.

80. Smith, *Civic Ideals,* 31.

81. Karst, *Belonging to America,* 43.

82. *Dred Scott v. Sandford,* 60 U.S. 393 (1856), http://laws.findlaw.com/us/60/393.html (accessed January 3, 2014). See also Smith, *Civic Ideals,* 263–41.

83. Karst, *Belonging to America,* 52. See also Kennedy, *"Dred Scott* and African American Citizenship," 101–21.

84. *Plessy v. Ferguson,* 163 U.S. 537 (1896), http://laws.findlaw.com/us/163/537.html (accessed January 8, 2014).

85. Smith, *Civic Ideals,* 310.

86. "Congressional Globe, 21st Congress, 1st Session, 148 (1830)," http://memory.loc .gov/cgi-bin/ampage?collId=llsl&fileName=004/llsl004.db&recNum=458 (accessed July 22, 2012).

87. "Civil Rights Act of 1866, 14 Stat. 27 (1866)," http://www.arch.ksu.edu/jwkplan/ law/civil%20rights%20acts%20of%201866,%201870,%201871,%201875.htm (accessed July 22, 2012). Rogers Smith argues that according to the 1866 Civil Right Act, "native-born blacks were clearly designated nationally protected citizens; but they were not so clearly made equal citizens." Smith, *Civic Ideals,* 307.

88. Quoted in Maltz, "The Fourteenth Amendment and Native American Citizenship," 555. See also Smith, *Civic Ideals,* 308.

89. Tennant, "'Excluding Indians Not Taxed'"; Indian Citizenship Act of 1924, http:// www.nebraskastudies.org/0700/stories/0701_0146.html (accessed August 1, 2013).

90. Smith, *Civic Ideals,* 15.

91. Kennedy, "Dred Scott and African American Citizenship," 101–21.

92. "Transcript of Chinese Exclusion Act (1882)," *OurDocuments.gov,* http://www .ourdocuments.gov/doc.php?doc=47&page=transcript (accessed July 22, 2011).

93. "Geary Act of 1892," *SanFranciscoChinaTown.com,* http://www.sanfrancisco chinatown.com/history/1892gearyact.html (accessed August 12, 2011).

94. "First Congress, Sess. II., Ch. 3 (1790)" [Naturalization Act of 1790], http://rs6 .loc.gov/cgi-bin/ampage?collId=llsl&fileName=001/llsl001.db&recNum=226 (accessed July 4, 2011); "Third Congress, Sess. II, Ch. 19, 20 (1795)" [Naturalization Act of 1795], http://rs6.loc.gov/cgi-bin/ampage?collId=llsl&fileName=001/llsl001.db&recNum =537 (accessed July 4, 2011); "The Congressional Globe, 5177 (1870)" [Naturalization Act of 1870], http://memory.loc.gov/cgi-bin/ampage?collId=llcg&fileName=094/llcg094 .db&recNum=460 (accessed July 4, 2011).

95. "Public Laws, 57 Stat., Ch. 344, December 17, 1943" [Chinese Exclusion Repeal Act of 1943, also known as the Magnuson Act], http://library.uwb.edu/guides/USimmi gration/57%20stat%20600.pdf (accessed July 4, 2011).

96. Smith, *Civic Ideals,* 441–42; Daniels, *The Politics of Prejudice.*

97. *Toyosaburo Korematsu v. United States,* 323 U.S. 214 (1944), http://laws.findlaw .com/us/323/214.html (accessed July 12, 2011).

98. *U.S. v. Bhagat Singh Thind,* 261 U.S. 204 (1923), http://laws.findlaw.com/ us/261/204.html (accessed September 11, 2011).

99. Cott, "Marriage and Women's Citizenship in the United States," 1467. See also Bredbenner, *A Nationality of Her Own.*

100. Smith, *Civic Ideals,* 130–31. But see also the evidence provided by Jan Lewis that suggests that women were intended to be included in the term "persons," as it is used in the Constitution. Lewis, "Representation of Women in the Constitution," 23–25.

101. Cott, "Marriage and Women's Citizenship in the United States," 1451.

102. "66 Stat. 163, An Act to Revise the Laws Relating to Immigration, Naturalization, and Nationality; And for Other Purposes" [McCarran-Walter Act], *U.S. Government Printing Office,* http://www.gpo.gov/fdsys/granule/STATUTE-66/STATUTE-66-Pg163/ content-detail.html (accessed September 18, 2010). In addition to striking out the racial

qualifications for naturalization that had been in effect since 1790, this act instituted a quota system designed to restrict the number of legal immigrants from Asia and Eastern Europe. See also Glazer, "Reflections on Citizenship and Diversity," 85–100.

103. Oboler, "Redefining Citizenship as Lived Experience," 9–10.

104. Cisneros, *The Border Crossed Us;* Castañeda, "Roads to Citizenship"; Isaac West provides an engaging and thorough consideration of some of the citizenship issues implicated with LGBTQ identity. Oboler, "Redefining Citizenship as Lived Experience," 9–10. West, *Transforming Citizenships.*

105. Du Bois, *Souls,* 9.

106. *Brown v. Board of Education,* 347 U.S. 483 (1954), http://laws.findlaw.com/ us/347/483.html (accessed September 11, 2011).

107. Allen, *Talking to Strangers,* 3, 15.

108. Quoted in Asen, "A Discourse Theory," 202–3.

109. Scorza, *Strong Liberalism,* 99.

110. Lister, "Dialectics of Citizenship," 13. Emphasis as in original.

111. Allen, *Talking to Strangers,* 87–88.

112. Kateb, *The Inner Ocean,* 166.

113. This sort of hesitancy bears a resemblance, perhaps, to the "Fabianism" in Du Bois's political philosophy. Reed, *W. E. B. Du Bois and American Political Thought.* I am indebted to one of the anonymous reviewers of this manuscript for the suggestion to consider more carefully "moral hesitancy" as a citizenly resource.

114. Kateb, "Democratic Individualism and Its Critics," 304.

115. Zakaras, *Individuality and Mass Democracy,* 9.

116. Allen, *Talking to Strangers,* 127.

117. See also Arabella Lyon's discussion of "deliberative recognition." Lyon, *Deliberative Acts,* 48–59.

118. Allen, *Talking to Strangers,* 133–34.

119. Markovits, *The Politics of Sincerity,* 33.

120. Markovits, *The Politics of Sincerity,* 34.

121. Sandel, *Democracy's Discontent,* 65.

122. Balfour, *Democracy's Reconstruction,* 6–7.

123. Balfour, *Democracy's Reconstruction,* 13.

124. While Du Bois's references to "blood" may be understood as participating in nineteenth-century notions of racial genetics, Du Bois himself seems to suggest otherwise in his 1897 address to the American Negro Academy, *The Conservation of Races.* But see Appiah, "The Uncompleted Argument."

125. Levinson, *No Citizen Left Behind,* 85.

126. Stewart, *Strange Jeremiahs,* 235.

127. Stewart, *Strange Jeremiahs,* 233.

128. Sandel, *Democracy's Discontent,* 14.

129. Zamir, *Dark Voices,* 171.

130. Zamir, *Dark Voices,* 163.

131. Zamir, *Dark Voices,* 171. Zamir specifically is comparing Du Bois to Ralph Waldo Emerson and to William James. Du Bois deeply admired James while he was his student at Harvard, and Emerson used the term "double-consciousness" in his famous essay "The Transcendentalist," with which Du Bois surely was familiar. Zamir argues that Du Bois was influenced by these prominent figures but altered their ideas by turning them in a more politically and culturally engaged direction.

132. Rampersad, *Art and Imagination of W. E. B. Du Bois,* 73–74.

133. Gates, *The Signifying Monkey,* xxv.

134. Gates, *The Signifying Monkey,* 21, 128.

Chapter 3—A More Perfect Union

1. Portions of this chapter are developed from Terrill, "Unity and Duality."

2. Plouffe, *The Audacity to Win,* 142; Wolffe, *Renegade,* 96–103.

3. Quoted in Wolffe, *Renegade,* 102.

4. Plouffe, *Audacity to Win,* 157; Wolffe, *Renegade,* 104–19.

5. Plouffe, *Audacity to Win,* 173; Wolffe, *Renegade,* 200–2.

6. Plouffe, *Audacity to Win,* 179–80.

7. "Is Obama's Pastor a Liability?," *ABC News,* March 13, 2009, http://abcnews .go.com/GMA/video?id=4443230 (accessed September 23, 2012).

8. Plouffe, *Audacity to Win,* 162–63.

9. Remnick, *The Bridge,* 517–18. Obery M. Hendricks Jr. identifies the two speeches from which these excerpts were taken: "'The Day of Jerusalem's Fall,' delivered on September 16, 2001, and 'Confusing God and Government,' delivered on April 13, 2003." Hendricks, "A More Perfect (High-Tech) Lynching," 167.

10. These epithets and many others are collected in: Hendricks, "A More Perfect (High-Tech) Lynching," 160. See also Remnick, *The Bridge,* 519.

11. Adolph Reed Jr., "Obama No," *Progressive,* May 2008, http://www.progressive .org/mag_reed0508 (accessed: April 17, 2011).

12. Quoted in Amanda Ripley, "The Story of Barack Obama's Mother," *Time,* April 9, 2008 http://www.time.com/time/magazine/article/0,9171,1729685,00.html (accessed April 17, 2011).

13. Remnick, *The Bridge,* 175.

14. Manya A. Brachear and Bob Secter, "Race Is Sensitive Subtext in Campaign: South Side Church's Tenets Spark Criticism of Obama by Some Conservatives," *Chicago Tribune,* February 7, 2007, http://articles.chicagotribune.com/2007–02–06/news/ 0702060164_1_black-family-presidential-campaign-black-advancement (accessed June 15, 2011).

15. Obama actually called Wright twice that day, February 9, 2007. The first time, he warned him not to say anything to "upset those Iowa farmers" that Obama would be addressing when he began campaigning in earnest immediately after throwing his hat into the ring. Remnick, *The Bridge,* 468–69.

16. The key text in this tradition generally is considered to be Cone, *Black Theology and Black Power.* See also Cone, *A Black Theology of Liberation,* 169–73.

17. Sharpley-Whiting, "Chloroform Morning Joe!," 7. See also Remnick, *The Bridge,* 520.

18. Hendricks, "A More Perfect (High-Tech) Lynching," 164.

19. Quoted in Walker and Smithers, *The Preacher and the Politician.*

20. "What We Believe," *The United Church of Christ,* http://www.ucc.org/about-us/ what-we-believe.html (accessed October 8, 2010); "The Early Church," *The United Church of Christ,* http://www.ucc.org/about-us/short-course/the-early-church.html (accessed October 8, 2010).

21. Geneva Smitherman provides a useful explanation of the jeremiad as a preaching form and a thumbnail sketch of its adaptation by African American preachers. Smitherman, "'It's Been a Long Time Comin," 184–204. See also Hendricks, "A More Perfect

(High-Tech) Lynching," 166–68. A longer and more detailed discussion of the jeremiad and African American preaching traditions is provided in Walker and Smithers, *The Preacher and the Politician*. All of those discussions rely, as must any informed discussion of the African American jeremiad tradition, on Bercovitch, *The American Jeremiad*, and Howard-Pitney, *The African-American Jeremiad*.

22. Walker and Smithers, *The Preacher and the Politician*, 26; Howard-Pitney, *The African-American Jeremiad*, 6. Also cited in Smitherman, "'It's Been a Long Time Comin'," 191–92. Interestingly, Howard-Pitney includes W. E. B. Du Bois among the practitioners of the African American jeremiad.

23. "7:30 am EST September 12, 2001 Fox News Broadcast," *YouTube.com*, September 12, 2001, http://www.youtube.com/watch?v=jtvOGk7BvcY (accessed March 12, 2010).

24. Reverend Jeremiah Wright, "The Day of Jerusalem's Fall," *Blakfacts*, September 12, 2001, http://blakfacts.blogspot.com/2008/03/day-of-jerusalems-fall.html.

25. Remnick, *The Bridge*, 517.

26. Remnick, *The Bridge*, 520–21.

27. Obama, "On My Faith and My Church," *Huffington Post*, March 14, 2008, http://www.huffingtonpost.com/barack-obama/on-my-faith-and-my-church_b_91623.html (accessed August 2, 2009).

28. "Obama Denounces Controversial Remarks," *YouTube.com*, March 14, 2008, http://www.youtube.com/watch?v=_7piGyou43c (accessed August 3, 2009).

29. Keith Olbermann, "Obama: 'Override Guilt by Association,'" *MSNBC.com*, March 15, 2008, http://www.msnbc.msn.com/id/23648883/ns/msnbc-countdown_with_keith_olbermann/t/obama-override-guilt-association (accessed October 21, 2008).

30. Hendricks, "A More Perfect (High-Tech) Lynching," 161.

31. Plouffe, *Audacity to Win*, 212.

32. Remnick, *The Bridge*, 522.

33. Plouffe, *Audacity to Win*, 212.

34. Allen, *Talking to Strangers*, 12.

35. Allen, *Talking to Strangers*, 87.

36. Frank similarly notes Obama's use of "elegant pairings of contraries" that challenge "the binary thinking at the root of racism and other pathologies." Frank and McPhail, "Barack Obama's Address to the 2004 Democratic National Convention," 579. Though the citation format makes it appear as though this article is traditionally cowritten, it actually is a highly innovative essay in which the two authors retain their individual voices, in a colloquy. As such, it can be said to enact the sort of discourse that democratic double-consciousness might foster.

37. George Lakoff describes Obama's stance toward Wright in parallel terms, casting it as a form of judgment. Lakoff, "What Made Obama's Speech Great," *Alternet.org*, March 25, 2008, http://www.alternet.org/story/80549 (accessed May 8, 2008). Frank, similarly, notes that Obama's critique of Wright is "two-fold," in that he both embraces the prophetic tradition within which Wright was preaching and recognizes that it is ill suited to the public sphere. Frank, "The Prophetic Voice," 184.

38. The passage that Obama reads is on page 294 of *Dreams from My Father*. For a description of attending Trinity United from the perspective of a not entirely sympathetic visitor, see Mansfied, *The Faith of Barack Obama*, 30–48.

39. Schultz, "His Grandmother, My Father, Your Uncle," 104–6.

40. Daniel, "Race, Multiraciality, and the Election of Barack Obama," 35.

41. Quoted in Wolffe, *Renegade*, 176.

42. The prepared text reads: "But we do need to remind ourselves that so many of the disparities that exist in the African-American community today can be directly traced to inequalities passed on from an earlier generation that suffered under the brutal legacy of slavery and Jim Crow." It may be that the references to disparities *within* the African American community was an error that Obama corrected in delivery. But, in any case, referring to inequalities *between* whites and blacks better fits the theme of the text.

43. It may be this quality, especially evident in this part of the speech, that Thomas L. Dumm is describing when he writes that Obama's speech was "as cool as the Wright video clip was hot, as deliberate as Wright's sermon was improvised, as quietly delivered as Wright's sermon was shouted, presented before a small and carefully chosen audience in a Philadelphia conference room, as opposed to the enormous sanctuary of Wright's Chicago church." Dumm, "Barack Obama and the Souls of White Folk," 318.

44. Maraniss, *Barack Obama*, xxii. Maraniss also notes that Obama's classmates at Occidental College "considered Obama 'a floater,' moving not only from culture to culture but also from political group to political group, dabbling, showing interest, but never staking a home, never grabbing hold of something and making it his." Maraniss, *Barack Obama*, 376. Jonathan Alter, referring specifically to Obama's first year in office, suggests that one of his challenges was "calibrating his detachment. Standing slightly apart from the action offered perspective and insulated him from the partisan clatter; standing above renewed charges that he lacked the human touch." Alter, *The Promise*, 140.

45. Frank, *Obama on the Couch*, 159.

46. David Brooks, "Where's the Landslide?," *New York Times*, August 5, 2008, A19.

47. The prepared text does not mention the beauty shop; Obama seems to have inserted that phrase in the moment of delivery.

48. Nunley, *Keepin' It Hushed*, 34. David A. Frank notes that Obama, because "of his mixed racial background . . . could move between the hush harbors of white and black worlds while retaining an identity in both." As such, perhaps he was especially well prepared to repair the breaching of the racial levees that separate black and white religious practices that had set off the controversy. Frank, "The Prophetic Voice," 182.

49. In the prepared text this passage positions Obama as an African American speaking to an African American audience: "it keeps us from squarely facing our own complicity in our condition."

50. Utley and Heyse, "Barack Obama's (Im)Perfect Union," 159–60; Mansbach, "The Audacity of Post-Racism."

51. "Obama does not equate the brutal legacies of slavery and segregation with the economic anxieties faced by the white community." Frank, "The Prophetic Voice," 185.

52. Mansbach, for example, argues that Obama speaks "the language of the emotional" in this passage, noting that Obama focuses on how people "feel." Mansbach, "The Audacity of Post-Racism," 75. But this assessment ignores the studied clinical distance from which Obama describes these feelings.

53. In the prepared text, the reference is to Obama's "single candidacy" rather than to Obama as the "single candidate."

54. Robert C. Rowland and John M. Jones note that this theme is present in Obama's 2004 DNC address as well, though they do not point out the supporting stylistic cues. Rowland and Jones, "Recasting the American Dream," 435.

55. Allen, *Talking to Strangers*, 105.

56. Aristotle, *The Nicomachean Ethics*, IX.ix.10, IX.vi.1–2. See also Berchman, "The Golden Rule."

57. Gates, *The Signifying Monkey*, 21, 128.

58. The word *trope*, of course, derives from the ancient Greek word for "turn" and generally is understood as referring to a turn of phrase. Tropes, in other words, twist or turn language away from some literal or denotative referent and toward a more figurative or connotative referent.

59. Jeffrey Wattles puts it this way, just before he quotes the passage from Du Bois's *Souls* referred to in the previous chapter: "The mature practice of the golden rule involves an identification with others that includes understanding plus an appropriate level of shared feeling plus an appropriate practical response." The understanding and shared feeling necessitate a doubled consciousness; the practical response finds its foundation in a doubled attitude. Wattles, *The Golden Rule*, 121.

60. Daniel, "Race, Multiraciality, and the Election of Barack Obama," 33.

61. Hendricks, "A More Perfect (High-Tech) Lynching," 178.

62. Quoted in Hendricks, "A More Perfect (High-Tech) Lynching," 159.

63. Reed, "Obama No." Reed refers to Booker T. Washington's famous address to the Cotton States Exposition, delivered in Atlanta, Georgia, on September 18, 1895.

64. Obery M. Hendricks Jr., suggests that "the Wright that he [Obama] refused to disown is apparently the Wright of the past, 'the man I met more than twenty years ago.'" Attending closely to which of Wright's qualities Obama places in the past and which of his qualities he places in the present, Hendricks argues that what Obama rejects is "Wright's prophetic ministry, Wright's incisive social commentary, the sincerity of Wright's struggle against injustice." Hendricks, "A More Perfect (High-Tech) Lynching," 178.

65. As I note in the next chapter, Obama had used the story about Ashley Baia in January 2008, in a speech he delivered at the historic Ebenezer Baptist Church in Atlanta; his chief speechwriter, Jon Favreau, recalls going "back and forth" with Obama about using it again but in the end deciding that "it was too perfect." Remnick, *The Bridge*, 522.

66. Lakoff, "What Made Obama's Speech Great." Emphasis as in original.

67. Wess, "Representative Anecdotes."

Chapter 4—The Confines of Race

1. Susanna Dilliplane concludes: "The themes sounded in Obama's March 18 speech may thus be understood as reverberating throughout diverse areas of his campaign rhetoric." While this may be true with regard to some "themes" in the March 18 speech, it is not true with regard to the manner in which he addressed race. Dilliplane, "Race, Rhetoric, and Running for President," 144.

2. Bitzer, "The Rhetorical Situation," 6.

3. Parts of this chapter are developed from a talk I gave at Lewis and Clark College in 2012, at the invitation of Mitch Reyes.

4. Sugrue, *Not Even Past*, 11. As Sugrue points out, the origin of this poem has not been established, but it became widespread after this report was broadcast on National Public Radio: Melissa Block, "St. Louis Voters Discuss Struggles, Election Hopes," *National Public Radio*, October 28, 2008, http://www.npr.org/templates/story/story.php?storyId=96215190 (accessed November 8, 2008).

5. Fleming, *Yes We Did?*, 238.

6. Quoted in Sugrue, *Not Even Past*, 12.

7. Quoted in Sugrue, *Not Even Past*, 12. In an online photo essay, *Time* declared that "the civil rights movement culminates in the election of America's first black president."

"From Emmett Till to Barack Obama," *Time,* http://www.time.com/time/photogallery/ 0,29307,1866753,00.html (accessed April 8, 2010).

8. Abramsky, *Inside Obama's Brain*, 5.

9. James Oliphant, "A Victory That Revolutionizes Civil Rights," *Chicago Tribune,* November 9, 2009, http://articles.chicagotribune.com/2008–11–09/news/0811080292_1 _gay-marriage-bans-same-sex-marriage-african-american (accessed September 3, 2010).

10. Remnick, *The Bridge,* 575.

11. Remnick, "The President's Hero," *The New Yorker,* February 2, 2009 http://www .newyorker.com/talk/comment/2009/02/02/090202taco_talk_remnick (accessed March 8, 2009).

12. Sugrue, *Not Even Past,* 40.

13. Sugrue, *Not Even Past,* 47.

14. Sugrue, *Not Even Past,* 48.

15. Remnick, *The Bridge,* 362.

16. Ford, "Barack Is the New Black," 39.

17. Toni Morrison, "The Talk of the Town: Comment," *The New Yorker,* October 5, 1998, http://www.newyorker.com/archive/1998/10/05/1998_10_05_031_TNY_LIBRY _000016504 (accessed February 15, 2011).

18. Quoted in Remnick, *The Bridge,* 491.

19. Quoted in: Wolffe, *Renegade,* 144.

20. Remnick, *The Bridge,* 462. That such fears were not entirely unfounded was made evident in October 2008, when white supremacists were foiled in an alleged attempt to assassinate Barack Obama. Jack Date, "Feds Thwart Alleged Obama Assassination Plot," *ABC News,* October 27, 2008, http://abcnews.go.com/TheLaw/Vote2008/ story?id=6122962 (accessed March 12, 2009). This website keeps track of "predictions" of Obama's assassination: "ObamaCSI: Exposing the Future Assassination of Barack Obama," https://sites.google.com/site/csiobama/PREDICTORS-OF-ASSASSINATION (accessed March 15, 2014).

21. Goldberg, *The Threat of Race,* 345, 360.

22. Enck-Wanzer, "Barack Obama, the Tea Party, and the Threat of Race," 28.

23. Sugrue, *Not Even Past,* 48–49.

24. Dumm, "Barack Obama and the Souls of White Folk," 319.

25. Sharpley-Whiting, "Chloroform Morning Joe!," 7. See also Remnick, *The Bridge,* 520.

26. Sugrue, *Not Even Past,* 49–50; Miller, "On Martin Luther King, Jr.," 167–83.

27. Steele, *A Bound Man,* 18.

28. Remnick, *The Bridge,* 78.

29. Remnick, *The Bridge,* 316.

30. Steele, *A Bound Man,* 126.

31. Verna Gates, "Clintons, Obama Cross Paths in Selma," *Time,* March 4, 2007, http://www.time.com/time/nation/article/0,8599,1595866,00.html (accessed June 15, 2012); Hillary Clinton, "Remarks on the 42nd Anniversary of Bloody Sunday in Selma, Alabama," Gerhard Peters and John T. Woolley, *The American Presidency Project,* March 4, 2007, http://www.presidency.ucsb.edu/ws/?pid=77047 (accessed September 26, 2011).

32. A second march, on March 9, was led by King himself and turned around at the Pettus Bridge, in compliance with a restraining order. James Reeb, a white Unitarian preacher from Boston, was beaten after the march and died from his wounds. The third march began on March 21, was again led by King, and succeeded in reaching Montgomery,

escorted by a phalanx consisting of thousands of members of the U.S. Army, the Alabama Nation Guard, federal marshals, and FBI agents.

33. Barack Obama, "Selma Voting Rights March Commemoration Speech," *American Rhetoric*, March 4, 2007, http://www.americanrhetoric.com/speeches/barackobama/ barackobamabrownchapel.htm (accessed January 24, 2012). Artur Davis was a member of the U.S. House of Representatives from 2003 to 2011, representing Alabama's 7th congressional district. At the time of Obama's speech, Keith Ellison had just been elected to the U.S. House, in November 2006, representing Minnesota's 5th congressional district.

34. Many critics suggested that Hillary Rodham Clinton also adjusted her dialect when delivering her speech in Selma.

35. Darsey, "Barack Obama and America's Journey," 93.

36. Murphy, "Barack Obama, the Exodus Tradition, and the Joshua Generation," 402–3.

37. As one of the reviewers of this manuscript pointed out, Clinton's position was constrained by race as well; white people were on that bridge in Selma in 1965, but playing a role with which Clinton would not want to associate herself.

38. Remnick, *The Bridge*, 33–36. See also Maraniss, *Barack Obama*, 116, 139, 150; Falk, *The Riddle of Barack Obama*, 29–30.

39. Murphy, "Barack Obama, the Exodus Tradition, and the Joshua Generation," 394.

40. Barack Obama, "Remarks at the Howard University Convocation in Washington, D.C.," in Gerhard Peters and John T. Woolley, *The American Presidency Project*, September 28, 2007, http://www.presidency.ucsb.edu/ws/?pid=77014 (accessed July 12, 2011). For partial video of the address that shows the reaction of the crowd, see Barack Obama, "Howard University Opening Convocation," *YouTube.com*, September 28, 2007, http:// www.youtube.com/watch?v=E15OCktLU68 (accessed September 1, 2009).

41. Barack Obama, "Ebenezer Baptist Church Address," *American Rhetoric*, January 20, 2008, http://www.americanrhetoric.com/speeches/barackobama/barackobama ebenezerbaptist.htm (accessed April 12, 2010).

42. The quotation is from Martin Luther King Jr., "Address to the First Montgomery Improvement Association (MIA) Mass Meeting," *Martin Luther King, Jr., and the Global Freedom Struggle*, December 5, 1955, http://mlk-kpp01.stanford.edu/index .php/encyclopedia/documentsentry/the_addres_to_the_first_montgomery_improvement _association_mia_mass_meeting (accessed May 4, 2010).

43. Barack Obama, "Remarks by the President at the NAACP Centennial Convention," *Whitehouse.gov*, July 17, 2009, http://www.whitehouse.gov/the-press-office/remarks -president-naacp-centennial-convention-7162009 (accessed March 5, 2012).

44. Stephanie Li provides insightful commentary on Geraldine Ferraro's widely circulated and criticized remark that Obama was "lucky to be who he is" as another instance of policing the boundaries of race talk: Li, *Signifying without Specifying*, 5–6.

45. Barack Obama, "News Conference by the President," *Whitehouse.gov*, July 22, 2009, http://www.whitehouse.gov/the_press_office/News-Conference-by-the-President -July-22–2009 (accessed December 22, 2009).

46. "Fox Host Genn Beck: Obama Is a 'Racist,'" *Huffington Post*, August 28, 2009, http://www.huffingtonpost.com/2009/07/28/fox-host-glenn-beck-obama_n_246310.html (accessed October 10, 2009).

47. Barack Obama, "Statement by the President," *Whitehouse.gov*, July 24, 2009, http://www.whitehouse.gov/the_press_office/Statement-by-the-President-in-the-James-S-Brady-Briefing-Room (accessed August 15, 2009).

48. John Lucaites, "President Obama's Teachable Moment," *No Caption Needed*, August 2, 2009, http://www.nocaptionneeded.com/?p=3538 (accessed September 9, 2009). See also Krista Ratcliffe's discussion of a "rhetoric of dysfunctional silence": Ratcliffe, *Rhetorical Listening*, 84–93.

49. "Obama: Trayvon Martin Case Is a 'Tragedy,'" *Associated Press, YouTube.com*, March 23, 2012, http://www.youtube.com/watch?v=ueWsjzbwOxQ (accessed January 6, 2013). See also Jackie Calmes and Helene Cooper, "A Personal Note as Obama Speaks on Death of Boy," *New York Times*, http://www.nytimes.com/2012/03/24/us/politics/obama-talks-of-tragedy-not-race-in-florida-killing.html (accessed December 2, 2012).

50. Devin Dwyer and Elicia Dover, "Gingrich Calls Obama's Trayvon Martin Remarks 'Disgraceful,'" *ABCNews.com*, March 23, 2012, http://abcnews.go.com/blogs/politics/2012/03/gingrich-calls-obamas-trayvon-martin-remarks-disgraceful (accessed July 23, 2013).

51. Maggie Haberman, "Santorum Hits Obama's Trayvon Comments to Conservative Talkers, Not National Ones," *Politico.com*, March 26, 2012, http://www.politico.com/blogs/burns-haberman/2012/03/santorum-hits-obamas-trayvon-comments-to-conservative-118669.html (accessed June 22, 2013). For an aggregation of many such remarks, see Aliyah Shahid, "Conservatives Blast President Obama's Remarks on Trayvon Martin: He's Race Baiting!," *New York Daily News*, March 24, 2012, http://www.nydailynews.com/news/politics/conservatives-blast-president-obama-remarks-trayvon-martin-race-baiting-article-1.1050298 (accessed June 22, 2013).

52. Michelle Malkin, "The Trayvon Martin Racial Litmus Test—and the Blame Game Bonanza," *Michelle Malkin*, March 23, 2012, http://michellemalkin.com/2012/03/23/the-trayvon-martin-racial-litmus-test-and-the-blame-game-bonanza (accessed February 12, 2013).

53. Abigail Thernstrom, "Obama's Mistake on Trayvon Martin Case," *CNN .com*, July 15, 2013, http://www.cnn.com/2013/07/15/opinion/thernstrom-trayvon-martin-obama/index.html (accessed July 17, 2013).

54. Barack Obama, "Remarks by the President at the Martin Luther King, Jr. Memorial Dedication," *Whitehouse.gov*, October 16, 2011, http://www.whitehouse.gov/the-press-office/2011/10/16/remarks-president-martin-luther-king-jr-memorial-dedication (accessed May 3, 2012).

55. Zamir, *Dark Voices*, 171.

56. It might also be argued that the memorial dedication is the most clearly epideictic or ceremonial address of those analyzed in this chapter and that the traditional emphasis of epideictic oratory on reiterating cultural values might account for the differences among the addresses. But all of the addresses analyzed in this chapter are epideictic to some degree, even those delivered during the campaign, and all of them reiterate cultural values. The difference lies in the quality of the values being articulated.

57. Obama, *Dreams from My Father*, 85–86.

58. Obama, *Dreams from My Father*, 197–98.

59. Remnick, *The Bridge*, 232–33.

60. Branch, *Parting the Waters; Pillar of Fire; At Canaan's Edge*.

Chapter 5—Beyond the Veil

1. Du Bois, *Souls*, xxxi, 3, 47, 58, 80–81.

2. Balfour, *Democracy's Reconstruction*, 6.

3. Obama, *Dreams from My Father*, 189.

4. Obama, *Audacity of Hope*, 22–23.

5. Obama, *Audacity of Hope*, 183.

6. Obama, *Audacity of Hope*, 184–85.

7. Barack Obama, "Official Announcement of Candidacy for U.S. President," *American Rhetoric*, February 10, 2007, http://www.americanrhetoric.com/speeches/barack obamacandidacyforpresident.htm (accessed May 12, 2009).

8. Barack Obama, "Iowa Caucus Victory Speech," *American Rhetoric*, January 3, 2008, http://www.americanrhetoric.com/speeches/barackobama/barackobamaiowavictory speech.htm (accessed May 12, 2009).

9. Barack Obama, "Democratic Nomination Victory Speech," *American Rhetoric*, June 3, 2008, http://www.americanrhetoric.com/speeches/barackobamademocraticnomi nationvictoryspeech.htm (accessed May 12, 2009).

10. Barack Obama, "Remarks by the President on the Economy," *Whitehouse.gov*, April 14, 2009, http://www.whitehouse.gov/the-press-office/remarks-president-economy -georgetown-university (accessed July 12, 2013).

11. Barack Obama, "Remarks by the President at the Opening of the White House Forum on Health Reform," *Whitehouse.gov*, March 5, 2009, http://www.whitehouse.gov/ the-press-office/remarks-president-opening-white-house-forum-health-reform (accessed June 4, 2012).

12. Barack Obama, "Remarks by the President at the Annual Conference of the American Medical Association," *Whitehouse.gov*, June 15, 2009, http://www.whitehouse.gov/the -press-office/remarks-president-annual-conference-american-medical-association (accessed July 13, 2013).

13. Conservative bloggers and Tea Party activists posted schedules of these town hall meetings, with locations and times: "Town Hall Events to Counter Protest," *Tea PartyPatriots.org*, *Internet Archive Wayback Machine*, August 9, 2009, http://web.archive .org/web/20090809111502/http://www.teapartypatriots.org/townhalls.aspx (accessed June 17, 2011); Michelle Malkin, "Protest a Health Care Town Hall: More Scenes from the Counterinsurgency," *Michellemalkin.com*, August 4, 2009, http://michellemalkin .com/2009/08/04/protest-a-health-care-town-hall (accessed June 17, 2011). Glenn Beck compared the proposals for health care reform to eugenics in Nazi Germany: "GlennBeck Eugenics part 1 Short History," *YouTube.com*, August 12, 2009, http://www.youtube.com/ watch?v=OTwRLbgcdOE (Accessed June 17, 2011).

14. "Dueling Protesters Disrupt Carnahan Forum on Aging: Six Arrested as People on Both Sides of Health Care Debate Square Off," *Business Highbeam*, August 7, 2009, http://business.highbeam.com/435553/article-1G1-205306662/dueling-protesters-disrupt -carnahan-forum-aging-six (accessed October 4, 2011).

15. Matthew Bigg and Nick Carey, "Protestors Disrupt Town-Hall Healthcare Talks," *Reuters*, August 8, 2009, http://www.reuters.com/article/2009/08/08/us-usa-healthcare -townhalls-idUSTRE5765QH20090808 (accessed October 4, 2011).

16. "Health Care Town Halls Turn Violent in Tampa and St. Louis," *Fox News*, August 7, 2009, http://www.foxnews.com/politics/2009/08/07/health-care-town-halls-turn -violent-tampa-st-louis (accessed October 4, 2011).

17. "CNN Story on the 'Obama Joker' Phenomenon," *YouTube.com*, August 4, 2009, http://www.youtube.com/watch?v=GStMLFMdRcQ (accessed October 19, 2011).

18. Enck-Wanzer, "Barack Obama, the Tea Party, and the Threat of Race," 26.

19. Brian Ross, Ann Schecter, and Megan Chuchmach, "Fear for Obama's Safety Grows as Hate Groups Thrive on Racial Backlash," *ABC News*, August 14, 2009, http://abcnews.go.com/Blotter/story?id=8324481 (accessed April 9, 2011).

20. Barack Obama, "Weekly Address: President Obama Says Health Reform Will Put Patients' Interests Ahead of Insurance Company Profits," *Whitehouse.gov*, August 15, 2009, http://www.whitehouse.gov/the-press-office/weekly-address-president-obama-says-health-reform-will-put-patients-interests-ahead (accessed February 12, 2011). The next day, an editorial written by Obama was published in the *New York Times* that used essentially the same language. Barack Obama, "Why We Need Health Care Reform," *New York Times*, August 15, 2009, http://www.nytimes.com/2009/08/16/opinion/16obama.html (accessed November 1, 2009).

21. Maraniss, *Barack Obama*, xxii; David Brooks, "Where's the Landslide?," *New York Times*, August 5, 2008, A19.

22. "Poll: More Wary of Obama on Health Care," *CBS News*, October 14, 2009, http://www.cbsnews.com/2100-500160_162-5280373.html (accessed February 12, 2010).

23. Talea Miller, "President Prepares for Pivotal Health Care Speech," *PBS Newshour*, September 9, 2009, http://www.pbs.org/newshour/updates/health/july-dec09/obama_09-09.html (accessed July 10, 2012).

24. David Corn, "Obama's Anger Problem?," *PoliticsDaily.com*, August 3, 2009, http://www.politicsdaily.com/2009/08/03/obamas-anger-problem (accessed July 1, 2013). During the 2012 presidential election, Corn was responsible for publicizing a videotape, made covertly, that showed Obama's opponent, Mitt Romney, telling supporters at a fundraising event: "There are 47 percent of the people who will vote for the president [Obama] no matter what. All right, there are 47 percent who are with him, who are dependent upon government, who believe that they are victims, who believe that government has a responsibility to care for them, who believe that they are entitled to health care, to food, to housing, to you name it. That that's an entitlement. And the government should give it to them. And they will vote for this president no matter what." "Full Transcript of Mitt Romney Secret Video," *Mother Jones*, September 19, 2012, http://www.motherjones.com/politics/2012/09/full-transcript-mitt-romney-secret-video (accessed April 19, 2013).

25. "Fired Up and Ready to Go: The President Weighs In on Health Reform," *The Economist*, September 10, 2009, http://www.economist.com/node/14419387?story_id=14419387 (accessed January 12, 2012). Dan Balz, in the *Washington Post*, understood that Obama "tried to set himself as the midpoint in a debate between a single-payer system run by the government and the abandonment of the existing employer-based system, although neither has been a real option in the discussion this year." Balz, "With Health-Care Reform on the Line, Obama Reframes Critical Debate," *Washington Post*, September 10, 2009, http://www.washingtonpost.com/wp-dyn/content/article/2009/09/09/AR2009090903464.html (accessed February 1, 2012).

26. Black, "The Second Persona," 111–13.

27. Allen, *Talking to Strangers*, 127–34.

28. Allen, *Talking to Strangers*, 105.

29. In the end, of course, Congress did pass a health care reform bill, officially titled the "Patient Protection and Affordable Care Act." A complete review of the legislative

process of this bill is beyond the scope of my argument and indeed might fill several books the length of this one, so a brief synopsis will suffice to suggest that the tumult of the town hall meetings continued, in only a somewhat muted fashion, in the halls of Congress. A version of the bill, which included a so-called public option, passed the House of Representatives in November 2009, by a vote of 220–15, with thirty-nine Democrats voting against and only one Republican voting in support. The next month, on Christmas Eve, the Senate passed a version of health care reform that did not include a public option, also along party lines, 60–39. In January 2010, in a special election, Scott Brown, a Republican, was elected to fill Ted Kennedy's vacant Senate seat, thereby depriving Democrats of the solid sixty-vote majority they would need to overcome a Republican filibuster; this caused party leaders to set aside their efforts to merge the House and Senate versions of the bill. In February 2010, Obama did what many of his supporters had advised him to do initially, which was to propose his own draft legislation; it relied heavily on the Senate version of the bill. After high-profile meetings with ranking leaders of both parties and the making of various deals and counterdeals, the House passed the Senate version of the bill, with a proviso that the bill would be immediately amended through a process called "reconciliation," which allowed only budgetary but not substantive changes. Obama signed the bill into law on March 23, 2010, and the amendment bill a week later, on March 30. In a coda, on June 28, 2012, the Supreme Court upheld the constitutionality of the so-called individual-mandate portion of the health care reform legislation.

30. Mettler, *The Submerged State*, 4, 6.

31. The effectiveness of Obama's orchestration of mood is perhaps indicated by some of the reactions in the press. Joe Klein, writing in *Time,* called the speech "powerful," yet seems to focus on the long middle section of the speech in which Obama described his plans and principles "clearly, concisely, using language that was mostly jargon-free— a triumph of speechwriting on this mind-numbing issue." Klein, "Obama's Appeal: A Test of National Character," *Time,* September 10, 2009, http://www.time.com/time/magazine/article/0,9171,1921599,00.html (accessed January 12, 2010). The *Economist,* on the other hand, attending particularly to Obama's reading of Kennedy's letter, argued that the address, coming "after a legislative recess in which his efforts were demonised [*sic*] at town hall meetings across the country," provided a needed "passionate" counterpart to the often "professorial, even pedantic" tone Obama had taken in other addresses on the issue. "Fired Up and Read to Go: The President Weighs In on Health Reform," *The Economist,* September 10, 2009 www.economist.com/node/14419387?story_id=14419387 (accessed January 12, 2010).

32. Mark Thompson, "Obama Accepts the Nobel Prize: 'Surprised and Deeply Humbled,'" *Time,* October 9, 2009, http://www.time.com/time/nation/article/0,8599,1929447,00.html (accessed January 13, 2011). The section of this chapter that focuses on Obama's Nobel Prize Lecture is developed from Terrill, "An Uneasy Peace."

33. Dan Lothian, "Obama: Nobel Peace Prize Is 'Call to Action,'" *CNN,* October 9, 2009, http://www.cnn.com/2009/WORLD/europe/10/09/nobel.peace.prize/index.html (accessed January 14, 2011).

34. "A Wide Range of Reactions," *Washington Post, HighBeam.com,* October 10, 2009, http://http://www.highbeam.com/doc/1P2–20868583.html (accessed July 24, 2012).

35. Ronald D. Rotunda and J. Peter Pham, "An Unconstitutional Nobel," *Washington Post,* October 16, 2009, A23.

36. "RNC Statement on President Obama's Nobel Peace Prize Award," October 9, 2009, *GOP.com,* http://www.gop.com/index.php/news/comments/rnc_statement_on_president

_obamas_nobel_peace_prize_award (accessed November 1, 2009). Responding to these negative reactions, Brad Woodhouse, communications director for the Democratic National Committee, noted that "The Republican Party has thrown in its lot with the terrorists—the Taliban and Hamas this morning—in criticizing the president for receiving the Nobel Peace Prize." Sam Stein, "Obama's Nobel Prize Inspires Conservative Outrage and Confusion," *Huffington Post,* October 9, 2009, http://www.huffingtonpost .com/2009/10/09/obamas-nobel-prize-inspir_n_315167.html (accessed November 1, 2009).

37. Adam Nagourney, "An Honor for Intangibles Complicates a Presidency in Search of Success," *New York Times,* October 10, 2009, A08.

38. Lynn Sweet, "Premature Honor a Potential Liability: Opens Door for Critics to Mock President," *Chicago Sun Times,* October 10, 2009, 9.

39. Doug Saunders, "He Rejected Missile Defense and Urges Disarmament, but Does Obama Really Deserve the Nobel Peace Prize? Yes." *The Globe and Mail* (Canada), October 10, 2009, A1.

40. Sweet, "Premature Honor a Potential Liability: Opens Door for Critics to Mock President." Recall that Sweet was the reporter who asked Obama, during a briefing on health care, the question about the arrest of Henry Louis Gates Jr.

41. The text of the speech contains approximately 4,300 words. After about three hundred words of introduction, in which Obama addresses the various controversies surrounding the award, he spends roughly two thousand words talking about war and then another two thousand talking about peace.

42. Barack Obama, "Remarks by the President at the Acceptance of the Nobel Peace Prize," *Whitehouse.gov,* December 10, 2009, http://www.whitehouse.gov/the-press-office/ remarks-president-acceptance-nobel-peace-prize (accessed January 1, 2011).

43. Mark Evans provides a brief summary of just-war theory, in outline form. Evans, "Introduction: Moral Theory and the Idea of a Just War," 12–13. For a thorough analysis of the just-war tradition in light of Obama's address, see Reeves and May, "The Peace Rhetoric of a War President," 623–50.

44. Michael Walzer notes that some version of just-war theory is now expected to be evoked in almost any justification for war. Walzer, *Arguing about War,* 3–22.

45. Carlson, "The Morality, Politics, and Irony of War," 620. It should be noted that Carlson was writing before Obama's Nobel Prize speech.

46. McKeogh, *The Political Realism of Reinhold Niebuhr,* 38, 42.

47. Here Obama may be channeling more directly Kennedy's speech at American University, evoking what James J. Kimble describes as a more belligerent "masculine style" in concert with his outline for a just peace. Kimble, "John F. Kennedy."

48. Obama would also refer to this passage of King's Nobel Prize lecture two years later, in his remarks at the dedication of the King memorial on the National Mall.

49. Brokaw and Cooper are quoted in Susan Davis, "Reactions to Obama's Nobel Peace Prize Lecture," *Wall Street Journal,* December 10, 2009, http://blogs.wsj.com/ washwire/2009/12/10/reactions-to-obamas-nobel-peace-prize-lecture (accessed October 15, 2010). Vanden Heuvel and Fineman are quoted in "Reaction to Obama's Nobel Speech," *National Public Radio,* December 10, 2009, http://www.npr.org/templates/story/ story.php?storyId=121304855 (accessed October 21, 2010).

50. Barack Obama, "Against Going to War With Iraq," *Information Clearinghouse,* February 28, 2008, http://www.informationclearinghouse.info/article19440.htm (accessed October 20, 2010). No video exists of the event, a fact often lamented by his 2008 campaign staff. See also Obama, *Audacity of Hope,* 47, 293–95.

51. Obama, quoted in David Brooks, "Obama, Gospel and Verse," *New York Times,* April 26, 2007, http://select.nytimes.com/2007/04/26/opinion/26brooks.html (accessed June 8, 2011).

52. For a compelling and thorough discussion about the relationship between rhetoric and peace, see Ivie, *Dissent from War.*

53. Reeves and May, "The Peace Rhetoric of a War President," 640.

54. Financial Crisis Inquiry Commission, "The Financial Crisis Inquiry Report: Final Report of the National Commission on the Causes of the Financial and Economic Crisis in the United States," *U.S. Government Printing Office,* February 25, 2011, http://www.gpo.gov/fdsys/pkg/GPO-FCIC/pdf/GPO-FCIC.pdf (accessed August 14, 2013), xi, xv, xvi; United State Senate Permanent Subcommittee on Investigations, "Wall Street and the Financial Crisis: Anatomy of a Financial Collapse," *U.S. Government Printing Office,* April 13, 2011, http://www.hsgac.senate.gov/download/report-psi-staff-report-wall-street -and-the-financial-crisis-anatomy-of-a-financial-collapse (accessed August 14, 2013), 1.

55. During these months Obama frequently described his purpose in terms of delivering information or correcting misconceptions. Barack Obama, "Remarks by the President on the Economy," *Whitehouse.gov,* August 7, 2009, http://www.whitehouse.gov/the-press -office/remarks-president-economy-rose-garden (accessed December 12, 2010).

56. The GOP emerged from the elections with a gain of sixty-three seats in the U.S. House of Representatives and six seats in the Senate. It also had control of twenty-five state legislatures and twenty-nine of the fifty governorships. At a morning-after press conference, Obama described the election results as a "shellacking" but also suggested that "this is something that I think every president needs to go through" because presidents may "lose track of . . . folks that got us here in the first place." "Obama: Dems Took a 'Shellacking,'" *YouTube.com,* November 3, 2010, http://www.youtube.com/watch? v=5kXjC2mZTfA (accessed October 1, 2011).

57. Barack Obama, "Remarks by the President on the Economy in Winston-Salem, North Carolina," *Whitehouse.gov,* December 6, 2010, http://www.whitehouse.gov/the-press -office/2010/12/06/remarks-president-economy-winston-salem-north-Carolina (accessed May 15, 2011); Barack Obama, "Remarks by the President in State of Union Address," *Whitehouse.gov,* January 25, 2011, http://www.whitehouse.gov/the-press-office/2011/01/25/ remarks-president-state-union-address (accessed January 26, 2011).

58. Chris Weigant, "Obama's New Theme: A Sputnik Moment," *Huffington Post,* December 6, 2010, http://www.huffingtonpost.com/chris-weigant/obamas-new-theme-a -sputni_b_792890.html (accessed December 10, 2010).

59. Barack Obama, "Remarks by the President on Fiscal Policy," *Whitehouse.gov,* April 13, 2011, http://www.whitehouse.gov/the-press-office/2011/04/13/remarks-president -fiscal-policy (accessed April 22, 2011).

60. Explicitly courting comparisons, the Obama administration posted a transcript of Roosevelt's speech on the White House website: "From the Archives: President Teddy Roosevelt's New Nationalism Speech," *Whitehouse.gov,* December 6, 2011, http://www .whitehouse.gov/blog/2011/12/06/archives-president-teddy-roosevelts-new-nationalism -speech (accessed March 8, 2012).

61. David Jackson, "Obama Seeks to Imitate Teddy Roosevelt," *USA Today,* December 5, 2011, http://content.usatoday.com/communities/theoval/post/2011/12/obama-seeks -to-imitate-teddy-roosevelt (accessed July 20, 2012).

62. Quoted in Scott Horsley, "In Kansas, Obama Invites Teddy Roosevelt Analogies," *National Public Radio,* December 6, 2011, http://www.npr.org/2011/12/06/143178163/

in-kansas-obama-seeks-teddy-roosevelt-comparisons (accessed July 22, 2012). See also Brands, *TR: The Last Romantic*, 675–77. Jean M. Yarbrough provides an informative reading Roosevelt's speech, especially focusing on his references to Lincoln. Yarbrough, *Theodore Roosevelt*, 211–20.

63. The factory in Wichita where Obama's grandmother worked was "essential to American military air strategy," built to produce the most advanced bomber of its time, the B-29 Superfortress. Obama's grandmother "was one of 29,795 workers at the plant, which had become the largest employer in Kansas." She worked as an inspector on the assembly line. Obama's grandfather, Stanley, was assigned to the 1830th Ordnance Supply and Maintenance Company, which eventually was attached to various temporary airfields constructed as Allied forced pushed through France in 1944. Sergeant Stanley Dunham was a "special services" officer whose duties included keeping "the men in his unit informed and entertained." Maraniss, *Barack Obama*, 72–73, 76–77.

64. John Cassidy, "Invoking Teddy Roosevelt, Obama Finds his Voice," *The New Yorker*, December 6, 2011, http://www.newyorker.com/online/blogs/johncassidy/2011/12/invoking-teddy-roosevelt-obama-finds-his-voice.html (accessed July 24, 2012).

65. Joshua D. Hawley, "Undoing Osawatomie," *Weekly Standard*, December 19, 2011, http://www.weeklystandard.com/articles/undoing-osawatomie_611849.html (accessed July 23, 2011).

66. Kloppenberg, *Reading Obama*, 183.

67. Obama, *Audacity of Hope*, 150–51.

68. Bitzer, "The Rhetorical Situation," 6.

69. Aune, *Selling the Free Market*.

70. It also turns out, apparently, that "Osawatomie" was the name of a newsletter published by the Weather Underground; for some conservative bloggers, this shores up their assertions of a close relationship between Obama and former members of the Weather Underground, such as Bill Ayers. Trevor Loudon, "The Osawatomie Coincidence," *TrevorLoudon.com*, December 8, 2011, http://www.trevorloudon.com/2011/12/the-osawatomie-coincidence (accessed March 10, 2012).

Chapter 6—Citizenship and Duality, Rhetoric and Race

1. Douglas E. Schoen, "Newsweek/Daily Beast Poll Finds Majorities of Americans Think Country Divided by Race," *Daily Beast*, April 7, 2012, http://www.thedailybeast.com/articles/2012/04/07/newsweek-daily-beast-poll-finds-majorities-of-americans-think-country-divided-by-race.html (accessed June 8, 2012).

2. Lucas, "Justifying America," 85.

3. The next section of the speech strongly echoes the "we will not be satisfied" section of King's "I Have a Dream" speech, as Obama repeats five times the anaphora "our journey is not complete." For a discussion of the "journey" metaphors in Obama's address, see Darsey, "Barack Obama and America's Journey," 88–103.

4. One of the anonymous reviewers of this manuscript reminded me that Barack Obama is only the second president to have taken the oath four times, twice in 2009 (because the first one was flubbed slightly) and twice in 2013 (because January 20 fell on a Sunday).

5. Burke, *Attitudes toward History*, 229; Jasinski, *Sourcebook on Rhetoric*, 89–90.

6. Meyers, *Civic War*, 4, 241.

7. Balfour, *Democracy's Reconstruction*, 6.

8. Black, "The Second Persona."

9. Recall that John McCain's tour bus during the 2008 presidential campaign was called the "Straight Talk Express."

10. Markovits, *The Politics of Sincerity*, 34.

11. Haiman, *Talk Is Cheap*, 101.

12. Markovits, *The Politics of Sincerity*, 33.

13. Meyers, *Civic War*, 258.

14. Walzer, "Teaching 'Political Wisdom,'" 113.

15. Connolly, *The State of Speech*, 2.

16. Young, *Inclusion and Democracy*, 65.

17. Hauser, *Vernacular Voices*, 33.

18. Allen, *Talking to Strangers*, 171.

19. Allen, *Talking to Strangers*, 153.

20. Connolly, *The State of Speech*, 135.

21. Walker, *The Genuine Teachers of This Art*, 83; Isocrates, "Panathenaicus," 200.

22. Walzer, "Teaching 'Political Wisdom,'" 115.

23. Walker, *The Genuine Teachers of This Art*, 103.

24. Sloane, *On the Contrary*, 3.

25. Sloane, *On the Contrary*, 30.

26. Jasinski, *Sourcebook on Rhetoric*, 201.

27. Quintilian, *The Orator's Education*, X.v.4–5.

28. Corbett, "The Theory and Practice of Imitation," 245.

29. Burke, *A Rhetoric of Motives*, 55.

30. Burke, *A Rhetoric of Motives*, 21. See also Arabella Lyon's discussion of the problematics of Burkean "identification" and Dana Anderson's thorough investigation of the concept. Lyons, *Deliberative Acts*, 59–65; Anderson, *Identity's Strategy*.

31. Burke also alerts us to the fundamental duality of "The Four Master Tropes"—metaphor, metonymy, synecdoche, and irony. Metaphor, Burke explains, "is a device for seeing something *in terms of* something else." He then notes that metonymy conveys "some incorporeal or intangible state in terms of the corporeal or tangible," that the prototype synecdoche presents an interchangeability between "microcosm" and "macrocosm," and that irony, the "perspective of perspectives," "arises when one tries, by the interaction of terms upon one another, to produce a *development* which uses all the terms." In each case, the tropological effect is to invite the hearer to attend to two perspectives, two concepts, or two categorical registers at the same time, not so that they merge but so that attention shifts back and forth between them in a way that generates another meaning.

32. Ford, "Barack Is the New Black," 40.

33. Ford, "Barack Is the New Black," 40.

34. Frank and McPhail, "Barack Obama's Address to the 2004 Democratic National Convention," 572–72, 586.

35. Enck-Wanzer, "Barack Obama, the Tea Party, and the Threat of Race," 24.

36. Li, *Signifying without Specifying*, 19.

37. Utley and Heyse, "Barack Obama's (Im)Perfect Union," 159, 162.

38. Balfour, *Democracy's Reconstruction*, 74.

Epilogue

1. Barack Obama, "Statement by the President," *Whitehouse.gov*, August 14, 2014, http://www.whitehouse.gov/the-press-office/2014/08/14/statement-president (accessed October 30, 2014); Barack Obama, "Statement by the President," *Whitehouse.gov*, August

18, 2014, http://www.whitehouse.gov/the-press-office/2014/08/18/statement-president (accessed October 30, 2014). Because these two addresses are both relatively brief, are substantially similar, and were delivered only days apart, I treat them together in this analysis as a single text.

2. A third mention of Ferguson came in Obama's address to the United Nations General Assembly on September 24, 2014. In a speech focused mainly on the leadership role of the United States in international affairs, Obama acknowledged that "America has plenty of problems within its own borders" and that "in a summer marked by instability in the Middle East and Eastern Europe . . . the world also took notice of the small American city of Ferguson, Missouri—where a young man was killed, and a community was divided. So, yes, we have our own racial and ethnic tensions." The negative reaction was quick and vehement, similar to that which followed his remarks about the arrest of Henry Louis Gates, Jr., and the shooting of Trayvon Martin. Barack Obama, "Remarks by President Obama in Address to the United Nations General Assembly," *White house.gov*, September 24, 2014, http://www.whitehouse.gov/the-press-office/2014/09/24/remarks-president-obama-address-united-nations-general-assembly (accessed November 1, 2014).

3. Jay Nixon, "Ferguson Commission Announcement," *Office of Missouri Governor Jay Nixon*, October 21, 2014, http://governor.mo.gov/news/speeches/ferguson-commission -announcement (accessed October 30, 2014).

Bibliography

Abramsky, Sasha. *Inside Obama's Brain*. New York: Portfolio, 2009.

Allen, Danielle S. *Talking to Strangers: Anxieties of Citizenship since* Brown v. Board of Education. Chicago: University of Chicago Press, 2004.

Allen, Ernest, Jr. "Du Boisian Double-Consciousness: The Unsustainable Argument." *Black Scholar* 33.2 (2003): 25–43.

Allen, Ernest, Jr. "Ever Feeling One's Twoness: 'Double Ideals' and 'Double-Consciousness' in *The Souls of Black Folk*." *Critique of Anthropology* 12.3 (1992): 261–75.

Alter, Jonathan. *The Promise: President Obama, Year One*. New York: Simon & Schuster, 2010.

Anderson, Dana. *Identity's Strategy: Rhetorical Selves in Conversion*. Columbia: University of South Carolina Press, 2007.

Appiah, Anthony. "The Uncompleted Argument: Du Bois and the Illusion of Race." *Critical Inquiry* 12 (1985): 21–37.

Aristotle. *The Nicomachean Ethics,* translated by H. Rackham. Cambridge, Mass.: Harvard University Press, 1926.

Asen, Robert. "A Discourse Theory of Citizenship." *Quarterly Journal of Speech* 90.2 (2004): 189–211.

Aune, James Arnt. *Selling the Free Market: The Rhetoric of Economic Correctness*. New York: Guilford, 2001.

Bakhtin, Mikhail. "Discourse in the Novel." In *The Dialogic Imagination: Four Essays By M. M. Bakhtin,* edited by Michael Holquist, translated by Caryl Emerson and Michael Holquist, 259–422. Austin: University of Texas Press, 1981.

Balfour, Lawrie. *Democracy's Reconstruction: Thinking Politically with W. E. B. Du Bois*. Oxford: Oxford University Press, 2011.

Beasley, Vanessa B. "The Rhetoric of Ideological Consensus in the United States: American Principles and American Pose in Presidential Inaugurals." *Communication Monographs* 68.2 (2001): 169–83.

Berchman, Robert M. "The Golden Rule in Greco-Roman Religion and Philosophy [1]." In *The Golden Rule: Analytical Perspectives,* edited by Jacob Neusner and Bruce Chilton, 9–44. Lanham, Md.: University Press of America, 2009.

Bercovitch, Sacvan. *The American Jeremiad*. Madison: University of Wisconsin Press, 1978.

Bitzer, Lloyd F. "The Rhetorical Situation." *Philosophy and Rhetoric* 1.1 (1968): 1–14.

Black, Edwin. "The Second Persona." *Quarterly Journal of Speech* 56.2 (1970): 109–19.

Branch, Taylor. *At Canaan's Edge: America in the King Years, 1965–1968*. New York: Simon & Schuster, 2006.

Branch, Taylor. *Parting the Waters: America in the King Years, 1954–1963*. New York: Simon & Schuster, 1988.

Bibliography

Branch, Taylor. *Pillar of Fire: America in the King Years, 1963–1965*. New York: Simon & Schuster, 1998.

Brands, H. W. *TR: The Last Romantic*. New York: Basic Books, 1997.

Bredbenner, Candice Lewis. *A Nationality of Her Own: Women, Marriage, and the Law of Citizenship*. Berkeley: University of California Press, 1998.

Bruce, Dickson D., Jr. "W. E. B. Du Bois and the Idea of Double Consciousness." *American Literature* 64.2 (1992): 299–309.

Burke, Kenneth. *Attitudes toward History*. Berkeley: University of California Press, 1984. First published 1937.

Burke, Kenneth. "The Four Master Tropes." In *A Grammar of Motives*, edited by Kenneth Burke, 503–17. Berkeley: University of California Press, 1969. First published 1945.

Burke, Kenneth. "Literature as Equipment for Living." In *The Philosophy of Literary Form*, edited by Kenneth Burke, 293–304. Berkeley: University of California Press, 1973. First published 1941.

Burke, Kenneth. *A Rhetoric of Motives*. Berkeley: University of California Press, 1969. First published 1950.

Campbell, Karlyn Kohrs. "Agency: Promiscuous and Protean." *Communication and Critical/Cultural Studies* 2.1 (2005): 1–19.

Campbell, Karlyn Kohrs, and Kathleen Hall Jamieson. *Deeds Done in Words: Presidential Rhetoric and the Genres of Governance*. Chicago: University of Chicago Press, 1990.

Carlson, John D. "The Morality, Politics, and Irony of War: Recovering Reinhold Niebuhr's Ethical Realism." *Journal of Religious Ethics* 36.4 (2008): 619–51.

Cashill, Jack. *Deconstructing Obama: The Life, Loves, and Letters of the First Postmodern President*. New York: Threshold Editions, 2011.

Castañeda, Alejandra. "Roads to Citizenship: Mexican Migrants in the United States." In *Latinos and Citizenship: The Dilemma of Belonging*, edited by Suzanne Oboler, 143–66. Gordonsville, Va.: Palgrave Macmillan, 2006.

Charland, Maurice. "Constitutive Rhetoric: The Case of the Peuple Québécois." *Quarterly Journal of Speech* 73.2 (1987): 133–50.

Cisneros, Josue David. *The Border Crossed Us: Rhetorics of Borders, Citizenship, and Latina/o Identity*. Tuscaloosa: University of Alabama Press, 2014.

Cohen, Elizabeth F. *Semi-Citizenship in Democratic Politics*. Cambridge: Cambridge University Press, 2009.

Cone, James H. *Black Theology and Black Power*. Maryknoll, N.Y.: Orbis, 1969.

Cone, James H. *A Black Theology of Liberation*. Philadelphia: Lippincott, 1970.

Conley, Donovan S. "Virtuoso." *Communication and Critical/Cultural Studies* 5.3 (2008): 307–11.

Connolly, Joy. *The State of Speech: Rhetoric and Political Thought in Ancient Rome*. Princeton: Princeton University Press, 2007.

Copeland, Rita. *Rhetoric, Hermeneutics, and Translation in the Middle Ages*. Cambridge: Cambridge University Press, 1991.

Corbett, Edward P. J. "The Theory and Practice of Imitation in Classical Rhetoric." *College Composition and Communication* 22.2 (1971): 243–50.

Corsi, Jerome R. *The Obama Nation: Leftist Politics and the Cult of Personality*. New York: Threshold Editions, 2008.

Cott, Nancy F. "Marriage and Women's Citizenship in the United States, 1830–1934." *American Historical Review* 103.5 (1998): 1440–75.

Bibliography

Crowley, Sharon. *The Methodical Memory: Invention in Current-traditional Rhetoric.* Carbondale: Southern Illinois University Press, 1990.

Crowley, Sharon. "Rhetoric, Literature, and the Dissociation of Invention." *Journal of Advanced Composition* 6 (1987): 17–32.

Daniel, G. Reginald. "Race, Multiraciality, and the Election of Barack Obama: Toward a More Perfect Union?" In *Obama and the Biracial Factor: The Battle for a New American Majority,* edited by Andrew J. Jolivette, 31–59. Chicago: Policy Press, 2012.

Daniels, Roger. *The Politics of Prejudice: The Anti-Japanese Movement in California and the Struggle for Japanese Exclusion.* Berkeley: University of California Press, 1999.

Darsey, James. "Barack Obama and America's Journey." *Southern Communication Journal* 74.1 (2009): 88–103.

Dilliplane, Susanna. "Race, Rhetoric, and Running for President: Unpacking the Significance of Barack Obama's "A More Perfect Union" Speech." *Rhetoric & Public Affairs* 15.1 (2012): 127–52.

D'Souza, Dinesh. *The Roots of Obama's Rage.* Washington, D.C.: Regnery, 2010.

Du Bois, W. E. B. *The Conservation of Races.* Washington, D.C.: American Negro Academy, 1897.

Du Bois, W. E. B. *The Souls of Black Folk.* New York: Bantam Books, 1989. First published 1903.

Dumm, Thomas L. "Barack Obama and the Souls of White Folk." *Communication and Critical/Cultural Studies* 5.3 (2008): 317–20.

Enck-Wanzer, Darrel. "Barack Obama, the Tea Party, and the Threat of Race: On Racial Neoliberalism and Born Again Racism." *Communication, Culture & Critique* 4.1 (2011): 23–30.

Evans, Mark. "Introduction: Moral Theory and the Idea of a Just War." In *Just War Theory: A Reappraisal,* edited by Mark Evans, 1–21. Edinburgh: Edinburgh University Press, 2005.

Falk, Avner. *The Riddle of Barack Obama: A Psychobiography.* Santa Barbara, Calif.: Praeger, 2010.

Fleming, Cynthia Griggs. *Yes We Did? From King's Dream to Obama's Promise.* Lexington: University Press of Kentucky, 2009.

Ford, Richard Thompson. "Barack Is the New Black: Obama and the Promise/Threat of the Post-Civil Rights Era." *Du Bois Review* 6.1 (2009): 37–48.

Frank, David A. "Obama's Rhetorical Signature: Cosmopolitan Civil Religion in the Presidential Inaugural Address, January 20, 2009." *Rhetoric & Public Affairs* 14.4 (2011): 605–30.

Frank, David A. "The Prophetic Voice and the Face of the Other in Barack Obama's 'A More Perfect Union' Address, March 18, 2008." *Rhetoric & Public Affairs* 12.2 (2009): 167–94.

Frank, David A., and Mark Lawrence McPhail. "Barack Obama's Address to the 2004 Democratic National Convention: Trauma, Compromise, Consilience, and the (Im)possibility of Racial Reconciliation." *Rhetoric & Public Affairs* 8.4 (2005): 571–94.

Frank, Justin A., M.D. *Obama on the Couch.* New York: Free Press, 2011.

Gaonkar, Dilip Parameshwar. "Object and Method in Rhetorical Criticism: From Wichelns to Leff and Mcgee." *Western Journal of Speech Communication* 54.3 (1990): 290–316.

Garsten, Bryan. *Saving Persuasion: A Defense of Rhetoric and Judgment.* Cambridge, Mass.: Harvard University Press, 2006.

Bibliography

Gates, Henry Louis, Jr. "Introduction: Darkly, as Through a Veil," in W. E. B. Du Bois, *The Souls of Black Folk,* vii–xxx. New York: Bantam, 1989.

Gates, Henry Louis, Jr. *The Signifying Monkey: A Theory of African-American Literary Criticism.* New York: Oxford University Press, 1988.

Gencarella, Stephen Olbrys. "Purifying Rhetoric: Empedocles and the Myth of Rhetorical Theory." *Quarterly Journal of Speech* 96.3 (2010): 231–56.

Gilroy, Paul. *The Black Atlantic: Modernity and Double-consciousness.* Cambridge, Mass.: Harvard University Press, 1993.

Glazer, Nathan. "Reflections on Citizenship and Diversity." In *Diversity and Citizenship: Rediscovering American Nationhood,* edited by Gary Jeffrey Jacobsohn and Susan Dunn, 85–100. Lanham, Md.: Rowman & Littlefield, 1996.

Goldberg, David Theo. *The Threat of Race: Reflections on Racial Neoliberalism.* Oxford: Wiley-Blackwell, 2009.

Haiman, John. *Talk Is Cheap: Sarcasm, Alienation, and the Evolution of Language.* New York: Oxford University Press, 1998.

Hariman, Robert. "Allegory and Democratic Public Culture in the Postmodern Era." *Philosophy and Rhetoric* 35.4 (2002): 267–96.

Hauser Gerard A. *Vernacular Voices: The Rhetoric of Publics and Public Spheres.* Columbia: University of South Carolina Press, 1999.

Hendricks, Obery M., Jr. "A More Perfect (High-Tech) Lynching: Obama, the Press, and Jeremiah Wright." In *The Speech: Race and Barack Obama's "A More Perfect Union,"* edited by T. Denean Sharpley-Whiting, 155–83. New York: Bloomsbury, 2009.

Holt, Thomas C. "The Political Uses of Alienation: W. E. B. Du Bois on Politics, Race, and Culture, 1903–1940." *American Quarterly* 42.2 (1990): 301–23.

Howard-Pitney, David. *The African-American Jeremiad.* Philadelphia: Temple University Press, 1990.

Isocrates. "The Panathenaicus." In *Isocrates II 229,* edited by Jeffrey Henderson, translated by George Norlin, 368–541. Cambridge, Mass.: Harvard University Press, 2000. First published 1929.

Ivie, Robert L. *Dissent from War.* West Harford, Conn.: Kumarian Press, 2007.

Ivie, Robert L. "Productive Criticism." *Quarterly Journal of Speech* 81.1 (1995): n.p.

Ivie, Robert L. "Productive Criticism Then and Now." *American Communication Journal* 4.3 (2001). http://ac-journal.org/journal/vol4/iss3/special/ivie.pdf (accessed January 23, 2010).

Jasinski, James. *Sourcebook on Rhetoric: Key Concepts in Contemporary Rhetorical Studies.* Thousand Oaks, Calif.: Sage, 2001.

Jasinski, James. "The Status of Theory and Method in Rhetorical Criticism." *Western Journal of Communication* 65.3 (2001): 249–70.

Jun, Helen Heran. *Race for Citizenship: Black Orientalism and Asian Uplift from Pre-Emancipation to Neoliberal America.* New York: New York University Press, 2011.

Karst, Kenneth L. *Belonging to America: Equal Citizenship and the Constitution.* New Haven: Yale University Press, 1989.

Kateb, George. "Democratic Individualism and Its Critics." *Annual Review of Political Science* 6 (2003): 275–305.

Kateb, George. *The Inner Ocean: Individualism and Democratic Culture.* Ithaca: Cornell University Press, 1992.

Keith, William, and Roxanne Mountford. "The Mt. Oread Manifesto on Rhetorical Education 2013." *Rhetoric Society Quarterly* 44.1 (2014): 1–5.

Bibliography

Kennedy, George A. *A New History of Classical Rhetoric.* Princeton: Princeton University Press, 1994.

Kennedy, Randall. "Dred Scott and African American Citizenship." In *Diversity and Citizenship: Rediscovering American Nationhood,* edited by Gary Jeffrey Jacobsohn and Susan Dunn, 101–21. Lanham, Md.: Rowman & Littlefield, 1996.

Kimble, James J. "John F. Kennedy, the Construction of Peace, and the Pitfalls of Androgynous Rhetoric." *Communication Quarterly* 57.2 (2009): 154–70.

Kitwana, Bakari. "Between Expediency and Conviction: What We Mean When We Say 'Post-Racial.'" In *The Speech: Race and Barack Obama's "A More Perfect Union,"* edited by T. Denean Sharpley-Whiting, 85–101. New York: Bloomsbury, 2009.

Kloppenberg, James T. *Reading Obama: Dreams, Hope, and the American Political Tradition.* Princeton: Princeton University Press, 2011.

Kock, Christian, and Lisa S. Villadsen. "Introduction: Citizenship as a Rhetorical Practice." In *Rhetorical Citizenship and Public Deliberation,* edited by Christian Kock and Lisa S. Villadsen, 1–10. University Park: Pennsylvania State University Press, 2012.

Lanham, Richard A. *Analyzing Prose.* New York: Continuum, 2003.

Lanham, Richard A. *A Handlist of Rhetorical Terms.* Berkeley: University of California Press, 1991.

Lape, Susan. *Race and Citizen Identity in the Classical Athenian Democracy.* New York: Cambridge University Press, 2010.

Leeman, Richard W. *The Teleological Discourse of Barack Obama.* Lanham, Md.: Lexington Books, 2012.

Leff, Michael. "Hermeneutical Rhetoric." In *Rhetoric and Hermeneutics in Our Time,* edited by Walter Jost and Michael J. Hyde, 196–214. New Haven: Yale University Press, 1997.

Leff, Michael. "The Idea of Rhetoric as Interpretive Practice: A Humanist's Response to Gaonkar." In *Rhetorical Hermeneutics: Invention and Interpretation in the Age of Science,* edited by Alan G. Gross and William M. Keith, 89–100. Albany: State University of New York Press, 1997.

Levinson, Meira. *No Citizen Left Behind.* Cambridge, Mass.: Harvard University Press, 2012.

Lewis, David Levering. *W. E. B. Du Bois: A Biography.* New York: Holt, 2009.

Lewis, Jan. "Representation of Women in the Constitution." In *Women and the United States Constitution,* edited by Sibyl A. Schwarzenbach and Patricia Smith, 23–33. New York: Columbia University Press, 2003.

Li, Stephanie. *Signifying without Specifying: Racial Discourse in the Age of Obama.* New Brunswick, N.J.: Rutgers University Press, 2012.

Lincoln, C. Eric. "The Du Boisian Dubiety and the American Dilemma: Two Levels of Lure and Loathing." In *Lure and Loathing: Essays on Race, Identity, and the Ambivalence of Assimilation,* edited by Gerald Early, 194–206. New York: Allen Lane/Penguin, 1993.

Lister, Ruth. "Dialectics of Citizenship." *Hypatia* 12.4 (1997): 6–26.

Lucas, Stephen E. "Justifying America: The Declaration of Independence as a Rhetorical Document." In *American Rhetoric: Context and Criticism,* edited by Thomas W. Benson, 67–130. Carbondale: Southern Illinois University Press, 1989.

Lyon, Arabella. *Deliberative Acts: Democracy, Rhetoric, and Rights.* University Park: Pennsylvania State University Press, 2013.

Lyon, Arabella. "Rhetoric and Hermeneutics." In *Perspectives on Rhetorical Invention,* edited by Janet M. Atwill and Janice M. Lauer, 36–52. Knoxville: University of Tennessee Press, 2002.

Bibliography

Maltz, Earl M. "The Fourteenth Amendment and Native American Citizenship." *Constitutional Commentary* 17.3 (2000): 555–74.

Mansbach, Adam. "The Audacity of Post-Racism." In *The Speech: Race and Barack Obama's "A More Perfect Union,"* edited by T. Denean Sharpley-Whiting, 69–84. New York: Bloomsbury, 2009.

Mansfied, Stephen. *The Faith of Barack Obama.* Nashville, Tenn.: Thomas Nelson, 2008.

Maraniss, David. *Barack Obama: The Story.* New York: Simon & Schuster, 2012.

Markovits, Elizabeth. *The Politics of Sincerity: Plato, Frank Speech, and Democratic Judgment.* University Park: Pennsylvania State University Press, 2008.

McCormick, Samuel. "Earning One's Inheritance: Rhetorical Criticism, Everyday Talk, and the Analysis of Public Discourse." *Quarterly Journal of Speech* 89.2 (2003): 109–31.

McGee, Michael C. "In Search of 'the People': A Rhetorical Alternative." *Quarterly Journal of Speech* 61.3 (1975): 235–49.

McGee, Michael Calvin. "Text, Context, and the Fragmentation of Contemporary Culture." *Western Journal of Communication* 54.3 (1990): 274–89.

McKeogh, Colm. *The Political Realism of Reinhold Niebuhr.* New York: St. Martin's Press, 1997.

McKeon, Richard. "The Methods of Rhetoric and Philosophy: Invention and Judgment." In *Rhetoric: Essays in Invention & Discovery,* edited by Mark Backman, 56–65. Woodbridge, Conn.: Ox Bow Press, 1987.

McKerrow, Raymie E. "Critical Rhetoric: Theory and Praxis." *Communication Monographs* 56.2 (1989): 91–111.

McPhail, Mark Lawrence. "Double-Consciousness in Black and White: Identity, Difference, and the Rhetorical Ideal of Life." Van Zelst Lecture in Communication, Northwestern University School of Speech, Evanston, Illinois, April 12, 2001.

Medhurst, Martin J. "Barack Obama's 2009 Inaugural Address: Narrative Signature and Interpretation." In *Making the Case: Advocacy and Judgment in Public Argument,* edited by Kathryn M. Olson, Michael William Pfau, Benjamin Ponder, and Kirt H. Wilson, 191–229. East Lansing: Michigan State University Press, 2012.

Mettler, Susanne. *The Submerged State: How Invisible Government Policies Undermine American Democracy.* Chicago: University of Chicago Press, 2011.

Meyers, Peter. *Civic War and the Corruption of the Citizen.* Chicago: University of Chicago Press, 2008.

Miller, Keith. "On Martin Luther King, Jr., and the Landscape of Civil Rights Rhetoric." *Rhetoric & Public Affairs* 16.1 (2013): 167–83.

Moses, Wilson J. "Ambivalent Maybe." In *Lure and Loathing: Essays on Race, Identity, and the Ambivalence of Assimilation,* edited by Gerald Early, 274–90. New York: Penguin, 1993.

Murphy, John M. "Barack Obama, the Exodus Tradition, and the Joshua Generation." *Quarterly Journal of Speech* 97.4 (2011): 387–410.

Norton, Anne. "Seeing in the Dark." *Theory & Event* 10.1 (2007).

Nothstine, William L., Carole Blair, and Gary A. Copeland. *Critical Questions: Invention, Creativity, and the Criticism of Discourse and Media.* New York: St. Martin's Press, 1994.

Nunley, Vorris L. *Keepin' It Hushed: The Barbershop and African American Hush Harbor Rhetoric.* Detroit: Wayne State University Press, 2011.

Obama, Barack. *The Audacity of Hope: Thoughts on Reclaiming the American Dream.* New York: Three Rivers Press, 2006.

Bibliography

Obama, Barack. *Dreams from My Father: A Story of Race and Inheritance*. New York: Three Rivers Press, 1995.

Oboler, Suzanne. "Redefining Citizenship as Lived Experience." In *Latinos and Citizenship: The Dilemma of Belonging,* edited by Suzanne Oboler, 3–30. Gordonsville, Va.: Palgrave Macmillan, 2006.

Ono, Kent A., and John M. Sloop. "Commitment to Telos—a Sustained Critical Rhetoric." *Communication Monographs* 59.1 (1992): 48–60.

Ono, Kent A., and John M. Sloop. "The Critique of Vernacular Discourse." *Communication Monographs* 62.1 (1995): 19–46.

Plouffe, David. *The Audacity to Win: The Inside Story and Lessons of Barack Obama's Historic Victory*. New York: Viking Press, 2009.

Quintilian. *The Orator's Education (Institutio Oratoria)*. Edited and translated by Donald A. Russell. Cambridge, Mass.: Harvard University Press, 2001.

Rampersad, Arnold. *The Art and Imagination of W. E. B. Du Bois*. New York: Schocken Books, 1990.

Ratcliffe, Krista. *Rhetorical Listening: Identification, Gender, Whiteness*. Carbondale: Southern Illinois University Press, 2005.

Reed, Adolph, Jr. "Du Bois's 'Double Consciousness': Race and Gender in Progressive Era American Thought." *Studies in American Political Development* 6 (1992): 93–139.

Reed, Adolph, Jr. *W. E. B. Du Bois and American Political Thought: Fabianism and the Color Line*. New York: Oxford University Press, 1997.

Reeves, Joshua, and Matthew S. May. "The Peace Rhetoric of a War President: Barack Obama and the Just War Legacy." *Rhetoric & Public Affairs* 16.4 (2013): 623–50.

Remnick, David. *The Bridge: The Life and Rise of Barack Obama*. New York: Vintage, 2011.

Roman, Ediberto. *In Citizenship and Its Exclusions: A Classical, Constitutional, and Critical Race Critique*. New York: New York University Press, 2010.

Romano, Carlin. *America the Philosophical*. New York: Knopf, 2012.

Rowland, Robert C., and John M. Jones. "Recasting the American Dream and American Politics: Barack Obama's Keynote Address to the 2004 Democratic National Convention." *Quarterly Journal of Speech* 93.4 (2007): 425–48.

Ryan, Halford. *The Inaugural Addresses of Twentieth-Century American Presidents*. Westport, Conn.: Praeger, 1993.

Sandel, Michael J. *Democracy's Discontent: America in Search of a Public Philosophy*. Cambridge: Belknap Press, 1996.

Schiappa, Edward. *The Beginnings of Rhetorical Theory in Classical Greece*. New Haven: Yale University Press, 1999.

Schultz, Connie, "His Grandmother, My Father, Your Uncle. . . ." In *The Speech: Race and Barack Obama's "A More Perfect Union,"* edited by T. Denean Sharpley-Whiting, 102–12. New York: Bloomsbury, 2009.

Scorza, Jason A. *Strong Liberalism: Habits of Mind for Democratic Citizenship*. Medford, Mass.: Tufts University Press, 2008.

Sharpley-Whiting, T. Denean. "Chloroform Morning Joe!" In *The Speech: Race and Barack Obama's "A More Perfect Union,"* edited by T. Denean Sharpley-Whiting, 1–15. New York: Bloomsbury, 2009.

Shklar, Judith N. *American Citizenship: The Quest for Inclusion*. Cambridge, Mass.: Harvard University Press, 1991.

Simonson, Peter. "The Streets of Laredo: Mercurian Rhetoric and the Obama Campaign." *Western Journal of Communication* 74.1 (2010): 94–126.

Bibliography

Sloane, Thomas O. *On the Contrary: The Protocol of Traditional Rhetoric.* Washington, D.C.: Catholic University of America Press, 1997.

Smith, Rogers M. *Civic Ideals: Conflicting Visions of Citizenship in U.S. History.* New Haven: Yale University Press, 1997.

Smitherman, Geneva. "'It's Been a Long Time Comin, But Our Change Done Come.'" In *The Speech: Race and Barack Obama's "A More Perfect Union,"* edited by T. Denean Sharpley-Whiting, 184–204. New York: Bloomsbury, 2009.

Steele, Shelby. *A Bound Man: Why We Are Excited about Obama and Why He Can't Win.* New York: Free Press, 2008.

Stewart, Carole Lynn. *Strange Jeremiahs: Civil Religion and the Literary Imaginations of Jonathan Edwards, Herman Melville, and W. E. B. Du Bois.* Albuquerque: University of New Mexico Press, 2010.

Sugrue, Thomas J. *Not Even Past: Barack Obama and the Burden of Race.* Princeton: Princeton University Press, 2010.

Tennant, Brad. "'Excluding Indians Not Taxed': *Dred Scott, Standing Bear, Elk* and the Legal Status of Native Americans in the Latter Half of the Nineteenth Century." *International Social Science Review* 86.1&2 (2011): 24–43.

Terrill, Robert E. "An Uneasy Peace: Barack Obama's Nobel Peace Prize Lecture." *Rhetoric & Public Affairs* 14.4 (2011): 761–79.

Terrill, Robert E. "Going Deep." *Southern Communication Journal* 71.2 (2006): 165–73.

Terrill, Robert E. "Learning to Read." *Rhetoric & Public Affairs* 13.4 (2011): 689–97.

Terrill, Robert E. "Mimesis, Duality, and Rhetorical Education." *Rhetoric Society Quarterly* 41.4 (2011): 295–315.

Terrill, Robert E. "Unity and Duality in Barack Obama's 'A More Perfect Union.'" *Quarterly Journal of Speech* 95.4 (2009): 363–86.

Terrill, Robert E., and Eric King Watts. "W. E. B. Du Bois, Double-Consciousness, and Pan-Africanism in the Progressive Era." In *A Rhetorical History of the United States: Vol 6. Rhetoric and Reform in the Progressive Era,* edited by J. Michael Hogan, 269–309. East Lansing: Michigan State University Press, 2002.

Terrill, Robert E., and Michael C. Leff. "The Polemicist as Artist: W. E. B. Du Bois's 'of Mr. Booker T. Washington and Others.'" *Argumentation and Values: Proceedings of the Ninth SCA/AFA Conference on Argumentation* (1995): 230–36.

Utley, Ebony, and Amy L. Heyse. "Barack Obama's (Im)perfect Union: An Analysis of the Strategic Successes and Failures in His Speech on Race." *Western Journal of Black Studies* 33.3 (2009): 153–63.

Vaughn, Justin S., and Jennifer R. Mercieca. *The Rhetoric of Heroic Expectations: Establishing the Obama Presidency.* College Station: Texas A&M University Press, 2014.

Walker, Clarence E., and Gregory D. Smithers. *The Preacher and the Politician: Jeremiah Wright, Barack Obama, and Race in America.* Charlottesville: University of Virginia Press, 2009.

Walker, Jeffrey. *The Genuine Teachers of This Art: Rhetorical Education in Antiquity.* Columbia: University of South Carolina Press, 2012.

Walzer, Arthur E. "Teaching 'Political Wisdom': Isocrates and the Tradition of Dissoi Logoi." In *The Viability of the Rhetorical Tradition,* edited by Richard Graff, Arthur E. Walzer, and Janet M. Atwill, 113–24. Albany: State University of New York Press, 2005.

Walzer, Michael. *Arguing about War.* New Haven: Yale University Press, 2004.

Watson, Walter. "Invention." In *Encyclopedia of Rhetoric,* edited by Thomas O. Sloane, 360. Oxford: Oxford University Press, 2001.

Wattles, Jeffrey. *The Golden Rule*. New York: Oxford University Press, 1996.

Wess, Robert. "Representative Anecdotes in General, with Notes toward a Representative Anecdote for Burkean Ecocriticism in Particular." *K. B. Journal On-Line* 1.1 (2004). http://www.kbjournal.org/node/54.

West, Isaac. *Transforming Citizenships: Transgender Articulations of the Law*. New York: New York University Press, 2014.

Wichelns, Herbert A. "The Literary Criticism of Oratory." In *Studies in Rhetoric and Public Speaking in Honor of James Albert Winans,* edited by A. M. Drummond, 181–216. New York: Russell & Russell, 1962.

Wilson, Kirt H. "The Racial Contexts of Public Address: Interpreting Violence during the Reconstruction Era." In *The Handbook of Rhetoric and Public Address,* edited by Shawn J. Parry-Giles and J. Michael Hogan, 205–28. Malden, Mass.: Blackwell, 2010.

Wolffe, Richard. *Renegade: The Making of a President*. New York: Crown, 2009.

Yarbrough, Jean M. *Theodore Roosevelt and the American Political Tradition*. Lawrence: University Press of Kansas, 2012.

Young, Iris Marion. *Inclusion and Democracy*. Oxford: Oxford University Press, 2000.

Zakaras, Alex. *Individuality and Mass Democracy: Mill, Emerson, and the Burdens of Citizenship*. Oxford: Oxford University Press, 2009.

Zamir, Shamoon. *Dark Voices: W. E. B. Du Bois and American Thought, 1888–1903*. Chicago: Chicago University Press, 1995.

Index

Abramsky, Sasha, on Obama's associations with civil rights movement, 77; on Obama's duality, 20, 21

active voice, use of in "A More Perfect Union," 59–63, 68

African American church: as a hush harbor, 66; as influential institution in black community, 53; and the jeremiad tradition, 55–56; and the most segregated hour of American life, 66

African American culture: and democratic double-consciousness, 75–76; and jeremiadic preaching, 55–56

African Americans: and alienation, 44; and citizenship, 36–37, 39; and Du Bois and double-consciousness, 91–92; and first black U.S. president, 1, 138, 151–52; and the Fourteenth Amendment, 36; identity and Du Bois's view on double-consciousness, 28.

alienation: and democratic citizenship, 43, 44; and double-consciousness, 27, 28, 29, 48, 81; and the price of citizenship, 26–27; and the promise of citizenship, 27–28

Allen, Danielle: on Aristotle's notion of civic friendship, 42; on civic friendship, 112; on effective citizenship, 148; on the mode of citizenship, 59; on race and citizenship, 34, 39–40

ambiguity, in double-consciousness, 27, 29

antithesis: in Obama's second inaugural address, 139; use of, in John F. Kennedy's inaugural address, 15; use of, in Barack Obama's inaugural address, 15–16

Aristotle: and notion of civic friendship, 42–43; and the "second self," 70

Asen, Robert, on rhetorical citizenship, 13, 14

Ashley story, the, 88–89; citizenly discourse and, 72–73; as an exemplary mode of address, 103

Audacity of Hope, The (Obama), 20, 21; double-consciousness as a collective adaptation, 29; and the parallels with Obama's economy address, 133–34

authenticity, 65

Balfour, Lawrie: on democratic citizenship, 143; double-consciousness and seeing the darkness, 30; Du Bois and democratic citizenship, 43; on mixed inheritance, 34

beer summit. *See* Henry Louis Gates Jr. incident

biracial, identity and Obama's duality, 18–19, 62–63, 67, 72, 74, 85, 127

black authenticity, 19

Black, Edwin, and rhetorical address, 14

Bloody Sunday. *See* Brown Chapel Address

Brands, H. W., on Obama's economy address, 126–27

Brooks, David (*New York Times*), on Obama as detached observer, 65

Brown Chapel Address (Selma, Alabama, March 4, 2007): and the birth narrative in, 84; and comparison with "A More Perfect Union," 85, 86; and the Moses-Joshua story line in, 84–85; and Obama's use of metaphorical devices, 83–85. *See also* campaign, 2008 presidential

Brown, U.S. Justice Henry Billings, on civil rights and citizenship, 36–37

89; and the ethic of reciprocity, 88–89; exemplified in Obama's "A More Perfect Union," 103, 143–44; fundamental qualities of, 142; and the Golden Rule, 70–71, 74; and individual responsibility, 88; inventional resources of, 134–37; limitations of, in Obama's Nobel Peace Prize Lecture, 116, 122–23; and and moral hesitancy, 65, 107; and Obama's response to the Jeremiah Wright controversy, 63–68; and the price of citizenship, 68; and the promise of citizenship, 68; and public discourse, 100; resources of, 99; and rhetorical invention, 148; variation and limitation of, 145. *See also* double-consciousness

dissoi logoi, in Isocrates's teachings, 149

double-consciousness, 24–30; as agent for proliferation of voices and perspectives, 31–32, 49; and alienation, 27, 28, 43, 44, 48, 81; the burden of, 120, 142; and casuistic stretching, 30, 142; and citizenship, 141–46; and the color line, 65–67; dispassionate, 106, 113–14; and dual commitment to citizenship, 40–43; Du Bois and, 19, 24–30, 31, 32–34, 46–47, 75, 91–92, 137, 152; evolution of, 28; as gift of second sight, 28; and the Golden Rule, 70–71; as an inventional resource for democratic citizenship, 76, 98–99; and the limitations on race rhetoric, 99; as mode of address among citizens, 31–32, 49; and moral hesitancy, 42, 65, 107; and Obama's embodiment of, 52, 59–63; and the price of citizenship, 3, 4, 26–27, 43; and the promise of citizenship, 3, 4, 27–28, 43; reflection on, as a racialized trope, 151–54; as resource for public citizenship, 31–32, 49; in *Souls of Black Folk, The*, 25–26. *See also* democratic double-consciousness

doubled address: in "A More Perfect Union," 68–71; and the past and the future, 69, 70. *See also* public address

doubled figures, as inventional resources, 121

doubled gaze: and the color line, 67, 69; and democratic citizenship, 153; and

the doubled perspective, 64, 67; and the notion of civic friendship, 42–43; and Obama's response to Jeremiah Wright controversy, 63–68; and the refuge of the hush harbor, 66

doubled persona, observations on Obama's, 20–22

doubled perspectives: and the color line, 67; as contributing to democratic citizenship, 52; and democratic double-consciousness, 73–74; as a productive model of citizenship, 61–62

doubled speech, as mode of address, 46–48

doubled tropes, 152; and African American literature, 47. *See also* chiasmus; isocolon; metaphor; paradox; parallelism; parataxis

Dowd, Maureen (*New York Times*), on Obama's duality, 21

Dreams from My Father (Obama), 18; and double-consciousness, 28–29; and Malcolm X, 18, 99–100; and Trinity United Church of Christ, 62

Dred Scott decision, 36

D'Souza, Dinesh, on Obama's public discourse, 4–5

duality: and the capacity for impassioned, 111; citizenship and, 40–45; and the Jeremiah Wright controversy, 61–62; non-dialectical, 20–24; and Obama's biracial identity, 18–19, 20–22, 59–60, 62–63, 67, 72, 74, 85, 127; passionate, 113–14; and rhetoric, 146–51, 153. *See also* double-consciousness; parataxis

dual perspectives: as articulated in "A More Perfect Union," 88, 89; and Henry Louis Gates Jr. incident, 93

Du Bois, W. E. B.: and African Americans and citizenship, 39; on alienation, 44, 81; and Aristotle's notion of civic friendship, 42–43; on the burdens of citizenship, 143; and the color line, 138; and democratic double-consciousness, 31–34, 142–42; and double-consciousness, 19, 24–30, 32–34, 46–47, 48, 75, 91–92, 137, 152; and the "gift" of exclusion, 62; and the Golden Rule, 120; and

Index

About the Author

ROBERT E. TERRILL is an associate professor of communication and culture at Indiana University, Bloomington. He earned his Ph.D. at Northwestern University in 1996 and focuses on the rhetorical criticism of African American public address. Terrill is the author of *Malcolm X: Inventing Radical Judgment* and editor of *Cambridge Companion to Malcolm X*. His work has appeared in *The Quarterly Journal of Speech, Rhetoric & Public Affairs, Rhetoric Society Quarterly, Critical Studies in Media Communication,* and *Southern Communication Journal.*